WRITING FEATURE STORIES

WRITING FEATURE STORIES

How to research and write newspaper and magazine articles

Matthew Ricketson

ALLEN&UNWIN

Every effort has been made by the author and publisher to contact copyright holders of materials quoted extensively. Unacknowledged copyright holders should contact the publisher with any queries.

First published in 2004
Copyright © Matthew Ricketson 2004

Allen & Unwin
83 Alexander Street
Crows Nest NSW 2065
Australia
Phone: (61 2) 8425 0100
Fax: (61 2) 9906 2218
Email: info@allenandunwin.com
Web: www.allenandunwin.com

National Library of Australia
Cataloguing-in-publication entry:

Ricketson, Matthew, 1958–
    Writing feature stories: how to research and write
    newspaper and magazine articles.

Includes index.
ISBN 978 1 86508 732 0

1. Authorship 2. Feature writing. I. Title.

808.066

Typeset in 11/14 pt RotisSerif by Midland Typesetters
Printed and bound by Griffin Press

MIX
Paper from
responsible sources
FSC
www.fsc.org
FSC® C009448

The paper in this book is FSC® certified. FSC® promotes environmentally responsible, socially beneficial and economically viable management of the world's forests.

20 19 18 17 16 15 14 13 12

CONTENTS

ACKNOWLEDGEMENTS

This book has been a long time coming. I remember solemnly promising to write it during the interview for my current job—in 1995. Other things got in the way—another book, a masters degree—but with the gentle prodding of colleagues in other journalism schools and Elizabeth Weiss at Allen & Unwin, it is finally finished. It is a truism that books are collaborative projects in disguise, but for a book about writing this is especially true. To begin with, I'd like to acknowledge Geoff Slattery whose sports journalism (particularly a profile of Lou Richards) first showed me what was possible in journalistic writing. Peter Ellingsen introduced me to Murray Smith who had been his first editor, and became mine, at the then Standard Newspapers in Cheltenham. Murray is a superb suburban editor and one of the nicest blokes you could hope to meet in a newsroom. Three other editors who helped me a lot were Neil Mitchell at *The Age*, Steve Foley at *The Australian* and Jeff Penberthy at *Time Australia*. I have been fortunate to work with and learn from many fine journalists, beginning with fellow cadets at *The Age* in 1982, and later including: Paul Austin; Paul Chadwick; Philip Chubb; Debi Enker; Gideon Haigh; Phillipa Hawker; Damien Murphy; Andrew Rule; John Schauble; Cameron Stewart; Ros Smallwood and Jane Sullivan.

At RMIT University, the considerable support granted to me by the School of Applied Communication provided time to write the book. I appreciate the university's commitment to encouraging staff to reflect on their craft and their profession and to pass on findings in books such as this, which, it is hoped, will help strengthen links between industry and the academy. Many students in many feature writing classes have influenced this book through their questions, their ideas and their candidly expressed views about my stories. Colleagues in the Journalism program team have taken a keen interest, especially fellow feature writing lecturers, John Hurst, who generously lent me his own extensive work on the area, and Sybil Nolan and Muriel Porter, who both read the manuscript and made valuable comments. I would like to thank the six journalists (Pamela Bone, David Brearley, Jon Casimir, Fiona Hudson, Garry Linnell and Kimina Lyall) who gave permission for their features to be reproduced in this book and who contributed the excellent stories behind their stories. Sarah Hudson and Chris Tatman also provided stories about their stories, but in the end, for space reasons, I was unable to include them. Thanks nevertheless.

At Allen & Unwin, thanks go to in-house editor, Catherine Taylor, and to the educational publisher, Elizabeth Weiss, for her support and her coolly incisive intelligence. At home, thanks as always go to my children Gemma, Hayley and Josh and my darling wife Gill.

INTRODUCTION

A writer says: read what I have written
An historian says: listen to my lecture
A critic says: listen to what I think
A journalist says: let me tell you a story.

Gideon Haigh

Novelists know the terror of the blank page; journalists know the terror of deadlines. Novelists have to create something out of nothing; without their imagination the page remains blank. Journalists have to find the news and test its accuracy; miss the deadline and they may as well have stayed in bed. And feature writers—what about feature writers? Wherever they turn they see paradox. They're not novelists but they are asked to do something more than simply report the news of the day. They are given licence to be creative but they are still journalists and are still writing about the real world. They have to meet deadlines but not necessarily daily deadlines. Is it any wonder people get confused about feature writing?

As a young journalist I vividly remember feeling confused when I was first asked to write features. I had grasped the essentials of the news story ('The Prime Minister yesterday called an election, after weeks of intense speculation . . .') but that was only after it was drilled into me by dint of repeated practice in a newsroom. Now editors were asking for pieces much longer than the customary 600-word (or 'twelve snappy pars' as they were called) news stories. They told me they wanted background, they wanted colour, they wanted to run 'long reads'. So I started gathering more information, reading reports, visiting places, interviewing people, and much of what I gathered was good stuff. I enjoyed interviewing and most people seemed happy enough to talk. I loved words and I had this idea I could write. The problem was, I had no idea how to put together a feature, no idea how to start it and no idea how to order the mass of raw material that sprawled across my desk and onto the floor.

Nowhere was this more painfully evident than in writing a profile of Frank Vitkovic, the 22-year-old man who in 1987 walked into the

Australia Post building in Queen Street, Melbourne, armed with a sawn-off M1 carbine, and killed eight innocent people and then himself. I covered the coronial inquest the next year, taking notes on the 115 witnesses' evidence and writing daily news stories for *The Australian*, where I was on staff. I was asked by the editor of the newspaper's colour magazine to profile Vitkovic for the first anniversary of the shootings. By the end of the coronial inquest I had filled five notebooks and separately interviewed several key players, including coroner Hal Hallenstein, QC. In the newsroom I could speak authoritatively about the inquest's every detail but when I sat down to write I was struck dumb.

Swimming in information, I was clueless about structuring the story. The factual material should have been like an anchor—essential equipment to be stowed so the story could set sail. Trouble was, the anchor was snagged on the seabed. When the ship finally got going, it seemed someone had left the compass onshore and the story proceeded painfully, frequently banging into sharp unseen objects. When land was finally sighted the captain hadn't the faintest notion how he had reached his destination, and so was no wiser for the next feature writing journey.

This went on for some years, sad to say. I did turn out some reasonable features but I still approached each one filled with anxiety and I still found the writing process bafflingly difficult. Paradoxically, it was only after leaving my last mainstream media job, at *Time Australia* magazine, to teach journalism that I finally found out how to write a feature. This may not be as strange as it sounds. Journalism, with its constant deadlines and yen for the new, is notoriously unreflective. As a journalist with 11 years' experience on local and metropolitan print media, I was seen as qualified to teach feature writing, yet I rarely had had the time nor was I encouraged to articulate how I did what I did. Then I found a book entitled *The Art and Craft of Feature Writing* by William Blundell, a veteran journalist at *The Wall Street Journal*, and suddenly the fog lifted. So, this is how you do it. His book was chockfull of insight and advice, grounded in his experience and expressed in vigorous, drum-tight prose.

As well as setting his book for students, I drew on it for features I was contributing to newspapers and magazines, and it helped a lot. A profile I did of the eminent and controversial historian, Geoffrey Blainey, also published in *The Weekend Australian Magazine*, won the 1994 George Munster prize for freelance journalism. In the years since I have written numerous features. I still face the squalls and heavy seas inherent in crafting any piece of writing, but at least I have a compass, which has made the whole process clearer, not to mention enjoyable.

Of course, different people learn how to write features in different ways. For a few gifted people it comes easily, while others are fortunate enough to be taken in hand by an old wise sub-editor. *The Sydney Morning Herald* and *The Age* have formalised this process as a mentor scheme for their incoming trainees, but this is the exception rather than the rule in the Australian media. Many have to find their own way and the evidence is that many are equally at sea as I was. If you don't believe me ask yourself how often are you really impressed by a feature story? Or, an even simpler question: how often do you read a feature story through to the end? Not often at all is the most likely answer.

A readership survey done by Quadrant Research for News Limited in 1995 found only one in three people read most of the copy in editorial items—and that included shorter news stories as well as features.[1] Why is this? It may have something to do with the sheer volume of media people consume today. Not only is there print and broadcast media, but pay TV's 24-hour news channels, videos, computer games and the Internet, with its cornucopia of information, blogs and chat rooms. It may also have something to do with the fact that many journalists, pre-occupied first with getting the news, then with comprehending the often complex issues they cover, have little time to make their features readable, let alone memorable. Shortage of time is a perennial lament in newsrooms but it is probably true that the average journalist is expected to write more stories per week than their counterpart 20 years ago.

Amid the rush it is easy for journalists to forget that people read newspapers and magazines to be entertained and moved as much as to be informed. They want to be told stories. They need to be told stories, you might argue. Storytelling is common across cultures and ages; it begins with saucer-eyed children at bedtime and ends only with death or dementia. It is a way of making sense of the world and a way of enabling people to identify with and perhaps understand other people's lives. Journalists, along with novelists, artists and film-makers, are among those members of society whose role it is to tell stories. Should journalists insist on their duty as objective seekers after the facts, let them look to their own vernacular where they talk about getting a 'story' or a 'yarn'. Where journalists do differ from novelists is that the stories they tell are true—or as true as they can make them in the time available.

The demands of researching and writing a series on, say, the illegal export trade in Australian wildlife may be of a different order to compiling a list of Adelaide's ten best ice creameries, but once journalists venture beyond the familiar inverted pyramid formula of the basic news story they need to be more conscious of their role as storytellers. Readers will put up with the hard news format for a 600-word news story but not for a 2000-word piece.

The core messages of this book, then, are threefold:

1. FEATURE WRITING IS FUN

Many students and journalists find the form of the straight news story rigid and impersonal. Writing features offers the opportunity to be creative. You can find your own journalistic voice, you can write with zest and bite and, in varying degrees, you can express your views. After several years, many working journalists also find the nature of straight news constricting. The same stories seem to keep coming round year after year and they want to explore a news event or an issue in more depth. The way to do that is through feature stories.

2. FEATURE WRITING IS HARD WORK

Many think creativity in journalism means you kick back in your chair, call on the muse for some incandescent prose and wait for the Walkley awards to roll in. This notion is as misplaced as it is persistent; sadly, you can't keep a good myth down. To write a compelling feature story requires more research than most news stories, with more care and attention paid to the writing.

3. FEATURE WRITING IS IMPORTANT

It was the English media baron, Lord Northcliffe, who said, 'It is hard news that catches readers. Features hold them.' Just what he meant will be discussed in the next chapter, but before that read this opening to a feature on the weird and wonderful world of bodybuilding headlined 'The power and the gory'.

Half the world was in mortal terror of him. He had a sixty-inch chest, twenty-three-inch arms, and when the Anadrol and Bolasterone backed up in his bloodstream, his eyes went as red as the laser scope on an Uzi. He threw people through windows, and chased them madly down Hempstead Turnpike when they had the temerity to cut him off. And in the gym he owned in Farmingdale, the notorious Mr America's, if he caught you looking at him while he trained, you generally woke up, bleeding, on the pavement outside. Half out of his mind on androgens and horse steroids, he had this idea that being looked at robbed him of energy, energy that he needed to leg-press two thousand pounds.

Nonetheless, one day a kid walked up to him between sets and said, "I want to be just like you, Steve Michalik. I want to be Mr America and Mr Universe."

"Yeah?" said Michalik in thick contempt. "How bad do you think you want it?"

"Worse than anything in the world," said the kid, a scrawny seventeen-year-old with more balls than biceps. "I can honestly say that I would die for a body like yours."

"Well, then you probably will," snorted Michalik. "Meet me down at the beach tomorrow at six a.m. sharp. And if you're even half a minute late . . ."

The kid was there at six a.m. pronto, freezing his ass off in a raggedy hood and sweats. "What do we do first?" he asked.

"Swim," grunted Michalik, dragging him into the ocean. Twenty yards out, Michalik suddenly seized the kid by his scalp and pushed him under a wave. The kid flailed punily, wriggling like a speared eel. A half-minute later, maybe forty-five seconds, passed before Michalik let the kid up, sobbing out sea water. He gave the kid a breath, then shoved him down again, holding him under this time until the air bubbles stopped. Whereupon he dragged him out by the hood and threw him, gasping, on the beach.

"When you want the title as bad as you wanted that last fucking breath," sneered Michalik, "then and only then can you come and talk to me."

Who wouldn't read on after that? Paul Solotaroff's article first appeared in the *Village Voice*, an American weekly newspaper, in 1991, and has been widely anthologised.[2] Apart from the crackerjack opening, Solotaroff's story reveals how Michalik and his ilk destroy their bodies even as they build them. It is a story whose power has less to do with its newsworthiness—bodybuilder confesses to using drugs; gosh, I had no idea—than with the compelling level of detail, the revulsion the reader feels at the toxic effects of drugs, and the sheer verve of the writing. It is an advanced feature story that shows the suppleness of journalism as a form and as an activity.

HOW TO USE THIS BOOK

Writing Feature Stories works on three different levels:

1. It offers a method of researching and writing elementary feature stories.
2. It offers a method of researching and writing more sophisticated feature stories.
3. It offers reflections on the nature, role and impact of feature stories.

The reflections infuse the entire book and the method of researching and writing feature stories contains the following topics, in the following chapters:

- generating fresh ideas (chapter four)
- organising limited time efficiently (chapter five)
- gathering information, whether factual or personal (chapters six to eight)
- sifting and sorting to find the most relevant material (chapter nine)
- finding the most interesting way to tell the story (chapter nine)
- writing the story (chapters ten and eleven)
- editing and proofreading the story (chapter twelve)
- working with editors (chapter twelve)

The method applies to both elementary and more sophisticated feature stories because they differ in degree rather than nature. It may be possible to put together a simple lifestyle feature or write up a celebrity interview without learning this method but beyond those you will probably struggle. Learning this method will enable you to write sharper, fresher lifestyle features and will give you the tools to tackle more complex features that engage readers' minds and emotions.

You may wonder why writing the story is only one of the eight topics. Typing words onto a computer screen is part of a process, and a late part at that. Many students mistakenly believe the writing is all, and many textbooks repeat the mistake, solemnly reiterating injunctions—prefer the active to the passive voice, use adjectives sparingly—that have been included in almost every book about writing since the original publication of William Strunk's *The Elements of Style* in 1918. This book is as much about how the words get onto the page as the words themselves, a field far less frequently tilled. Even William Blundell in *The Art and Craft of Feature Writing*, who identifies smart ways to generate ideas, admits he 'conveniently vaults over the disorder' of a journalist researching a feature. It is this disorder, though, that is not only as important to features as the writing, it also fills many journalists with dread. How do I report 'colour' and 'atmosphere' as well as facts? How do I persuade people to talk to me? And, how do I stop them from rambling when they do?

Chapters one and two of this book define the nature and variety of feature stories, outline where features conform and where they diverge from news values and set them in their context in Australian newspapers and magazines. Chapter three offers a method of analysing feature stories that helps students think like practitioners and practitioners sharpen their own practice. Chapters four to twelve as discussed above walk through the creation of a feature from initial idea to edited article. These chapters assume the reader is working on their own feature. They can be used profitably if readers are not but work better if they are. Chapter thirteen offers a glimpse at the advanced feature writing that Paul Solotaroff and others practise, which shows the vast potential of journalism. The final chapter provides a list of must-read pieces and books. Sprinkled among the chapters are four feature stories originally published in Australian newspapers and magazines, each accompanied by the journalist's story behind their story. At the end of each chapter are discussion questions about the issues raised in feature stories, and exercises to help prepare readers as they do their own features.

WHO IS THIS BOOK FOR?

Anyone, of course, is welcome to draw on ideas they find useful, but the express aim of this book is to help journalists research and write feature stories for publication in Australian newspapers and magazines. The groups most likely to gain something from *Writing Feature Stories* are tertiary students of journalism and professional writing; journalists working in the industry who are being asked to write features; and freelance journalists.

Before moving on to the first chapter, let me squelch two of the great myths of writing books and writers of writing books. The first is that by reading this book you will automatically become a great feature writer. If you are going to be a great feature writer it is you who will make that happen. This book can help you sidestep various reportorial briar patches and literary quicksands, and it can stimulate you to think more deeply about writing feature stories, and the role of journalism in society. The second myth is that the writing teacher is some kind of god. God knows I'm not god, and if she is off-duty I only have to look at my published features to confirm my ordinariness. But here is a heretical thought—I don't think that matters. It is only important that a writing teacher is god if you think they are the source of your success, and as I have said, they aren't.

There are many outstanding journalists who are unwilling or unable to explain clearly what they do or to reflect on why they do what they do. Similarly, there are many excellent academic teachers who have little, if any, experience as a working journalist. What I offer you is a combination of journalistic and teaching experience, fired by a passion for journalism, an activity that is fun, is fascinating and, no matter what politicians, academics or public relations spin doctors tell you, does make an impact. In the month-long Gulf War of 2003 at least ten journalists died doing their job. How many PR officers died doing theirs?

A celebrity is a person who works hard all his life to become well known, and then wears dark glasses to avoid being recognised.

Fred Allen

DISCUSSION QUESTIONS AND EXERCISES

1. Survey the day's newspapers and find the longest hard news story you can. How long is it, and how readable is it?
2. List three feature articles that made an impression on you. Describe and analyse why you remember them.

WHAT EXACTLY IS A FEATURE STORY?

It is hard news that catches readers. Features hold them.
Lord Northcliffe

The feature writer's aim is the dramatist's aim: make 'em laugh; make 'em weep.
Mary J.J. Rimm,
***The Elements of Journalism* (1929)**

CHAPTER SUMMARY

Feature stories are defined as articles containing emotion and analysis as well as information, compared to hard news stories that are first and foremost about information. Feature stories are asserted to be an essential part of Australian newspapers and magazines. Their development is briefly charted. The relationship between news and features is explained by analysing which news values apply to features and in what circumstances.

One simple definition of feature stories is 'everything in the newspaper that is not news', but that is of little help. Not only is it better to define something by saying what it is rather than what it isn't, the definition above would include cartoons, reviews, gardening columns and everything in between. It would also exclude magazines, most of which run more features than news. If you find the relationship between news and features confusing, don't worry. Many working journalists use the term loosely, and know little about the history of what they do, but a brief backward glance can help you understand not only the relationship between news and features but the value of both.

The modern media's unceasing production of words and images swamps the reader's sense of history, of the way things change. Look at any newspaper in Australia today and news is written to the inverted pyramid formula, with the most significant piece of information first followed by data in descending order of importance. It looks logical and it is easy to think news has always been presented this way. It isn't and it hasn't. For instance, think of the familiar phrase 'Dr Livingstone, I presume'. Livingstone was a renowned Scottish explorer who in 1871 had been missing in Africa for at least two years. Henry Stanley, a fellow explorer and journalist, was sent by *The New York Herald* to track down Livingstone. Stanley's dispatch about his mission's success dawdled to the news:

. . . There is a group of the most respectable Arabs, and as I come nearer I see the white face of an old man among them. He has a cap with a gold band around it, his dress is a short jacket of red blanket cloth, and his pants—well, I didn't observe. I am shaking hands with him. We raise our hats, and I say:

"Dr Livingstone, I presume?"

And he says, "Yes."[1]

Nor is this an isolated example of a piece not in the inverted pyramid style. In the mid-19th century the American president's state of the union address used to be reprinted in its entirety; *The New York Times'* 1852 news story, if we can call it that, of that event began: 'It is a bright and beautiful day, and the galleries of the House are crowded with ladies and gentlemen; all is gaiety.'[2] The idea of highlighting the most significant piece of information from the address had not yet crystallised. The reasons behind the development of the inverted pyramid are more complicated than merit discussion here; the point is that history shows us the notion of the objective journalist simply reporting the facts is at best misleading, at worst a dangerous myth.[3]

Writing a news lead is an act of selection, not stenography. Any news story we read today has inbuilt assumptions about what is important and what isn't. This does not mean they are right or wrong, just that the assumptions rest on a set of values seldom articulated or debated. Even leaving aside contentious issues such as race or gender, the basic news story puts information in pride of place. And it puts certain kinds of information in pride of place—election results, earthquakes, murders, gold medals, stock movements, scientific breakthroughs and so on. This is a drop in the ocean of information flowing through society. Much of the remainder is interesting and illuminating; much of it is unknown to readers, and much of it finds its way into feature articles.

Stories written to the inverted pyramid formula are known in the industry as hard news. The more information, the harder the story. Emotions are hived off into soft news. In newsrooms the term hard news connotes importance and seriousness, while soft news connotes the reverse. It is a testosterone-fuelled worldview, one satirised in the Australian series about television current affairs programs, *Frontline*, where any journalist flinching from the most intrusive or inflammatory stories was labelled a 'soft-cock'. Newspaper offices share many of the same values. Driven by information, hard news excludes a good deal, with strange results. There are more things in heaven and earth than are dreamt of in a news editor's philosophy. To continue the Shakespearean analogy, consider the world's most famous play, *Hamlet*, rendered as news. The lead might be: 'Fortinbras, the Prince of Norway, is tipped to become the next King of Denmark after the entire Danish Royal family was slaughtered by its own members during a night of revenge killings and cruel mishaps . . .' Something is missing, and it is not just the blank verse.

News presented in the terse, impersonal inverted pyramid format is highly efficient at conveying information; in the hundred plus years since its development, no one has come up with a better method. Even the most recent media form, online news, all speed and McNugget-sized stories, draws on the inverted pyramid. Where the inverted pyramid flounders is in conveying anything other than information. It corrals emotions into dry phraselets such as 'visibly upset'. It is unable to set events in context; in the words of Norman Mailer, news is forever 'munching nuances like peanuts'.[4] Feature stories on the other hand flesh out the daily news skeleton by revealing the emotions inherent in news stories and clothe it by backgrounding and analysing the meaning of news events. To do that requires a different format from the inverted pyramid. Stories presented in straight news style usually run between 500 and 600 words, rarely longer than 800, but newspaper and magazine feature articles start at about 1000 words and range up to 3000 words (and occasionally longer). A feature does need information but it should also convey emotion and atmosphere and analyse events and issues. A feature needs a coherent structure, with an arresting opening, well-organised material and an ending that, in direct contrast to the hard news story, reaches a satisfying conclusion.

A first-rate feature can add almost as much to a newspaper as a breaking news story. This may seem an outlandish claim. By definition, news is central to a newspaper but just as editors ignored for years many Australians' habit of reading the sports pages first, so the value of features has been overshadowed by the imperative of finding news. There is no doubt the act of breaking news should remain a newspaper's most prized asset, but the investment in it, in resources and energy, obscures how little the impact made by a news story may be. Out of the thousands and thousands of news stories published last year, try remembering 50. You can probably come up with a dozen off the top of your head. Not much of a return. Information overload is at work here, and so is the essence of news, which is preoccupied with the day to day. Readers will always be interested in the day to day, but they have other needs too. Features are aimed at some of those needs, and a well-written feature connects with readers more fully than the average news story.

Features play to the two advantages newspapers and magazines have over radio and television: the ability to analyse and literary quality. The first means the print media is better equipped to drill down deep into complicated issues; the second means the reader is more likely to be moved, whether to outrage or sympathy or laughter. Feature stories that win Walkleys, the most prestigious awards in Australian journalism, are the result of weeks, even months, of work by experienced journalists. Inexperienced journalists are not expected to produce work at this level, but award-winning articles give an idea of what is possible in feature writing.

Any definition of feature stories, such as the one above, is likely to be leaky. It would be easy to find material in the print media that does not fit this book's definition. That says something about the media and about textbooks; the imperatives of the media—space to fill, limited time—override almost everything else. An editor may assign a journalist to write a feature, but equally journalists do not always begin work knowing the form their story will take. They may end up writing a news story or a feature or may have only a tidbit to pass on to the gossip columnist. What the journalist finds dictates the form of the story. So too does the nature of the medium; newspapers are published daily and with online news and 24-hour TV news channels, print journalists may need to do more than simply report the news of the day. They might pitch the story forward, they might analyse the implications of the news or they might tell a story.

This was illustrated at the 2002 Commonwealth Games in Manchester. Because of the time difference between Australian and England, most events occurred overnight, the dead zone of newspapers. Everybody in Australia wanted to see Cathy Freeman run. It was her first major competition since winning gold at the Olympics two years before, and she was running only in the 4×400 metres relay, only after her husband, Sandy Bodecker, ill with cancer, encouraged her to compete. The physically underprepared Freeman ran well below her best time but the team still managed to win gold early on the morning of 1 August. Nothing appeared in that day's newspapers but radio and television covered the win in detail. The next day Peter Wilson of *The Australian* pitched the story forward, suggesting the medal would encourage Freeman to get back into peak physical condition for the coming world championships. In the *Herald Sun* Shaun Phillips and Damian Barrett told the story of 'Cathy's love dash: track star's race for sick Sandy' while Greg Baum of *The Age* combined analysis with storytelling in his piece headlined 'Freeman reignites flame'.

Print journalists need to be aware of their roles as storytellers and analysts when covering daily news even though the bulk of news will still be covered in the conventional inverted pyramid form. This kind of messy reality can be acknowledged in a textbook, but that is all; textbooks always contain a degree of artificiality because it is their job to break things down into parts so they can be understood. Newsrooms contain a degree of artificiality too, breaking down the world into various sections and rounds. There is nothing wrong with that, but features, like news, can be written about any and every subject. There may be issues specific to writing about politics or sport or business or entertainment but the core elements of journalistic work apply to all these areas, even if many journalists prefer to see their specialty as unique. A successful feature about, say, the Australian film industry needs the same elements of content and structure as one about federal politics. With this in mind, let's look at where features fit into Australian newspapers and magazines which, despite the high profile of television and radio, employ five out of every six journalists who are members of the Media Entertainment & Arts Alliance.[5]

NEWSPAPERS

Australia has two national daily newspapers, ten other metropolitan dailies, 37 regional dailies, 250 weekly suburban papers and 66 multicultural papers, and each capital has a Sunday newspaper.[6] Suburban and regional papers carry a small amount of feature material, mostly in the weekend editions of regional dailies, some of which include colour magazines. The bulk of feature stories run in metro dailies. Of them, five are broadsheet in size, and seven are tabloid. One, *The Australian*, is aimed at the nation and another, *The Financial Review*, is aimed at business around the nation; the others service a particular city or state. Common to all metro dailies and particularly relevant to features is the amount of material that is not hard news. The volume of feature material mushroomed in the 1960s. In the late 1970s and early 1980s, *The Age*, drawing on models from *The New York Times* and *The Los Angeles Times*, led the way in expanding its range of supplements and liftouts so there was at least one for each day of the week. Pioneering market research for the newspaper identified various types of readers whose personal interests could be catered for by the smorgasbord of supplements. Other metro dailies followed suit. These days the breakdown of *The Age* is as follows: Monday, education; Tuesday, the computer industry and food; Wednesday, homes and personal investment; Thursday, motoring, television, radio and personal computers; and Friday, entertainment.

Compare *The Age* today with the paper 50 years ago and the first thing you notice is how much larger it is. The average weekday edition—64 pages—is thicker than the Saturday edition of 1956, and the present Saturday edition is around 340 pages including the colour magazine, *Good Weekend*. What is most striking is the space allocated to hard news is not much more than it was 50 years before, despite the fivefold increase in the paper's size. Much of that extra space has been taken up by advertising, but the rest is editorial space. The Melbourne newspaper is the most dramatic example of a trend that appears to have occurred across the country—bigger newspapers, more advertising, more analysis and more features, particularly lifestyle features. I say appears because no comprehensive study has been done.[7]

MAGAZINES

The magazine market in Australia is huge. Over 3000 titles are available in the $1.35 billion annual market, according to David Hogan, the national sales manager for distributor Gordon and Gotch. Per head, Australians read more magazines than any other nation in the world.[8] 'There is a magazine for everyone and nearly everyone reads magazines,' says the Magazine Publishers of Australia Association. 'No other medium caters for the variety of interests and activities the way magazines do.'[9] It is not an idle boast. There are 51 broad categories of magazines listed in the Newsagency Council's publication *Title Tracker* and they include the most visible, such as women's interests and health, but also less visible fields such as electronics and woodwork. There are hundreds of titles to choose from in the most popular categories: food and wine

(520); motoring and transport (315); home, decor and design (310), and sport (290). *New Idea* celebrated its 100th birthday in 2002 but the average magazine has the life cycle of the march fly. *Title Tracker* is published twice yearly but is out of date days after its release.

Many magazines are imported, so they are unavailable as potential employers to local journalists, but there are two large local magazines companies, Australian Consolidated Press, owned by Kerry Packer, and Pacific Publications, owned by Kerry Stokes' Seven Network. Between them they account for 25 of the top 40 bestselling Australian magazines sold in Australia.[10] There are also smaller magazine companies, such as Media Giants, which produces glossy publications for Australian Rules football clubs. Where newspapers are driven by news, magazines are driven to meet the needs and desires of their readership, though newspapers are about more than news, as we have seen, and numerous magazines contain news elements.

There are two newsmagazines in Australia, *The Bulletin* and *Time Australia*. There is a handful whose focus is current affairs, such as *Quadrant, Eureka Street* and *Dissent*. Women's magazines, such as *The Australian Women's Weekly*, once covered news diligently—during World War II the magazine's Tilly Shelton-Smith became the first Australian woman to cover the war in Singapore and Malaya[11]—but in the past 15 years or so these magazines have been best known for extraordinarily intrusive exposes of royal foibles and celebrity failings, some of which according to media commentator Mark Day are completely made up.[12]

In areas such as business, music, sport and science, there are magazines that run substantial news and features about the fields they cover. *Business Review Weekly* could be called a business news magazine. *New Scientist* covers science news comprehensively, making considerable effort to be understood by non-scientists. *Rolling Stone* has a strong reputation for cultural criticism. Daniel Johns of silverchair chose to reveal his struggles with depression and bulimia in the local edition of the magazine, which has been running in Australia for over 30 years. *Inside Sport* has run numerous excellent features by top-flight sportswriters such as Gideon Haigh and Daniel Williams, alongside its glossy picture spreads of even glossier uberbabes. The great majority of magazine titles are aimed at special interests; they might contain news but not news that offends their readership or questions the activity covered by the magazine. *Off Road* rarely confronts the environmental damage caused by four-wheel-drive vehicles; likewise, *Grass Roots* rarely eulogises the pleasures of petrol hedonism.

NEWS VALUES AND FEATURE VALUES

Do news values apply to feature stories? Mostly. It is important to understand that news and features are not different worlds but different approaches to the same world. The eight most commonly identified news values—impact, relevance, proximity, prominence, timeliness, conflict, currency and the unusual—are just that, values. News does not consist of immutable laws. Many find that confusing, but there is by no means universal agreement within newsrooms about the definition of news either. People wonder why a newspaper can devote a dozen pages to an AFL footballer's extra-marital affair as the *Herald Sun* did with Wayne Carey early in 2002. They wonder why Australian newspapers carried detailed coverage of the remarkable rescue of nine miners trapped underground in the United States but virtually ignored the death of eighteen miners in China on the same day.[13] News values apply most strongly to those features tied to the news of the day and least to those features that are not. Some news values apply to features, but not as rigidly as for news, and some features are published without any connection at all to the daily news agenda.

1. IMPACT

News that has a big impact is rare. As Graham Perkin, former editor of *The Age*, once said, an important story has its roots in the past and a stake in the future.[14] News of this scale prompts numerous features because it bursts the bounds of the daily news story. The Human Rights and Equal Opportunity Commission's 1997 report on the Stolen Generations of Aborigines, 'Bringing them Home', is an example. It was impossible to evaluate the report without understanding the history of black–white relations in Australia; it was important the report be absorbed before shaping new policies.

2. RELEVANCE

Two tasks of feature stories are to explain the news and to personalise abstract issues, so the relevance news value applies to many features. Background pieces are explicitly written to ensure the reader understands the relevance of an issue, whether as a citizen or as a consumer. A backgrounder on the importance of the vote for independence in East Timor in 1999 is an example of the former; 'The GST: how it will affect you' is an example of the latter. The raison d'être of lifestyle features is their relevance to the reader's life.

3. PROXIMITY

Feature stories can erase the importance of proximity as a news value because they use a palette of colours (emotion, context, atmosphere, analysis) rather than the black and white of information. Each day people die on the nation's roads; most are given modest space in newspapers. Yet a journalist who tells the full human story of just one car crash and its impact on family and friends can leap over standard news boundaries.

4. PROMINENCE

Prominence pays heed to the public's fascination with the rich and powerful, and the notorious, as shown by the public resurrection of convicted criminal Mark 'Chopper' Read into bestselling author. Many features, whether interview pieces or profiles, are about famous people, and many media commentators wonder whether prominence has become disproportionately important, a point made in the American satirical newspaper, *The Onion*, with the headline: 'The rich and famous: do we know enough about their lifestyles?'[15]

5. TIMELINESS

The urgency of printing news as soon as it comes to hand applies only partly to features. It does apply to news features where journalists sometimes need to turn around a piece inside a day but more commonly within three or four days in readiness for the weekend newspaper. Timeliness also applies to interview pieces linked to the interview subject's new movie/book/CD/show, even though it need not apply so strictly. Interview pieces are published just before or just as the new movie/book/CD/show is released, meaning readers cannot have experienced it. Readers may well be interested in a new Hollywood blockbuster before its release; they will be more interested to know all about the film and its making after they have seen it, but by that time the interview piece with, say, Keanu Reeves will be in the recycling bin. More precisely, readers will be interested to know more if the movie is any good.

And that is the point: for interview pieces, timeliness is not so much a news value as a public relations value.

Feature stories may be published that do not relate to the daily news agenda, though journalists and editors usually find a news peg on which to hang the feature, such as Anzac Day or Christmas or an Ashes cricket series. Lifestyle features about, say, the quest for the perfect chocolate mudcake, are written with no thought for the news agenda. It is possible to write a general feature story that pays no heed to time-liness but it needs something else if it is to win a place in a newspaper or magazine. Australian novelist Helen Garner has written pieces about her visits to the morgue and the crematorium that have no news value whatsoever but are compelling reading because the topic—death—is of universal interest and, more importantly, because they are superbly written.[16]

6. CONFLICT

Conflict, antagonism and tension are the stuff of human drama, and human drama is the stuff of news. It is also the stuff of feature stories, and it is given fuller rein in features. Conflict referred to cryptically in basic news stories can be mined in depth in a feature, as was exemplified in the bitter ructions within the Labor Party over Simon Crean's leadership in 2003. Sometimes conflict is presented in a two-dimensional way, as in a piece about the visiting American psychic/medium John Edward in *The Daily Telegraph*. The piece was broken into two sections, one written by a supporter, Kylie 'The truth is out there' Keogh, the other by a detractor, Naomi 'I want to believe' Toy.[17] Conflict can also be set in context and analysed from a range of perspectives, as in two lengthy news features published in *The Weekend Australian* about the dispute between historians over whether there was a policy of genocide against Tasmanian Aborigines. The dispute was sparked by publication of Keith Windschuttle's *The Fabrication of Aboriginal History*.[18]

7. CURRENCY

Feature stories come into their own with the news value currency. When, for whatever reason, a news event or issue gains currency, readers become more interested. They want to know the background to an event, they want to know who is this person suddenly catapulted onto the national stage. They want to know if this particular news event is a one-off or part of a pattern. All these elements offer scope for the feature writer. This phenomenon is easily seen at work in major news events, such as the massacre of 35 people at Port Arthur by Martin Bryant in 1996, but it applies to less dramatic news too. A feature about how to read companies' annual reports is scarcely edge of the seat material, but soon after the scandal surrounding the collapse of American energy giant Enron and its auditors, Arthur Andersen, in 2001, just such a feature appeared in the business pages of one daily paper. If you were ever going to read such a piece, that was the time.

8. THE UNUSUAL

It was John B. Bogart of *The New York Sun* who in the 19th century coined the pithy definition of news: 'It's not news if a dog bites a man, but if a man bites a dog, then it's news.'[19] News is about what is new and different; it is also about the quirky, the odd. This news value applies mostly to human interest features. A daily paper recently ran on its front page a touching story about the public's response to the death of a homeless man who lived and slept at a bus shelter outside St Vincent's Hospital in Sydney. Bouquets and cards were left at the shelter, mourning the loss of a man who would help passengers find the right bus and would tell St Vincent's staff about other homeless people who might have got into difficulty.[20]

DISCUSSION QUESTIONS AND EXERCISES

1. Write up an episode of your favourite sitcom, such as *The Simpsons* or *Malcolm in the Middle*, as a straight news story. How did you choose the most significant event? What was left out in rendering it as hard news?

2. Visit the state library and examine how the daily newspaper/s in your capital city and *The Australian Women's Weekly* presented news and features in the past. Take a sample of a week's newspapers and two magazines from each decade since the 1950s. How do they differ from today's media? Compare prose styles, type size, layout, headlines, use of pictures and other graphics.

2 THE VARIETY OF FEATURE STORIES

Columnists usually start out full of juice, sounding like terrific boulevardiers and raconteurs, retailing in print all the marvellous mots and anecdotes they have been dribbling away over lunch for the past few years. After eight or ten weeks, however, they start to dry up. You can see the poor bastards floundering and gasping. They're dying of thirst. They're out of material. They start writing about funny things that happened around the house the other day, homey one-liners that the Better Half or the Avon lady got off, or some fascinating book or article that started them thinking, or else something they saw on the TV. Thank God for the TV! Without television shows to cannibalise, half of these people would be lost, utterly catatonic. Pretty soon you can see it, the tubercular blue of the 23-inch screen, radiating from their prose.

Tom Wolfe

CHAPTER SUMMARY

The variety of feature stories is broken down into twelve categories. Each is briefly described and set in its context in Australian newspapers and magazines. The audience appeal of each category is outlined and the practice issues for journalists in each are sketched. It is questionable whether three of the categories should be defined as features, but they are included because they contain feature elements.

Journalists have long been expected to write about a wide variety of subjects and in the 21st century they are also expected to write a wide variety of feature articles, ranging from lifestyle pieces to news backgrounders to profiles to multi-part series. This applies as much to specialist journalists covering politics, sport, business or entertainment, though the emphasis may vary. Political correspondents write more news features than lifestyle pieces, while for journalists covering the entertainment industries the reverse is true. Is a column a feature? What about an interview piece, or a review?

Columns, interview pieces and reviews can be found in almost every newspaper and magazine, and more often than they were even a decade ago. Journalists are routinely assigned interview pieces, many clamour to review their favourite bands and many aspire to writing a column. A lot of people in the media industry argue they are not features—interview pieces are one-dimensional, columns are a person's opinion and reviews are criticism—and this is true, but all three sub-genres contain feature elements. They have been overlooked in most Australian texts, and the methods outlined in this book can be usefully applied to them. What follows is a breakdown of the twelve most common types of article falling within the broad church of features.

COLOUR STORY

Sometimes known as a scene or a slice-of-life piece, the colour story's purpose is to provide the atmosphere or 'feel' of an event. Where hard news is about information, colour is about emotion. Its scope is limited and it does not aim to provide a comprehensive picture of an issue or event, but colour stories are deceptively difficult to do well because so much depends on the journalist's ability to observe and describe. There are two types of colour story.

The first is written as an adjunct to a news story, usually an important news event. At a major criminal trial, a royal commission, or an Olympic Games, say, the day's news will be covered by one journalist while a second conveys the atmosphere of the day. The second journalist does not repeat any more news information than is necessary for their story; instead, the aim is to answer the question, what was it like to be there? They observe events closely and describe how people look, what they are wearing, byplay between participants in the news event, dialogue and so on. If space is tight, the colour story will be dropped and only the news story run. The trial for war crimes of deposed Serbian leader, Slobodan Milosevic, was covered exhaustively in the world news pages. On 13 July 2002 *The Weekend Australian* magazine ran a piece in its 'Dispatches' column by Tracy Sutherland, which showed that far from being remorseful, Milosevic conducted his own defence in a theatrical and aggressively manipulative way, a picture difficult to convey in straight news.

The second kind of colour story contains no news at all. It wins a place in the paper purely on the strength of the atmosphere described. A journalist covering the magistrate's court might or might not find news to report, but on any given day they could give readers a sense of the everyday reality of the court by observing and describing the variety of cases, and the sort of people who find themselves in court and on what charges. They are offering a slice of life that the reader may well have not experienced. A variation of this is to squeeze the atmospheric juice from an undersized news event. Melissa Fyfe managed just that in her piece about the premiere of a Hollywood movie in Sydney. As news, it was gossamer thin—Hollywood stars walk along red carpet into cinema—but as colour, the attendance of stars Tom Cruise and Penelope Cruz and the absence of the former Mrs Cruise, Nicole Kidman, had possibilities that Fyfe wittily exploited, providing a mock breathless report on the all important question of whether Tom is taller than Penelope and whether Penelope is more beautiful than 'our Nicole'.[1]

HUMAN INTEREST STORY

When people think of feature stories, most often they are thinking of human interest features—ripping yarns of lost adventurers or cute tales of dogs who have lost their tails. That is fine; readers have always been fascinated by such stories. As with colour stories, human interest features are about emotion first and information second. As with colour stories, they don't provide a comprehensive picture of an event or an issue. Human interest stories are easier to write than colour stories—as long as you have a feel for people. There are two types of human interest stories.

The first clusters around dramatic events, such as Australian teenager Jesse Martin's record-breaking solo voyage around the world in 1999 or the remarkable rescue of Stuart Diver, 66 hours after he was buried alive at Thredbo in 1997. These are not everyday events fortunately, but the human thirst for intense emotion is slaked by sport, where triumphs and tragedies unfold weekly on the (relative) safety of the playing field. Examples abound, but recall the image of marathon walker Jane Saville's anguished face when she was disqualified within sight of the finish line and an Olympic gold medal in Sydney. Subsequently, she won Commonwealth Games gold in Manchester to, at least partly, put the nightmare behind her—and us.

The second kind of human interest feature taps less dramatic but similarly affecting material. Just as colour stories can mine the everyday, so do these types of stories, such as Chris Tatman's piece about a mother who lost a child soon after he was born with malformed internal organs, then gave birth to a disabled girl. Suburban newspapers do not run many features but this one in *The Bayside Advertiser* was simply written and it evoked a stronger response from readers than anything Tatman had written over a decade in local newspapers.[2] Robyn Riley wrote about a nine-year-old English boy with a rare brain tumour whose family flew him to Australia so he could have an operation pioneered at Melbourne's Alfred Hospital. The continual seizures Sebastian Selo suffered had prevented him from taking part in normal childhood activities. Riley's first story for the *Sunday Herald Sun* focused on 'the miracle operation', after which she was able to gain an interview with the family.[3] *The Weekly Times* is a well-established paper for country readers; it carried a story by Sandra Godwin about the plight of a dairy farming couple who had spent days searching for more than 80 top milking cows that had vanished from their Murrabit property. The couple had been planning to retire and had leased their farm to a company for a year before selling it. When they found the cows missing a dispute broke out that would probably end up in court.[4]

NEWS FEATURE

Probably the most common kind of feature story in newspapers, the news feature begins with the news of the day and develops it, either by explaining the meaning of the news or examining its implications. News features are written quickly, putting pressure on the journalists to convey more to the reader than a hard news story. For instance, when the second Gulf War ended in 2003, most daily newspapers swiftly provided news features asking how Iraq would be rebuilt, and whether the war would bring peace and democracy to the Middle East or plunge it into further war. Such pieces are usually written by specialist reporters because they require knowledge, good contacts and speed.

Most metro daily papers carry news features on weekends, and some have sections devoted to them with titles like 'Inquirer' (*The Weekend Australian*), or 'Inside Edition' (*The Daily Telegraph*), or 'Saturday Forum' (*The Canberra Times*) or 'Inside Mail' (*The Courier-Mail*). These sections are well read; weekend papers sell around one and a half times as many copies as weekdays papers, and *The Weekend Australian* more than doubles that paper's Monday to Friday circulation. Many readers struggle to find time to keep up with news daily and welcome articles summarising and explaining news events, a trend cemented with the arrival of the *Editor* section in *The Weekend Australian*. This is particularly true with court cases and royal commissions, which are usually long-running, complicated and written in the cryptic language of court reports. The royal commission into the collapse of the HIH insurance company in 2001 and the various parliamentary inquiries into the so-called 'children overboard affair', where the federal government was shown to have lied about whether asylum seekers threw their children off boats when confronted by the Australian navy, are two such examples.

Some newspapers have realised that to capture the attention of media-rich but time-poor readers they need to do more, not less. *The Age* rethought its coverage of the federal budget; for years it provided saturation coverage of the annual event but budgets are particularly impervious to explanation, not to mention readability. For its 2002 supplement *The Age* broke down the budget into portfolios (defence, health, education, etc.), then provided three articles per page about each portfolio. The first, labelled 'In context', explained the situation before the budget. The second reported the contents of the budget, and the third was an analysis by the newspaper's relevant roundsperson.

Sometimes newspapers provide news features in anticipation of events, such as a royal commission into police corruption in Western Australia.[5] Finally, a news feature may explore the implications of the news of the day. When Prime Minister John Howard celebrated his 63rd birthday he appeared at the peak of his political power; he had won a third term of office and the Labor opposition was floundering. Experienced political journalist, Mike Steketee, contrasted this with what he portrayed as the decrepit organisation of the Liberal Party at local branch level.[6]

BACKGROUNDER

A variation of the news feature, the backgrounder recognises that some news events and issues need to be explained to readers either because they are inherently complicated, because their significance is linked to past events, or because before the news broke no one had heard of them. An example of the first would be a major scientific breakthrough, such as the human genome project, or a change in Australia's labyrinthine superannuation laws. An example of the second was the war in Kosovo in 1999, which could not be understood without knowledge about the history of the break-up (and creation, for that matter) of the former Yugoslavia. An example of the third was the collapse of WorldCom in 2002. Few people outside the United States knew much about the Mississippi-based telecommunications company before its bosses committed a multi-billion dollar fraud. The English news magazine, *The Week*, chose to feature WorldCom's woes in its excellent briefing page, backgrounding the issue of the week, on 6 July 2002, providing answers to the questions on everybody's lips:

What is WorldCom? How was WorldCom able to grow so big? Why did things start to go wrong? and so on.

To succeed, a backgrounder must be clear and concise. This applies to all journalism, but is especially important in backgrounders because their implicit promise to the reader is to make the complicated simple. For this reason, most backgrounders are written by experienced journalists familiar with the topic at hand. Backgrounders used to be written in the form of a background briefing, but these days the question and answer form is common. The Internet, with its FAQs (frequently asked questions), has made this form popular; likewise, there are series of books that openly, even humorously, acknowledge we are drowning in information and need summaries to stay on top of subjects. These series have titles like *K.I.S.S* (keep it simple, stupid). Many deal with the arcane, such as *Lacan for Beginners*, but increasingly titles cover mundane topics, a trend epitomised by the appearance of *The Idiot's Guide to Pro Wrestling.*

LIFESTYLE FEATURE

Probably the fastest growing kind of feature, and the best place to break into the industry for freelancers, lifestyle pieces are 'news you can use'. They used to be known as service stories. News features revolve around conflict, or at least contention; lifestyle features provide entertaining information about life and how to live it more comfortably. Lifestyle features used to be the province of magazines but with the mushrooming growth of sections and supplements in newspapers, they are found in both print media. Subject matter ranges from the (literally) light and frothy—where to find the city's finest cafe latte—to critical household issues—should I buy a house or continue to rent? Subject matter is familiar to the readership, in contrast to much straight news, which zeroes in on the extraordinary rather than the ordinary (disasters, war, resignations, etc.). But the lifestyle feature must still offer readers something new. A piece about a day in the life of an airport arrival and departure lounge is familiar to most but will not deliver anything new or useful to readers no matter how well it is written.[7]

Lifestyle features are well read because they deliver information relevant to people's everyday lives in an entertaining way, and because they offer the simple pleasure of escapism. Many journalists lament the rise of lifestyle features, saying they are vehicles to deliver advertising revenue to companies hurt by falling circulation and they erode space for 'real' news. Others say modern readers are weary of being told what they should be interested in by crusty old editors and welcome information helpful for daily living. Contrary to what some journalists think, entertainment has always been a part of newspapers, not to mention magazines; it is also true that lifestyle journalism is fuelled by a media company's commercial needs. It is rare for a lifestyle feature in, say, the fashion page to question the industry it covers, but not unprecedented. Sharon Krum wrote a feature about a protest against the craze led by pop singer Britney Spears for blonde hair, bare midriff, skimpy shorts and halter tops. The protest was led by a group of teenage girls in Mesa, Arizona, who 'felt pressured by the MTV culture to become highly sexualised'.[8]

The real concern about lifestyle journalism is not its existence, but whether its growth is at the expense of investigative journalism. Again, no comprehensive data is available but journalists are as prone to the myth of the Golden Age as any group, perhaps more so, as English scribe Francis Wheen discovered when he re-read G.K. Chesterton's autobiography, which lamented the demise of 'ragged pressmen' wandering between pub and office and bemoaned the new quiet, businesslike newspaper office—in 1936.[9] If it is fair to observe that lifestyle supplements generate lots of revenue and few lawsuits while investigative journalism offers the reverse, it is equally fair to observe that there is still much more investigative journalism in newspapers today than there was in the 1950s.

There are three main types of lifestyle feature. The first revolves around a list, the second an issue and the third an idea. An example of the first, from *The Guardian* in England, was a test of 21 home hair-removal products, organised under categories such as price, pros, cons, technical data and score. Accompanying the piece were frequently asked questions, viz., 'How can I reduce the pain of waxing or epilating'. (Answer, for those interested: Take a warm bath beforehand and be sure to thoroughly towel off before doing the business.)[10]

Where the first type of lifestyle feature is aimed at the reader as consumer, the second picks up an issue in the news and presents it in an unthreatening way. It may be a routine news issue, such as a report on child care, which *Who Weekly* presented through the eyes of four different types of families, but it can also be a highly charged issue, such as Islam in Australia, which was seen from the perspectives of a Muslim family, a convert and a student in a double-page spread in the 'Life' section of *The Courier-Mail*.[11] Also included was a breakout box with facts and myths about Islam.

An example of the third type of lifestyle feature was a piece from the 'Weekend' section of the *Herald Sun*, about what makes a hit single, featuring interviews with Vika and Linda Bull, Shane Howard, Russell Morris and Ross Wilson.[12] The piece was idea driven but still familiar and unthreatening to readers.

TRAVEL STORIES

The idea of being paid to write about an overseas trip is nirvana to most journalists, which is why such assignments are sought after and why the best place to start is local travel. The same applies to freelance journalists, unless they happen to be travelling overseas; then it makes sense to talk to a travel editor and see if they might be interested in a story. As a genre travel writing has become popular; Bill Bryson, Tim Parks and Pico Iyer are well-known names. They are all talented and experienced writers. Travel writing these days is as much about the writer's internal journey as the actual trip, according to Ian Jack, the editor of *Granta*, the English magazine renowned for its travel writing.[13]

Travel sections have long been a staple of newspapers and there are around 50 travel and tourism magazines available in Australia. The great majority of features in travel sections are lifestyle pieces aimed at providing consumer information about travel destinations—where to go, how much will it cost, do they speak English—or providing a luxuriating read about an exotic location, accompanied by a luscious photo spread. Some newspapers, such as *The Sydney Morning Herald*, also provide columns with industry insider tips and invite readers to share their travel experiences, good and bad. *The Australian* asks its foreign correspondents to file colour stories for the 'Dispatches' column in its colour magazine and offbeat pieces for the 'Worldview' pages in its Monday edition.

The editorial integrity of travel sections has been clouded by the extent to which the travel industry underwrites journalists' travel, which was highlighted in the cash-for-comment scandal of 1999–2000. This began as an exposé of radio talkback king John Laws' habit of disguising paid advertisements as editorial comment but spread to newspaper travel sections. Since then some newspapers, such as *The Sydney Morning Herald*, have a policy of paying for travel, while others, such as *The Advertiser* in Adelaide, still accept courtesy flights but print a disclosure at the end of the article.

GENERAL FEATURE

There is some overlap between this and other categories, but it is worth plucking out the feature not driven by the daily news agenda but not necessarily soufflé light. From the outside it can be hard to distinguish these features in newspapers because the journalist or the editor will try and find a news peg on which to hang them. Travelling to work a journalist may have noticed teenage boys train surfing so then decides to investigate this social phenomenon, where people ride on top of train carriages, sometimes with fatal results. This story will take time to research. The editor may decide to run the story as soon as it is finished or may wait until a news development, such as another death or a community leader's call for a government inquiry. If the latter occurs, it would be easy to label the piece a news feature, but that would obscure the vital role played by journalists alert to potential stories.

News features win a place in the paper through their connection to the news, while general features must have intrinsic interest. For instance, Vanessa Walker told the story of an Albanian man who migrated to Australia in 1949 aged seventeen with few English language skills. He was admitted to a New South Wales psychiatric hospital for reasons that remain unclear; experts told Walker that in the 1950s it was far easier to admit people than it is today. Bexhet Hoxhaj's inability to speak English and the carelessness of officials conspired to imprison him in various hospitals for the next 50 years, effectively ruining his life.[14] The story of this lost migrant was poignant—I have not mentioned the efforts to reunite him with his family in Albania—and it raised questions about bureaucratic systems. Many general features do not contain such compelling material. An editor may ask a journalist to write an overview of an industry or issue. At *Time Australia* magazine in 1992, the then editor, Michael Gawenda, asked me to do a cover story on Australians' eating habits—and that's about as general as it gets—and the story duly ran.

Anniversaries are the oft-used—and flimsy—news peg for many general features, whether for annual events that loom large in the national psyche (Anzac Day) or as a means of revisiting an issue (the February 2003 issue of *The Australian Women's Weekly* devoted six pages to the 20th anniversary of the Ash Wednesday bushfires). There is nothing inherently wrong with a general overview or an anniversary piece, but many journalists forget that the absence of a strong news rationale actually puts them under more pressure to unearth interesting material.

INTERVIEW PIECE

Interview pieces are confined to an interview, often with a celebrity. The piece is not developed beyond that. In their simplest form they are run as a Q&A; that is, questions followed by the answers. The virtue of this form is that people can read the subject's own words; the vice lies in the form's laziness. Few people are endlessly quotable; nowhere is this clearer than in post-game interviews with stumble-tongued footballers. Even the virtue of the Q&A is outshone on television. It remains a journalistic staple, though, because it is so quick and easy to do.

Former footballer Peter 'Crackers' Keenan did a Q&A with one-time Collingwood ruckman, Damian Monkhorst, in his column in *The Geelong Advertiser* on 13 July 2002 while in the same paper on the same day Sally Stratton conducted a Q&A with former Boyzone star Ronan Keating. Where the latter interview was driven by an event—a new CD—others are designed to be quirky. The most famous Q&A of this kind is *Desert Island Discs*, a long-running feature on English radio where the guest is asked to nominate which records (that's how old it is) or books they would take if they were castaways. More promising, *The Sydney Morning Herald* runs each Saturday an interview with a prominent person on the premise, 'If I had one year to live'. It is possible to provide fascinating reading through Q&A interviews but it requires either a quirky idea or thorough research and smart questioning. *Rolling Stone* and *Playboy* interviews were renowned for these reasons.

You cannot make friends with the rock stars. If you're going to be a true journalist, a rock journalist, first you never get paid much, but you will get free records from the record company. God it's going to get ugly, man. They're going to buy you drinks. You're going to meet girls. They're going to fly you places for free, and offer you drugs. I know it sounds great but these people are not your friends. These are people who want you to write sanctimonious stories about the genius of rock stars. And they will ruin rock 'n' roll and strangle everything we love about it, right? And then it just becomes an industry of cool. You have to make your reputation on being honest and unmerciful.

Philip Seymour Hoffman, playing legendary rock critic Lester Bangs in *Almost Famous*

The next step up from this is to integrate the interview into a piece that has an engaging lead and describes the subject. The vast majority of such interview pieces are predicated on the release of a new CD/book/film/exhibition/opera/tour, etc. The journalist should research the subject before the interview but the pressure of time may hinder this as the majority of interview pieces are run in supplements, which are usually short-staffed. The interview piece is only marginally less lazy than the Q&A and these days it is primarily an extension of the PR industry, which not only coordinates national publicity tours for pop stars such as Ronan Keating, but deftly controls journalists' access to interviewees and the questions they will ask, as was satirised in the 2002 film *America's Sweethearts* starring Billy Crystal and Catherine Zeta-Jones. As with Q&A, it is possible to make interview pieces sing but again it takes strong research and questioning. Perhaps the best known exponent of the probing interview piece is English journalist Lynn Barber.[15]

PROFILE

The profile is one of the most popular kinds of features. As a journalistic form it was invented by *The New Yorker* magazine in the late 1920s to offer an arch, sidelong perspective of a subject, but the magazine's writers soon extended the form to mini-biographies that were exhaustively researched and elegantly written.[16] The profile distinguishes itself from the interview piece by providing a range of perspectives on the subject. To do it well, a profile writer also requires sound judgement of people, which means profiles tend to be done by more experienced journalists. The most common type of profile is of well-known people, mostly politicians, business leaders, sportspeople, criminals, actors, writers and musicians. The impetus for the piece is either a fresh achievement (or infamy for criminals), such as scientist Peter Doherty winning the Nobel Prize. Probably the most accomplished profile writer in Australia is David Leser, best known for his thoroughly researched and sharply written portraits of powerful figures such as radio shock jock Alan Jones, but he has also written lighter pieces, like one about the fantastically powerful figure of Xena, warrior princess, aka Lucy Lawless.

Sometimes an interesting public figure is publicity shy. The journalist may persuade them to be interviewed but if unsuccessful must choose between abandoning the story or writing what is known as a hostile profile, the equivalent of an unauthorised biography. The best known unauthorised biography in Australia actually began life as a hostile profile. Paul Barry released *The Rise and Rise of Kerry Packer* despite legal threats from the Packer camp; before that he had profiled Australia's richest man for ABC TV's *Four Corners* (profiles can be done in broadcast media too) and had likewise received no cooperation from his subject.

Not all profiles spring from a person's achievements or notoriety. Some aim to portray a particular job or group of people, one of whom is chosen as representative. War veterans are one such group and four days before one Anzac Day, John Hamilton told the story in the *Herald Sun* of 27-year-old Lieutenant Edward Henty, who died in the famous charge at the Nek at Gallipoli in World War I. The individual details of Henty's life were given full weight, but he was one of thousands who died in the war. The reader was implicitly being asked to allow his story to stand for them all.[17]

INVESTIGATIVE FEATURE

Investigative features are rare and like most investigative work are written by experienced journalists. Known as 'big hit' pieces in the industry, they win awards and make a major impact both on readers and those written about. An investigative feature places as much weight on news as on storytelling. Indeed, an investigative feature will have failed if it does not contain revelations. Sometimes newspapers will run a news story at the front and point to the feature inside. Much of the newsworthy information will be repeated inside but the feature's job is to set this information in context. For instance, Keith Moor wrote a three-part series in the *Herald Sun* about how Crown Casino courts high rollers and how it paid a triad gang boss $2.5 million while he was running an international drug trafficking business from suites in the casino's hotel. Each day there was a news story accompanied by a double-page spread containing two or more features.[18]

Other investigative features may not contain the kind of explosive relevations that Moor's did, but still contain revelatory material that is the result of solid investigative work. For instance, Pamela Williams of *The Financial Review* was given permission to be inside the Liberal Party's campaign headquarters throughout the 1996 federal election campaign. This was a rare opportunity—politicians are patrolled by a phalanx of image-makers and spin doctors—that produced a four-part series and was later expanded into book form.[19]

The strength of the investigative feature—it wraps the bite of revelation in a good read—is also its weakness, or at least its danger, as was well illustrated in Andrew Rule's story in *The Age* alleging that Geoff Clark, the chair of the Aboriginal and Torres Strait Islander Commission, had committed multiple rapes—an allegation Clark vehemently denied. The article was caught between being a profile and a news story. Allegations of rape are difficult to contain in a profile, which is usually written in narrative form. Originally, Rule wrote an accompanying news story containing the allegations. The news piece did not appear, however, because the editor believed it unnecessarily duplicated material in the profile, which he described not as a profile but a 'context news story'. The news story instead ran in *The Warrnambool Standard*, an affiliated paper in Clark's home town.[20]

Fellow Fairfax paper, *The Sydney Morning Herald*, ran the Rule story but removed the original feature-style lead to the article. It was an anecdote about another incident that cast Clark's character in a poor light; in the context of the rape allegations this lead came across as a personal dig at him. These questions, and others, such as the need for fuller disclosure about the detailed processes by which Rule investigated and the newspaper verified the women's accusations, do not negate the story's value but they did send readers misleading cues. To some these questions seem academic but matters of presentation, tone and style are important in investigative features because the stakes are so much higher than in standard daily journalism, and any error or misjudgement is magnified. These matters accounted for at least part of the controversy surrounding publication of Rule's article.

COLUMNS

In this celebrity-studded age it should not be surprising that columnists are the stars of print media, displacing foreign correspondents. A good columnist brings knowledge, wit and personality to their publication. Readers develop a relationship with them, as they do with radio presenters. Bad columnists, and sadly there are many, inflame prejudices rather than inspire debate. Charles Moore, editor of *The Daily Telegraph* in London, once observed that to write a successful column 'one was obliged not just to express an opinion but to shout it', which is why most columns are puffed with a certain theatricality that suffers from the law of diminishing returns.[21] As with lifestyle journalism, the question to ask is whether the number of columnists is growing at the expense of investigative or public service journalism. As before, there is no solid data.

There are five main varieties of columns. First, there are service and advice columns about gardening, beauty, travel, health, personal finance, pets, relationships, etc., usually written by well-known experts, such as veterinarian Dr Katrina Warren (from the TV program *Harry's Practice*) in *New Idea*. Within the column category, these equate to lifestyle features—same topics, same emphasis on meeting the reader's needs and desires. Second, there are gossip columnists, like Ros Reines at *The Sunday Telegraph*, and social diarists, like Lillian Frank at the *Herald Sun*. The latter trade in who has been seen with whom, the former in who's up who, and who is paying the rent. Composed of brief items, these columns are not features but do need smart, snappy writing. Lawrence Money's 'Spy' column in *The Sunday Age* has a lexicon of catchphrases for luminaries; the seasonally-sacked radio and TV star Derryn Hinch is called 'The Great Unwatched'.

The third category is the pundit, a Hindi word meaning learned and skilled; these days it is applied to senior newspaper people who pronounce regularly on any and every issue. Such columnists express their views freely and forcibly; readers want to know their opinion on an issue. Feature stories give journalists more scope to express themselves but it is still rare for a feature writer to express their opinion openly; the story, not them, remains the focus. Good pundits have strong followings and apply broad general knowledge and experience to the issues of the day. It has been forgotten that it was a columnist, Pamela Bone, who first drew public attention to the apparent anti-Semitism and slipshod historical research in the Miles Franklin award-winning novel, *The Hand that Signed the Paper*, by Helen Demidenko—later revealed as Helen Darville.[22]

Often, though, pundits are little more than crude opinion-mongers or, what Westbrook Pegler, himself a columnist, once described as, 'the deep-thinking, hair-trigger columnist who knows all the answers just offhand and can settle great affairs with absolute finality three or even six days a week'.[23] Their arrogance extends to their disdain for research, let alone getting out of the office to do any on-the-ground reporting work. P.P. McGuinness, the editor of *Quadrant*, has written columns for many newspapers over many years. He presents himself as a gadfly, fearlessly challenging received wisdom, but under pressure of time and the need to fill space, this has become a pose, a contrived contrariness. As issues arise in the news, McGuinness punches out formulaic opinions. Other well-known pundits include Piers Akerman (*The Daily Telegraph*), Andrew Bolt (*Herald Sun*), Peter Charlton (*The Courier-Mail*), Miranda Devine (*The Sydney Morning Herald*), Robert Manne (*The Age*) and Brian Toohey (*The Financial Review*).

Why do I have all these columnists? I have political columnists, guest columnists, celebrity columnists. The only thing I don't have is a dead columnist. You know what every columnist at this paper needs to do? Shut—the—fuck—up.

Robert Duvall, playing a managing editor in *The Paper*

The fourth category is growing faster than the Alien—the personal columnist. They may comment on the news of the day but more likely will regale you with the latest chapter in the dog-eared book of their life. Like pundits, they gain loyal readerships (including those who love to hate them), but where the former focus on the public world the latter turn their gaze inward. Good personal columnists are a delight to read; some still remember Charmian Clift's pioneering columns for *The Sydney Morning Herald* in the 1960s, which in 2001 were edited and re-released by her biographer, Nadia Wheatley, while others fondly recall Kaz Cooke's 'Keep yourself nice' columns of the early 1990s.

More recently, many find Danny Katz's columns in the Fairfax papers VERY FUNNY.

Many journalists are attracted to the prospect of personal columns; there is no messy research and you can say whatever you like about a topic you find endlessly fascinating—yourself. Tread carefully. Personal columns are deceptively difficult. Just as clowns may be the most skilled acrobats in the circus, so writing about your travails in an amusing or engaging way requires not less but more skill than the average news story. In the 1990s in England personal columns written by young women became staggeringly popular, epitomised by Helen Fielding whose column 'Bridget Jones's Diary' became a book then a movie.

Zoe Heller, who wrote one of these 'girl columns' for *The Sunday Times*, has reflected on her experience, beginning by outlining the three categories:

> There is the good-humoured 'home front' column in which a woman writes in a jolly, eye-rolling way about her accident-prone kids and lazy husband. ('Mum—Johnny's stuck a marble up his nose!') There is the stern comment piece, in which public affairs are examined from an admonitory, feminist point of view. ('When was the last time the Foreign Secretary changed a nappy?') And then there is the daffy 'girl' piece, in which a youngish single female confides the vagaries of her rackety personal life. ('Never try shaving your legs in a moving taxi.')[24]

In the end, Heller found the experience dispiriting. Writing a personal column from 'the female perspective' trapped her in a gender cage and reduced her to wrenching more and more tawdry details from her personal life to feed the media maw. She concluded it was far preferable to seek 'the wide open spaces and the simple pleasures of writing as a human'.

The fifth and final columnist is the specialist called on to write about a particular issue. Such columns are analogous to news features. They are prompted by a news event; they add expert knowledge and comment. These columnists stand a chance of not running out of steam because they write when they feel they have something to say and because most specialists are continually learning new things about their field. Not surprisingly, many specialist columnists are academics, such as international relations lecturer Scott Burchill who wrote several columns about the war in Afghanistan post-September 11 and the campaign against Saddam Hussein. The drawback is that many academics find it difficult to respond quickly and condense their knowledge into a readable 800-word opinion piece, as illustrated by the lead for an article about schools by educational psychologist Herb Marsh that appeared in *The Sydney Morning Herald*.[25]

> Entry into an academically selective school is an educational achievement that is highly valued by students and their parents. It is widely believed that selective schools will automatically advantage students in a wide array of academic outcomes; that putting together the brightest students encourages them to perform to their best. However, despite an almost complete lack of research by the NSW Education Department, there is some evidence to refute this.

... Sorry, I nodded off there for a while. An important topic, no question, but little thought has been given to the reader. The lead for an opinion piece can and should engage the reader's attention. Here is the 'Media' column in *Australian Book Review*, following a call by the Australian Broadcasting Authority head, David Flint, to abolish the cross-media ownership laws on the astonishing ground that the greatest influence on the media today is not media proprietors but journalists. The column began:

> There are watchdogs and there are lapdogs. Watchdogs are alert. At the slightest movement, they growl. When they bite it hurts. Lapdogs are alert—to their master's moods. At the slightest movement they yap. When they bite it tickles.[26]

It is more readable because the language is simple yet rhythmical. It also creates a sense of expectation by not referring to Professor Flint immediately.

REVIEWS

Reviews contain just as much opinion as columns but do not have the same profile because reviews do not exist without something to review—columnists, you may have noticed, can fill entire columns with the difficulties they faced filling their column. There are review sections in all metropolitan papers and specialist magazines devoted to literature, film, theatre, music, dance and art. Many reviewers are specialists in their field, working either as practitioners or in universities, but others are staff journalists with an interest and, it is hoped, a knowledge of the artform. A handful of reviewers become big names, usually because they treat reviewing as a blood sport. It is selfless work. At the other end of the spectrum is the equally poisonous problem of friends saying nice things about friends in reviews, partly because of the small number of Australian artists and partly because it seems endemic to public discussion of the arts. Many journalists want to review, particularly music, which they see as poorly served by the dinosaurs running the arts pages. Fair enough, but remember the advice legendary rock critic Lester Bangs gave Cameron Crowe in the movie *Almost Famous*: 'You cannot make friends with the rock stars ... You have to make your reputation on being honest and unmerciful.'

At its root the review is a piece of service journalism, informing people about which movies, say, have opened and whether they are worth seeing. They differ from previews and interview pieces in that the review is an independent assessment, which is its appeal and challenge. It is always and only one person's assessment. Reviewers should remember a few other tips: do not give away the ending, and make sure you actually read the book or attend the play. Sounds basic, but you would be surprised how often it does not happen. Equally important, a review should be entertaining as well as informative. It is not a university essay, though it covers similar terrain. It is essential to give the reader a clear idea of what the artist set out to do and whether, in your assessment, they succeeded. Whatever assessment is made should be supported by examples and evidence. In other words, it is not enough to simply say the band was crap. And remember, you might join a band yourself one day and suffer the ill-informed criticism of a pimply-faced prat.

DISCUSSION QUESTIONS AND EXERCISES

1. Buy three metro daily newspapers and three magazines (or look at them in your local library) and try and pick out examples of the different kinds of features. Justify your labelling by listing the defining elements of the various types of feature.

2. Using the same newspapers and magazines, see if some categories of features overlap. Do the twelve categories listed in the chapter cover all types of feature stories? If not, how would you characterise those stories?

3. CROSSING THE BRIDGE FROM MEDIA CONSUMER TO MEDIA PRACTITIONER

Journalists belong in the gutter because that is where the ruling classes throw their dirty secrets.

Gerald Priestland

The truth isn't always beautiful, but the hunger for it is.

Nadine Gordimer

CHAPTER SUMMARY

A valuable first step in learning how to write features is to analyse published pieces paragraph by paragraph. In this chapter two feature stories, one from a Melbourne tabloid, the other from a Sydney broadsheet, are reprinted and analysed. A second, equally powerful, tool is to learn the story behind a story's creation. These are provided by the two journalists who wrote the two feature stories discussed.

Is there anything easier in this world than criticising the media? Just throw a rock in the air and you'll hit something guilty, either a factual mistake, a typo or a beat-up.[1] It couldn't be hard to do a better job than the average hack, could it? Well, yes, it could, but few see that until they have tried for themselves, just as few journalists appreciate it is harder to run the nation than it is to tee off on the politicians who do. As one wag put it: 'All editorial writers ever do is come down from the hills after the battle is over and bayonet the wounded.'

If you want to write feature stories, though, it is essential to cross the bridge from being a consumer of the media to a practitioner; that is, get out of the armchair and have a go yourself. The same applies to news journalists being asked to write features; their information gathering and reporting muscles are well developed, their storytelling muscles less so. A good starting point is to rigorously analyse features paragraph by paragraph, asking these three questions:

- What works in the feature story, and why?
- What does not work in the feature story, and why not?
- How exactly would you improve the story, if you were doing it?

It might seem excessive to analyse a humble piece of journalism paragraph by paragraph; isn't this what literary critics call practical criticism, and isn't it more usually lavished on the epic poetry of John

Milton and his ilk? It is, which is why it is such a powerful tool. Literary criticism has changed too since I.A. Richards wrote *Practical Criticism* in 1929. Today's literary critic spends as much time watching *The Simpsons* as Shakespeare. By paying close attention to exactly how a piece of journalism works (or doesn't), you will begin to see what is required to do journalism. You will begin to see certain common ways of capturing the reader's attention, of organising the material so that it flows, and certain logjams that crop up in features. This is practical criticism of a practical kind. The third question is the hardest to answer. It is the question literary critics rarely consider, but it is the key one for a practitioner.

With this in mind, let's look at two common or garden features. In a book format, the text of the article can be reprinted, but not how it appeared in the newspaper or magazine, or if it is, only in condensed form. That does not mean these matters are unimportant. It is essential to analyse how an article was placed because much as writers hate to admit it, readers do not turn instantly to the words. They look at other things first such as:

- Who published the feature story, and what is their audience? *The Financial Review* is not the same as *The Gold Coast Bulletin*. Nor are people reading *Home and Garden* flipping through *Australian Bride* for the same reasons.
- Is the story accompanied by pictures? Are they effective? Do the captions draw the reader to the story?
- Is the story laid out well on the page? Is the headline appealing; does it match the story? Does the precede or standfirst that sits just below the headline entice you into the story?
- Are there breakout boxes or breakout quotes or other design features? Are they effective?

If all these elements are inviting, then the reader will start reading the story.

ANALYSIS: FEATURE STORY ONE

This piece was published in the *Weekend* magazine of the *Herald Sun* on Saturday 3 October 1998 and was written by Fiona Hudson, who has since become the paper's city editor. It is just under 1200 words.

BLAZING A TRAIL

[Precede] In the wilds of Wilsons Promontory, a group of men are building a track the hard way. Fiona Hudson and photographer Rob Baird hiked for hours to find them.

[1] A trail of pink ribbons is the first sign of life on the remote track. Flapping in blustery winds blowing off a restless Bass Strait, the ribbons carry neat markings in black texta: 100m. 200m. 300m.

[2] The fluorescent bows beckon onwards into the rugged Wilsons Promontory bush.

[3] 1400m. 1500m. 1600m.

[4] Through ferny glades and across trickling creeks.

[5] 2800m. 2900m. 3000m.

[6] Up steep, forested hills, along boulder-strewn stretches, and through muddy patches. Further, higher.

[7] 5200m. 5300m. 5400m.

[13] Their task is to forge a controversial seven-kilometre walking track through pristine bush from the Prom's lighthouse to Waterloo Bay on the south-east coast—by hand.

[14] "Welcome to the cutting edge," grins one of the whiskery men. He introduces himself as "Snapper" Hughes, the unofficial leader of this group of "trackies"—people who build or repair bush walking tracks.

[15] Parks Victoria have hired the six-man trackie crew—all from Tasmania—to carve this $260,000 track.

[16] As pioneers through virgin bush, the work Snapper and his crew are doing

"Welcome to the cutting edge," grins one of the whiskery men.

[8] One foot in front of the other we squelch. Pink ribbon after pink ribbon.

[9] And then, a tent, pitched in the bushes beside the gravel-smattered track. A stack of unwashed pots guards the door, but there's no one inside.

[10] 5900m. 6000m. 6100m.

[11] More tents, all empty. From ahead voices waft back along the track, and suddenly, we're upon them.

[12] The six men seem momentarily startled for a second to see human faces. And not surprisingly—they've been isolated here at the bottom of mainland Australia for five months.

is "cutting edge". The tools they are using certainly aren't.

[17] Trackie Colin Bradshaw is levering a lump of granite into position with a crowbar. Further along the shoulder-width trail, Richard Chin is wrestling a tree stump with a small hand-winch.

[18] Other tools strewn about include picks, mattocks, sledgehammers, secateurs and a wheelbarrow.

[19] "The more hand tools we use, the better the job," says Snapper. "We're handcraftsmen . . . and we want to do as little damage as possible."

[20] The art, fellow trackie Andrew Ferguson chips in, is to build a track people don't really notice.

[21] "The real skill in trackwork is disguise," he says. "You don't just cut a straight swathe through the bush—it has to be very carefully planned."

[22] The crew laughingly recall a recent visit from "head office". Crossing a creek on moss-covered, boulder-sized stepping stones, a "suit" said, "You were lucky to find those ones in place."

[23] In fact, the trackies had taken a full day to painstakingly hand-winch the boulders—including a three-tonne monster—into place.

[24] On a good day, the crew will progress up to 200m, following roughly the pink ribbon trail they marked on a reconnaissance through the area.

[25] On bad days, when the track requires stairs or rock work, they progress as little as 10m.

[26] It may be taking the team about six months to coax the track from the bush, but when finished, the walk will take hikers a mere three hours to complete.

[27] The group take pride in the fact they've used no introduced materials, despite initial plans for some wooden decking and a suspension bridge.

[28] It's a sign, says trackie and park ranger Rob Beedham, of the group's environmental sensitivity: "You'd be hard pressed to find a bunch of people with better green credentials."

[29] Other projects under their belt include work in Tasmania's World Heritage-listed Lake St Clair region, and on parts of Tassie's famed South Coast Track.

[30] Despite this, the Prom track has attracted widespread criticism, led by Victorian National Parks Association project officer Leslie Sorensen.

[31] "The area the new track goes through has remote qualities which should be protected, not opened up to incremental development," she says. "We haven't seen the track, and I can't comment on the trackies' work . . . but whether it is a good job or not, we still believe it shouldn't have gone in."

[32] But the job gets the thumbs-up from the trackies—an eccentric bunch, by their own admission. Some have been to university (one is a Cambridge drop-out). Others have a farming background. The rest simply love nature.

[33] "I love this because you get to see some of the most incredible, natural places in the world," says Ferguson, a trackie for nine years.

[34] The work is physically hard and tiring. And the weather can be beastly, but compared to Tasmania, the Wilsons Promontory weather has been kind—only four full days of rain since May, and no snow or sleet.

[35] Besides, says Ferguson, there's much to make up for any foul conditions they experience.

[36] Such as the spectacular, sweeping views of Bass Strait, the lighthouse and Waterloo Bay; the swooping sea eagles hooking fish straight from the sea; the small native animals.

[37] Shifts are nine days on, five days off, 7.30am to about 5pm.

[38] "By the end of day nine we can be sick of the sight of each other," says Bradshaw, scraping at his stubbled chin. "We have good days and bad days

... but there's a good enough rapport between us all."

[39] Nights are spent in individual tents pitched near each other. Meals consist of basic campers' fare—pasta, rice or other simple dishes. The men use the time at night to think, read, write, and watch the ships pass in the distance as lighthouse beams bounce off their tents.

[40] "It's a simple life—and some people just can't hack the isolation," says Ferguson.

[41] Asked about the effect of their job on their family and other relationships, he jams his hands deeper in his pockets and shuffles his feet in the dirt.

[42] "It's hard," he says quietly. "We've had some broken marriages, some broken relationships. It's very hard."

[43] Visitors along the new Wilsons Prom track are infrequent, but while *Weekend* is there, two red-faced walkers appear.

[44] The women have bush-bashed their way in from the unmade Waterloo Bay end of the track, following only the fluttering pink ribbons.

[45] "Couldn't wait for the blokes to finish it," they laugh.

[46] And as the job draws to an end, it seems neither can the blokes.

[47] "The best bit about the job," says Snapper, a pink ribbon marked 6300m fluttering beside his ear, "is knowing it has an end."

[48] The new track forms part of the Great Prom Walk and is expected to be completed by October 30. Parks Victoria is planning a fortnight of special walks and events to mark 100 years of Wilsons Promontory. Details: 13 19 63.

1. WHAT WORKS IN THE FEATURE STORY, AND WHY?

'Blazing a trail' is a straightforward general feature about the environment with a diverting blend of information and entertainment that would have appealed to *Herald Sun* readers. The track is not the issue; it is the people making the track who are the focus of the piece. Hudson has not simply offered an interview piece but has animated the feature with the hike she and the photographer made to reach the trackies. This is the real strength of the piece. The making of bush tracks is not a subject likely to set hearts racing, but by dramatising her hike (100m, 200m, 300m), Hudson is able to show her readers just how much work is needed to create a track. There is plenty of information in the piece about the track—how long it will take to build, how much it will cost, the difference between a good day and a bad day—and plenty of strong quotes from the trackies. Hudson's prose is, for the most part, clear and crisp, never more so than in paragraph 17 where she works her verbs as hard as the trackies are, 'levering a lump of granite' and 'wrestling a tree stump'.

2. WHAT DOES NOT WORK IN THE FEATURE STORY, AND WHY NOT?

Hudson has packed a good deal into a 1200-word feature and as a result a couple of sections, such as the discussion of the job's loneliness and the arrival of the two bushwalkers, seem underdone. The former comes as a bit of a jolt after the easygoing tone of the first three-quarters of the article and the latter is a development introduced just five paragraphs from the end. Similarly, paragraph 30 says there has been widespread criticism of the track but quotes only one person. There are a few stylistic lapses; there is a redundancy in paragraph 12 ('momentarily startled for a second'), an ambiguity caused by compression in paragraph 13 (was it stipulated they build a controversial track?), a grammatical error in paragraph 15 ('Parks Victoria have') and an ambiguity in paragraph 43 in describing the bushwalking women as 'red-faced', which might suggest they are embarrassed rather than tired.

3. HOW EXACTLY WOULD YOU IMPROVE THE STORY, IF YOU WERE DOING IT?

First, clean up the stylistic lapses. To show the bushwalking women's tiredness, for instance, Hudson could have reported if they were sweating, or breathing hard or could have simply said their faces were red with exertion. Apart from these easily fixed matters, the main improvement I suggest would be to strengthen the article's strength and jettison its underdeveloped sub-topics. The piece is freshest when it focuses on exactly how a bush track is made and how it affects the trackies. So include more on that; make room by cutting the discussion about the controversy surrounding the track, which does not seem to be overly urgent.

ANALYSIS: FEATURE STORY TWO

This second piece was published in the 'Metropolitan' section of *The Sydney Morning Herald* on Saturday 27 July 2002 and reprinted in the 'Agenda' section of *The Sunday Age* the following weekend. Written by Jon Casimir, it coincided with a tour by Kylie Minogue during which breathless interviews with the pop icon ran in almost all metropolitan dailies and numerous magazines. Headlined 'Bottoms up' in Sydney and 'The year her bum went psycho' in Melbourne, the piece contained 2400 words and a breakout box.

BOTTOMS UP

[Precede] If Russell Crowe was Maximus, then Kylie Minogue is Gluteus, a woman as famous for her rear end as her records. On the eve of her sold-out Australian tour, Jon Casimir toasts her success.

[1] In March this year, London newspaper *The Sun* sponsored a campaign to have Kylie Minogue's rear end heritage-listed, preserved for "posteriority" on the grounds that it's an Area of Outstanding Natural Beauty. The tabloid invited its readers to lobby the government to make sure Kylie's "bum remains in safe hands—by turning it into a national institution".

[2] The heritage listing has not yet been confirmed (how, exactly, would you go about preserving the area? Formaldehyde? Botox?), but *The Sun* is no doubt still hoping, if only because the resulting story would provide another excuse to run a circulation-boosting photo of Kylie bending over.

[3] For *The Sun*, the heritage campaign was just another in a long line of excitable Kylie stunts, coming only a fortnight after a story that suggested Kylie had undergone a bum lift, secret cosmetic surgery to enhance her pertness and "boost her appeal down under". Declaring its intention to uncover the source of the lift rumour, the paper said it was "trying to get to the bottom of the cheeky claims".

[4] This week, Madame Tussaud's unveiled its new Kylie exhibit, a model of the singer on all fours with backside provocatively raised. Such is the English fixation with Kylie's rear view that chat show host Johnny Vaughan recently commented that "if an alien landed on Earth he would think Kylie's arse is the world's leader".

[5] How quickly things change. Only three years ago, Kylie's career had its own postcode in the doldrums. After her *Impossible Princess* album (retitled *Kylie Minogue* for the Brits after Diana's death) stiffed in the UK, she was written off by media and industry alike. Now she is England's most beloved pop star.

[6] And certainly, she *is* an English pop star. To consider what makes her career work, you must first accept that she made one single, "Locomotion", in Australia before relocating to London. Nothing about her work—the sounds, the styles, the fashions, the context—is Australian. We may love her and she us, but we are not her core audience, financially or creatively.

[7] The greatest career resurrection of recent times is most often attributed to the pair of gold leather hotpants (famously bought in an op shop for 50 pence by stylist Will Baker) that Kylie wore in the video for "Spinning Around", her 2000 single. The song's clip, the closest TV has come to lap dancing, did not pretend to be much more than a showcase for her rear, a casting decision Baker defended by saying, "Kylie's bottom is like a peach—sex sells and her best asset is her bum." Kylie's dry reply was, "You never know what the future holds. It could become a pear."

[8] "Spinning Around" went to No. 1 in the UK, her first chart-topper there in a decade. Since then, her career has exploded, moving beyond mere questions of chart placings, units shifted, dollars banked (*Business Review Weekly* estimated her 2001 earnings at $10 million, up from $2.1 million the previous year).

[9] Here she is, at the zenith of her success, 15 years after it began, dropping into Sydney to play six sold-out shows at the Entertainment Centre. After 40 weeks, her *Fever* album is still in the Top 10 and has sold more than 350,000 copies in Australia. Its lead-off single, "Can't Get You Out Of My Head", went to No 1 in 19 countries and even cracked the US Top Five.

[10] Yet, though Kylie can carry a tune, she can't carry one far. And even Baker was quoted last year as saying she can't really dance, though he later denied the comment.

[11] Neither of these flaws holds her back. Kylie works brilliantly within her limitations. Name one other act, just one, a band or a solo performer, whose comeback has been bigger than the initial wave of success. So how do you explain her revival? Here are a dozen reasons:

KYLIE LOVES THE CAMERA/THE CAMERA LOVES KYLIE

[12] Kylie tells a great story about the night she and her makeshift band of *Neighbours* cronies played "Locomotion" live for the first time, at a benefit for the Fitzroy Lions AFL club. After the song, someone told her she should record it as a single. Her first thought, she recalled last year, was not "I'd get to make a record." It was "I'd get to make a video."

[13] Kylie understands the packaging necessities of the modern pop star. Like Madonna before her she has, particularly of late, fashioned a career as much out of canny media manipulation as musical nous. In her recent videos and public appearances, she has carefully courted attention, knowing when to push boundaries and when to pull back.

KYLIE IS SEXY

[14] Look, it doesn't hurt that she flaunts the bod, but don't sell her short by reducing her success to skin alone. For one thing, Kylie's sexiness is not new. People have been commenting about her grown-up appeal since "Better The Devil You Know", the 1990 video that saw her abandon the perm and fairy floss image for something more slinky and stirring.

[15] What *is* new is the acreage of her flesh on display. The clip for "Can't Get You Out Of My Head" featured Kylie in a hooded, white outfit split up the thighs and down the torso. It left approximately nothing to the imagination—her nipples had to be taped to the inside of the fabric to keep them away from the lens.

[16] What works for Kylie is not the fact that she's sexy, but the kind of sexy she is. After all, there are plenty of female singers trading on their sultry looks. But Kylie is not a competitor with Britney; she's an antidote. She's no panting, try-hard adolescent, all hot and bothered for the camera.

[17] Kylie's sexiness is more contained and more of a game. Kylie delivers it with a wink. She knows the bum fixation is pure 1960s England, the latest manifestation of a never-far-from-the-surface fascination with knickers and

stocking-tops. She's a saucy seaside postcard. She's a *Carry On* gag. And this is at least partly because . . .

KYLIE IS TINY

[18] At 152cm, she's a whisker over five feet in the imperial measure. Her smallness makes her overt sexuality less threatening. No matter how much she bumps and grinds, she never quite seems aggressive or predatory. She is sexy to men and non-threatening to women. Smallness also makes her seem vulnerable. It helps her youngest fans relate to her. And her size makes her a perennial underdog. It's easy to barrack for Kylie and her career—she's the little engine that could.

KYLIE REALLY CAN ACT

[19] As long as she's playing Kylie, that is. And don't think for a second that Kylie is not a role (everyone close calls her Min; Kylie exists for the public). Read any Kylie interview. She is meticulously self-deprecating. She flirts, giving the impression of parting with confidences while never actually offering much of an opinion—let alone a revelation—on anything. Kylie presents as grounded, human and straightforward, never too big for her boots. Kylie is pretty much the Queen Mother of pop: a woman with longevity and the common touch, permanently in the public eye, ever gracious, ever aware that without the support of the people, she is nothing.

[20] All these things are no doubt partly true, but there is always a sense that she is withholding another self. This probably goes back to her initial mauling at the hands of the English press. Visiting South Africa in 1989, the year before Nelson Mandela was freed, she made things worse when she was asked what she thought of the situation in the country. "I think they should stop killing the rhinos," was her reply. Since that gaffe, Kylie has exerted an almost magisterial control over her persona.

KYLIE WORKS DAMN HARD

[21] It is, of course, possible to get to the top without talent. It happens all the time, through various permutations of marketing, coincidence and happy accident. But you don't get to stay at the top without having something. And what Kylie clearly has is tenacity.

[22] Read either of the two biographies published this year, *Kylie: Naked* and *Kylie Confidential.* Everyone who works with her seems to comment on her steely work ethic. She's conceded on many occasions that her "hideous professionalism" comes before her life and has pushed herself to breakdown point more than once.

KYLIE FOUND HER IRONY

[23] For a long time, it appeared that Kylie had no sense of humour. Then, in 1996, with Nick Cave urging her on, she took the stage at the Poetry Olympics in London and recited, with mock seriousness, the lyrics of "I Should Be So Lucky". Subsequent live tours have included torch-song versions of the single. Kylie learned to laugh at herself, to embrace the kitsch part of her career for which her fans maintain affection. Now that she knows that we know that she knows it's all just pop music, the whole shebang is a lot more fun.

AMBITION FIRST, EGO SECOND

[24] After breaking away from the Stock, Aitken and Waterman hit factory in 1992, Kylie set out to find herself as an artist. The wonderful "Confide In Me" single was an early flowering, but it was *Impossible Princess* she really poured herself into—the first time she really committed her thoughts to paper, declared herself in the lyrics (Will Baker says anyone wanting to understand her should read them).

[25] The fact the Big Personal Statement tanked (it performed respectably here, but disappeared in the UK) could have destroyed a bigger ego, but Kylie appears to have taken what she could from the experience and moved on. If confession wasn't what the people wanted, then she'd give them what they did. Which leads us to . . .

KYLIE HAS COME FULL CIRCLE

[26] Kylie has used her hard-earned pop puppet skills to fashion her recent career. In essence, she has become her own puppeteer. She's a packaged, marketed, targeted commodity again, but this time, the calculating is all her own.

[27] Here she is in 2002 offering what is essentially the music that made her famous: upbeat, uplifting pop. Make no mistake, her new songs have a greater hip quotient but the same old formula: tunes you can hum, cheerful sentiment, unchallenging lyrics. She is fluffy Kylie again, showgirl Kylie, good-time Kylie. In a recent attempt at derision, David Bowie labelled her a cruise ship entertainer. Yes, and his point was?

[28] You can't beat good songs. "Spinning Around" was written by Paula Abdul for her own, aborted comeback. Kylie snapped it up and the rest is history. And when you choose songs rather than write them, as Kylie does, success breeds success. With every degree your star ascends, the choice improves. Right now, Kylie will have her pick of the work from the best songwriters around.

TIMING. OH, AND SEPTEMBER 11

[29] Kylie suits the new millennium. Good-time pop music is what sells right now. Post-September 11, this trend has been even stronger. We're looking for things that make us feel better about ourselves and our world. That's part of the reason the World Cup soccer was so huge and it's part of the reason Kylie's surge continues. She combines forward-looking optimism with comfortable nostalgia. Her current career phase will last as long as these values are saleable.

KYLIE'S GAY AUDIENCE

[30] While it's true that Kylie's gay audience has been incredibly and impressively loyal, it's not the audience as much as the aesthetic that is most important. To look at Kylie now is to see a drag act. She has never lost the sense of being a little girl playing dress-ups, vamping and pouting for all it's worth. The *Fever* tour includes: torch singer Kylie, New York cop Kylie, Barbarella Kylie and geisha Kylie, to name but a few.

THE X FACTOR

[31] In the end, there are always indefinables. Stand a few feet to the left and, when the bus crashes, it won't hit you. Kylie's career is a triumph of X factor. Though there are many reasons for her

success, they never add up neatly. As she has charitably pointed out, there are buskers with more talent. You need luck, you need timing, you need to know what to do when a door opens.

THE DERRIERE

[32] OK, it has to count for something. Though Robbie Millen, writing for *The Times*, recently observed that "her bottom will go the way of the Empire: overstretched and financially packing less of a punch, it will decline and fall", you'd have to bet it has a few years left in it yet. Kylie herself is clearly aware of its power. She's been selling underwear at her shows for years. She told the *Sunday People*, in her usual modest fashion, that her bottom "does what it's meant to do and it's in fairly good shape". At least all those hours in the gym aren't being wasted.

[33] When the *Fever* tour began in Cardiff at the end of April, *The Mirror*'s scribe, Richard Smith, amused himself by counting all the bum wiggles in the first show. He came up with a figure of 251, noting that Kylie averages two a minute and "even has two sorts of moves. Wiggle One is a full-on seductive sort whereas Wiggle Two is made up of a short, sharp hip thrust".

[34] And you always thought Wiggle Two was the purple one who sleeps a lot.

KYLIE'S BUM: WHAT THE CRITICS SAY

'Pert' *The Mirror*

'The best in the world' *Adelaide Advertiser*

'Terrific' *The Sun*

'Perfect' *The Glasgow Herald*

'To die for' *Sunday Times*

'The butt that rocked the world' *Daily Telegraph* (London)

'So famous that it has probably got its own agent' *The Express*

'Heat-seeking' *GQ*

'Award-winning' *Daily Telegraph* (London)

'The best known bum in Britain' *The Times*

'Sensational' *Daily Mail*

'Perfectly formed' *The Express*

'The world's most admired backside' *The Guardian*

'A wonderful thing—one of the cornerstones of our culture' *The Scotsman*

'Above-average' *The Australian*

1. WHAT WORKS IN THE FEATURE STORY, AND WHY?

In my view, this feature works well. It is thoroughly researched, appealingly structured and wittily written. The marketing of Kylie Minogue's 2002 Australian tour was as choreographed as one of her dance clips; many newspapers and magazines carried featherdown-light interview pieces with her that, as Jon Casimir noted, promised to reveal all but said little. Casimir decided to bypass Kylie, asking a good journalistic question: how is Kylie so successful when she is, by her own admission, only moderately talented? Casimir offered the reader an analysis of Minogue's success, which is a risky strategy given that most readers shun abstract pieces and many might ask, 'Why bother dissecting the success of a pop singer?'

There is more analysis, though, in *The Sydney Morning Herald* than in, say, *The Daily Telegraph* and Minogue has become one of the biggest names in a multi-billion dollar industry that touches most people's lives. To the best of my knowledge (I am not a Kylie aficionado), there has been little analysis of her success. In other words, Casimir is attempting to satisfy one of the criteria for news: tell me something I don't know. Casimir sugar-coated his analysis, in an easily digested structure that suited his subject matter—the dozen reasons format. He has also wrapped the intellectual muscle supporting his analysis in language as pert and perky as Kylie's much-applauded posterior. Note particularly his observations that Kylie's bum has become a national obsession in the land of the 'saucy seaside postcard', that her tininess makes her 'overt sexuality less threatening' and that her gay audience loves how 'she has never lost the sense of being a little girl playing dress-ups'. These are observations of a high order.

2. WHAT DOES NOT WORK IN THE FEATURE STORY, AND WHY NOT?

It is possible that fans might be annoyed or offended by the article's knowing attitude towards their Kylie. Is the article aimed at them? Not really. It seems to be aimed to be enjoyed by Kylie haters as well as Kylie lovers and by those indifferent to her charms. The article may well irritate fans but they would probably read it because they are fans; it would amuse the non-believers. It also stood as good a chance as any of drawing in the uninterested reader. Regardless of the reader's perspective on Kylie, though, it is likely some would have disliked the tone of the piece. To me, Casimir's tone was smart, but to others it might be smartarse. This is at least partly a matter of individual taste.

The order of most of the reasons for Kylie's success flows, strengthened by the direct links as between reasons two and three, but at times the order looks haphazard. There is also, dare I say it, a tad too much emphasis on Kylie's bottom. Casimir argues it is central to her success, but are twelve mentions (plus a box breakout devoted to her bottom) needed to make the case? When *The Sunday Age* ran the article it deleted the box breakout.

3. HOW EXACTLY WOULD YOU IMPROVE THE STORY, IF YOU WERE DOING IT?

There is not a lot I would have done differently, assuming I could have done the piece as well as Casimir in the first place. Certainly, no major changes are required. Those I would have made were suggested in the preceding section. The bottom references could be trimmed, particularly at the start where there is an over-reliance on bum jokes from *The Sun*, and the box breakout is not essential either. I would have slightly re-ordered the dozen reasons, especially in the middle where they jump back and forth between reasons tied to chronology and reasons tied to her qualities. Kylie's gay audience is mentioned late when it would appear to be more important than this weighting suggests (remembering that many people do not read articles to the end), but it is possible Casimir deliberately put it late so that readers looking for that reason would keep reading.

Evaluating a feature story in this way can be illuminating, and there is no shortage of available stories to evaluate. The limitation is you see only the published article. You can only glimpse at the work that preceded publication: where the idea came from, how the journalist gathered the material, how they structured it, the role of the editor, and so on. Yet it is this process that you need to see and understand in order to report and write your own feature stories. With this in mind, I asked Fiona Hudson and Jon Casimir to tell the stories behind their stories.

THE STORY BEHIND THE STORY

Fiona Hudson

It only took seven words for the *Weekend* liftout editor to hook me. Never mind that she hadn't explained the assignment at all. Her question was enough: 'Have you ever flown in a helicopter?' Two years out of my cadetship with the *Herald Sun* and only a few months into a stint in the features department, I was lucky to escape the office in a fleet car. 'I'll do it.'

The assignment turned out to be a trip into the wilds of Wilsons Promontory to meet a group of men carving a track through virgin bush. Parks Victoria had approached *Weekend* editor Allison Harding with the idea of visiting the men and reporting on their work. The report would be tied in to celebrations marking the 100th anniversary of the Prom. She jumped at the idea. Only recently appointed editor, she was keen to cover more local stories, and to shift the magazine away from profiles of Hollywood celebrities.

A quick call to the Parks Victoria public relations bloke and a date was locked in for a photographer and I to catch the chopper and fly in to meet the 'trackies'. It sounded a dream job. Fly in, interview the blokes over a sandwich, and be home in time for dinner. Too easy. Things unravelled the next day when my editor approached with another question: 'Er, Fiona, do you own a tent?' The bean counters had baulked at the cost of hiring a chopper. Instead the photographer and I arranged to drive to the Prom and hike—in borrowed boots—to meet the trackies. We'd then hike back out and spend a cold night at the lighthouse keeper's accommodation before driving home.

The trek began badly. We hadn't realised we'd have to walk for 40 minutes to even reach the start of the new track. Photographer Rob Baird was grumpy about lugging his gear into the bush, and not feeling chatty. His first word came five minutes along the track: 'Snake!' I caught a glimpse of the brown snake beside the slim track. We picked up pace for the next few kilometres, counting the pink ribbons marking the shoulder-width track.

The walk was tough, and made longer by regular smoko stops. Three hours and six kilometres into the walk, we came upon the trackies. Though friendly, they were shy. Questions were met with simple, short answers. Even the Cambridge drop-out could barely be coaxed into chatting.

In the end, some of the better quotes were taken from snatches of conversation between the men and Rob Baird as they shared a cigarette. A couple of good lines also slipped out as we sipped cups of tea and looked out over Bass Strait. (These few quotes were almost lost when rain smudged my pen ink. Luckily Rob lent me a pencil.) Both Rob and I were rapt when two women bush-bashed their way in from the unmade end of the track. The men were clearly thrilled to know future walkers would be saved the effort, and the conversation between the two groups garnered a few more quotes.

After spending a couple of hours with the blokes it was time to leave. Darkness, accompanied by a storm, arrived before we could trek out. We realised then how ill-prepared we were, without even a torch or umbrella. We stayed overnight, then hauled our stiff bodies up a steep climb.

The story needed a quick turnaround. After driving back to Melbourne, I had about a day to write—sandwiched between several other tasks. We'd paid so much attention to the fluttering pink ribbons on the walk that they seemed a natural narrative device to use. They really helped draw the reader into the journey. The foot-slogging was painful, but I reckon it made a huge difference to the piece.

The on-the-spot observation was essential, given the interviewees' reluctance to speak. Watching them said much more than they did. It's rare for me to feel such enjoyment writing a piece. It's a cliché, but the story almost wrote itself. The story raised no issues, other than my undiscovered fear of snakes. It's likely the subjects never read it. Parks Victoria wrote a letter of thanks, and I received a few comments from readers and colleagues.

Re-reading the piece recently, I realised there are a couple of things I'd change. The first is the tautology the subs introduced which saw the men 'momentarily startled for a second'. I'd also make a bit more of the controversy surrounding the track. The token comments from the National Parks Association officer hint at the criticism of the project, but really should have gone further. Then there's the journalist's constant lament: if only I'd had more space! Given more, I'd have fleshed out the effect of the job on the trackies' personal lives.

This article taught me the importance of logistics. These days I work out how long it will take me to get to a job, and how much time I'll spend there. And if I'm likely to encounter snakes.

THE STORY BEHIND THE STORY

Jon Casimir—the journalist interviews himself
So, Jon, what was the initial impetus for the story? Was it an assignment or was it your idea?
I'm glad you asked that, because it gives me a chance to talk, and I've always been fond of the sound of my own voice. Looking back, I seem to

recall the editor of the newspaper section furrowing his brow and saying something like, 'You wouldn't want to do something on Kylie, would you?' To which I replied, 'What, like an interview?' He said no, at which point I became interested.

I suppose, in all honesty, I wouldn't mind interviewing Kylie, but I can't remember ever reading or seeing an interview with her that was enlightening. She has long seemed an interview specialist to me, someone with a crack-free persona who never offers an accidental revelation or anything of the remotest possible interest. Her responses have all the vitality and humanity of the average computerised switchboard operator.

What, exactly, was the brief?
Well, I think it was pretty much along the lines of, 'There's a 2000-word hole right here that I want to put a photo of Kylie on top of. Can you fill it?' Half in jest, I suggested writing a piece about the British fascination with Kylie's arse. 'Good, good,' the editor muttered, 'I can have the headline, "The year my bum went psycho".' I'm not sure why he was so keen on that line, but he clearly was. [Perhaps because it is the title of a bestselling Australian children's book by Andy Griffiths. M.R.]

In his defence, I would like to point out that the no-brief brief is not as uncommon as you might think. Earlier in the year, I had another editor show me a photo and say, 'Can you write a cover story to go with this?' And just a few weeks ago, another editor handed me a photocopied catalogue of upcoming releases from a local publisher. One of the books was circled. 'Could you get this book and write 2000 words about it?' was the brief.

Some would argue these editors are not doing their job well. Certainly they're taking big risks by not really having much of an idea of what they want. But as the guy who keeps getting non-briefs, I kinda like it. At least you end up doing something that interests you, rather than fleshing out somebody else's half-arsed theories. My half-arsed theories suit me just fine. I'm the kind of feature writer that is happy to do interviews, but just as happy to go away and think for a living. And I have always thought that part of a journalist's job is to look at an event/person/thing and find what is interesting about it. Of course there should be a Kylie story to coincide with her tour and the increased public interest. The question is: what's the angle?

Did you have underlying premises or motives when approaching the story?
To not kick Kylie. The standard broadsheet line on Kylie is to see her as a

talentless poppet worthy only of mockery and derision. In short, we sneer. My feeling was that a demolition job was pretty much what every cynical reader of a paper like the *Herald* would expect. So to fulfil that expectation would be pointless. Sure, it would be easy. And fun. But it would still be pointless. What I wanted to do was a piece that might surprise and engage our readers, possibly even make them look at Kylie another way.

The truth is, broadsheets reflexively knock middlebrow and lowbrow culture. And they're wrong to do it. What they should do is find intelligent ways to engage with it. To explain it. To put it in context. To distil what is good while not denying what is bad. Broadsheet papers should review Celine Dion albums and Christopher Columbus films without just dumping on them.

How did the brief grow?
Actually, I ignored the psycho bum brief for a while and went off down another path. My first idea was that it might be fun to watch all of Kylie's music videos consecutively (what was I thinking?) and write about the changes evident in them. That would provide a chronological structure to the story and the opportunity to isolate themes as they arose (and the crucial opportunity to mock her eyeshadow choices). So I went shopping and bought her tapes, as well as two newish UK biographies, which struck me as bankably riveting weekend reading. I was, of course, horribly wrong.

The books—witless, clueless drivel—took about two hours to read and gave me precisely bugger all to work with. By the time I'd made it through them, I was starting to think that I couldn't possibly survive a day with all her videos.

So what happened then?
I procrastinated. I had a week up my sleeve before the story was due, so I put off watching the tapes and went to the library instead. There, I perused the clippings files on Kylie, confirming my idea that she never gave away much in interviews. I could also see the overall shape of her career coming through: the explosive early success, the wilderness years (much longer than her current bio makes them out to be) and the very recent upswing. I began to make notes of some of the things I wanted to say.

I saw a TV interview in which she made the comment about wanting to be in a music video. That struck me as symbolic of the pop career she's had:

one in which image and showpersonship is almost everything.

Gradually, I returned to the idea of Kylie's arse, because its deification amused me and I figure if I'm amused (even though my sense of humour is largely puerile), then the readers will be amused too. I asked the wonderful Fairfax librarians to run a Lexis-Nexis database search, looking for references to the arse in British papers in the preceding six months. It returned 196 matches. They turned up in everything from pop articles to gardening columns and political commentary. Clearly, the arse had achieved a kind of transcendence.

I printed a dozen or so of the key articles from the UK press and put together the breakout for the Kylie story: 'Kylie's bum: what the critics say'. The breakout is still my favourite part of the whole thing. It just makes me laugh. I was depressed when *The Age* syndicated the story but did not have room for the breakout.

How did you get from there to the story?

I had spotted *The Sun's* campaign to have the arse declared an area of natural beauty in one of the clippings. Clearly, this was the lead paragraph handed to me on the plate. After that, there had to be an extrapolation of the English fixation with the arse, setting out examples. These would obviously provide a good laugh and a way into whatever story I was going to write. The fact that the arse obsession (so *Carry On*, so Benny Hill) is peculiarly British led to the consideration that despite her origins, Kylie's career is particularly British too. I felt it was a really important point to make: though she's 'Our Kylie' and she loves us, she's sooooooooooo not an Australian pop star.

Then the through line struck me. Though many in England put her success down to her arse, a cute idea, this could not be true. Well, not wholly true anyway. So why not write a piece about the reasons for Kylie's success. This would allow me to look at the Kylie phenomenon without having to spend a lot of time on the 'Is her music good or bad?' question, which I really wanted to avoid.

How did you decide on structure?

I like list stories. I like making lists. They're wonderfully flexible. And done right, they're great for the reader, who always has a sense of what is being said and can skip easily and usefully back and forth through the copy. It also seemed to me, in this case, that pop success is the collision of a lot of reasons and circumstances, many of which have little to do with each other. A huge part of it is coincidence.

Writing a list story also means you don't have to worry about segues and linking material, so you can pack more information in, in a more staccato tone. I like a story that reads fast. And the section of the paper it was intended for, Saturday's 'Metropolitan', is very much a light read destination, a quality read, but an easy one. It would have been wrong to approach it in a cultural studies essay way.

I asked myself, could I come up with twelve reasons why Kylie is successful, and substantiate all of them? And with about two days left to write it in (I'd been distracted by navel fluff or footy tipping or something else early in the week), I just sat down and began to scribble notes.

For me, a lot of the joy of writing is the blank page itself. I love the responsibility of having to come up with my own ideas and answers to a question (Why Kylie?). I love sitting there at home (because it's quieter) and dreaming a story into existence. So yes, I made reference to clippings, to biographies, to TV specials, but the key part of the research involved just thinking. What are the patterns in her career? How did she behave in public? What were the pieces of luck she'd had, good and bad? What factors had contributed to her star power? Where is pop music at right now and what context does it provide for her?

Some of the reasons for Kylie's success were obvious. Some followed logically from others. Some had to be conjured to help the picture make sense. Some had to be carefully thought through. Reading the books and clippings was very helpful in the end. For two weeks I'd had Kylie thoughts and events sloshing around in my brain. When it came time to analyse them, it was surprisingly easy.

How long did it all take?
The piece took about a day to write and half a day to rewrite. Honestly, I was quite proud of it. I thought I'd come up with a number of ways of considering her that had not previously been put together.

I ran into the editor of the paper in the lift the day after. He said, 'What are you working on?' I told him about the Kylie story and he said I was too old to be writing things like that (I was 37). 'Actually,' I replied, 'I think I'm only just starting to understand this stuff'.

I gave the video tapes to someone I know who loves Kylie. I never watched them. I don't feel bad about that.

DISCUSSION QUESTIONS AND EXERCISES

1. Find two features, one that you think is good, the other bad, and evaluate them according to the three questions listed at the beginning of this chapter. Begin by analysing each article paragraph by paragraph to help you see exactly how the article flows, or doesn't, and whether there are obvious unanswered questions.

2. Evaluate two articles on the same topic or person. How are they similar, how are they different? Try and distinguish between differences owing to different publications and differences because of the individual journalist's work.

4 GENERATING FRESH STORY IDEAS

At a certain point you realise there's not enough happening to justify 24 hours of news. They should just show a snow cone melting until something happens.

Jon Stewart

CHAPTER SUMMARY

Feature writers need to be able to develop the news of the day; they also need to be able to generate fresh ideas. Various ways of dealing with the information overload and of putting yourself in the right place to pick up ideas are outlined in this chapter. Seven methods of generating ideas, derived from lateral thinking, are discussed, with examples.

E verybody knows we live in an age of information overload, but not everybody knows just how novel this situation is. Experts vary on when the information age began but even if you take an early date, such as that put forward by the inventor of the precursor to the Internet—1945—it still amounts to the tiniest fraction of the 100 000 plus years of human history.[1] Because people drown in information today, they have little idea how pervasive information scarcity has been in history—and how important. In 1814, to take a dramatic example, a peace treaty between England and America was signed in Belgium; in those days it took two months or more for news to travel across the ocean by ship. In the meantime the Battle of New Orleans was fought and 2000 soldiers died simply because they did not know of the treaty's signing.[2]

The journalistic models we have today were created for an information-scarce society. How well do they serve the readers of today? How important, for instance, is it to be first with the news when there is so much news around and, with rare exceptions, it is only journalists who notice who got it first? There is intense competition for readers' time and attention. 'A wealth of information creates a poverty of attention', as one commentator put it.[3]

Newspaper circulation has been declining slowly for decades; even the most popular Australian women's magazines, which used to boast circulations well over one million, have dropped in recent years. The total size of the newspaper and the magazine markets, though, has not declined. What newspaper and magazine editors have had to do is become more creative in finding ways to attract readers' attention. They have provided specialist material aimed at readers' particular interests, and they have paid more attention to entertaining readers, whether by introducing colour photos in newspapers, telling ripping yarns or retailing celebrity gossip. Newspapers and, to a lesser extent, magazines have also met the problem of information overload head-on by recognising their role in making sense of the mass of confusing news flying around.

Information overload affects journalists as well as readers. The articles in newspapers or magazines represent only a proportion of the total number of stories written and they in turn represent a fraction of the material sifted for potential stories. Each day, journalists and editors wade through wads of media releases, invitations, reports and tip-offs. At the *Herald Sun*, the chief of staff processes at least 500 items each day and a further 100 emails from people and organisations, all wanting coverage in the nation's highest circulating daily newspaper.[4] Some contain genuinely interesting news, but most amount to little or are self-promoting pap. Section editors are similarly beseiged. Part of their job is to generate story ideas, but time is always short, the number of blank pages long.

Journalists habitually gripe about their editors' impoverished imagination for story ideas. Why have I been lumbered with this lemon, they moan. How come I never get the good assignments? Sieving the sheer crush of material that rolls over an editor's desk is grinding work, which leaves little mental space for dazzling story ideas and helps explain why much of what is published is repeated across the media with little development of the source material. The sameness, not to mention lameness, of these stories is why the ability to generate fresh story ideas is essential for journalists, especially freelancers who do not have the luxury of a salary.

Fresh ideas, whether in journalism, literature, business and science among other fields, are always in short supply. The feature writer with bright ideas, then, is as rare and as valuable in a newsroom as the journalist who regularly breaks news stories. Editors know this and soon identify these fertile minds. They need not be so rare, though. Journalists are not expected to come up with ideas that no one has ever thought of; there are methods of thinking that can be applied to news events and issues of the day that yield fresh information and insight for readers.

TAKING CHARGE

A feature writer who relies on their editor for story ideas will rarely be given the juiciest assignments; they are also handing over control of a vital part of their job to a busy person who, in all likelihood, is not unduly worried about the feature writer's wellbeing. Why put your professional satisfaction in someone else's hands when you can take charge of it yourself? The first step is to develop habits, such as those outlined below, that over time put you in the right place, physically and mentally, to pick up ideas for stories.

DON'T STAND STILL

Anyone aspiring to get into the news media industry should be reading newspapers and magazines, listening to radio news, watching TV news and surfing the Net. In addition to keeping abreast of the news, working journalists spend time and energy each day sifting through media releases. This is necessary work but, for good journalism, insufficient because you are consuming what everyone else in the industry is consuming; it is stale air. If all you do is recycle it for readers they'll get legionnaire's disease.

READ VORACIOUSLY

This is unexceptionable advice in a writing textbook, but an alarming number think the two activities are unrelated. Supermodel Elle MacPherson was once quoted saying she did not read books but with her own she'd make an exception. Writing and reading are joined at the hip, as the prodigiously popular novelist Stephen King says: 'If you want to be a writer, you must do two things above all others: read a lot and write a lot.'[5]

- Read publications your audience would not regularly read as well as those they do. When editing *The Sydney Morning Herald*, John Alexander used to chide his reporters for listening to the ABC when they should have been tuned to Alan Jones on morning radio.[6]
- There are around 3000 magazine titles available in Australia. Try some of the 2995 you don't read regularly.

- Read trade journals, government reports and academic journals. They may be boring but that means few others will read them and they will have useful information and ideas buried in them.
- Read good literature, both for the writing and the ideas.
- Soak up mass culture, whether films, TV, live music or chat rooms.

TALK TO ANYONE AND EVERYONE

First and foremost, all good journalists possess a burning curiosity about the world around them and the people in it. Journalists develop contacts in the areas they cover, but you can pick up leads for stories wherever you go. In everyday life you meet a variety of people, doctors, greengrocers, video store assistants, bartenders and so on. Talk to them, show an interest in their lives, tell them about yours. You will be surprised where these conversations lead.

DRAW ON YOUR OWN EXPERIENCE

The question of when to put yourself in a feature story is discussed in chapter eleven, but it is entirely legitimate to draw on your own experience for story ideas. Every person's life opens up some possibilities even as it closes off others. You may come from a small country town; you may have grown up in a sports-mad family; your brother may be intellectually disabled; you may know everything about the roots of hip hop music. Any of these experiences would give a head start in writing a story about these issues. One of the first newspaper stories I wrote as a freelancer drew on my university holiday experience of working in a geriatric nursing home.

KEEP AN IDEAS FILE

One of life's pleasures is the idea that pops into your head; one of life's frustrations is how easily ideas pop out, never to be seen again. Catch them before they do, and jot them down in an ideas file. Don't make the note cryptic; otherwise, in a couple of weeks time you will need a cryptographer to understand it. Clip newspapers, magazines, journals, reports and the like for potential story ideas for your ideas file. Likewise, file ideas gleaned from conversations with sources. Left in your notebook, they will soon be overrun by the next dozen interviews. The ideas file should be organised so you can keep an eye on any that hinge on a particular future event (such as the 20th anniversary of the

Queen Street shootings in 2007) or relate to a news issue that is current and needs immediate attention.

WORK WITH YOUR EDITOR

No matter how many ideas you generate you will still be given assignments by editors. Discuss their ideas and yours; two minds can be better than one. An unnecessarily sharp divide has developed between journalists and editors in many newsrooms. Remember that most editors have been writers and have much to offer journalists during the reporting and writing and editing process.

THINK LATERALLY

The second step in taking charge of your career is to keep in mind the relationship between news and features—not different worlds but different approaches to the same world. There is no single definition of news, but a simple one is news is what is on society's mind.[7] Good journalists have a knack of writing about what is on society's mind. Ian Thorpe is a national icon these days, but when he streamed to prominence a year before the Sydney Olympics what did everyone talk about? Not just his ability; Australia is blessed with fine swimmers. No, it was his humungous size seventeen feet. Jacqueline Magnay made them the subject of a feature straight after Thorpe captured the nation's attention. Even better, she fed public curiosity with interesting information from experts about the extent to which the Thorpedo's feet gave him an advantage over his rivals.[8]

Good journalists also have a knack of writing about what is on society's mind even if society does not like to admit it. Yes, I am talking about sex and violence but not necessarily stag films and snuff movies. Questions of taste and censorship are important and complex but beyond the scope of this book; what journalists should understand is that at some stage of their career they will write about topics that displease their parents, and that this is entirely legitimate. News is not always, or even often, nice and polite. Feature stories about war or rape or child abuse are always going to be disturbing but clearly they are important topics.

There are also less obviously contentious topics that polite society would frown upon while furtively taking a peek. A stunning example of this was published in *Good Weekend*, the colour magazine inserted in *The Sydney Morning Herald* and *The Age*.[9] It was a history of the vibrator, which was invented in the 1890s and used by doctors to masturbate women to health. Cynthia King interviewed an American academic, Rachel Maines, who had spent 20 years researching vibrators and written a book entitled *The Technology of Orgasm*. It was a remarkable feature on several levels. First, it was news; how many histories of the vibrator have been published? Second, it was a deliciously impolite topic. And, third, the article contained interesting information that revealed as much about politics and social mores as about vibrators (though there was still plenty of nitty-gritty material about sizes, designs and gadgetry).

Victorian-era doctors believed the way to treat women they diagnosed as hysterical was to massage their genitals to 'hysterical paroxysm' but grew tired of performing this task manually. So Dr Joseph Mortimer Granville developed the first vibrator. Not that the doctors thought what they were doing was sexual. Maines is quoted saying, 'Well, we all know—with a capital K—that real sex is penetration to male orgasm. When there isn't penetration to orgasm, they figured, there isn't sex.' King, writing amid the scandal over American president Bill Clinton's 'sexual relations' with 'that woman', Monica Lewinsky, commented how little things had changed. Maines' research worried her university in New York, which summarily dismissed her.

Cynthia King's article points to another simple definition of news to keep in mind: tell me something I don't know. It is obvious that when a major news event breaks there will be demand for features; it is not obvious what to do for the vast majority of news events and issues. Think laterally. If you imagine the news and issues of the day as a river, look at it from all possible vantage points—in front, behind, underneath, above, up close, from afar and underwater.

EXTRAPOLATION: IF SOMETHING IS HAPPENING HERE, WHAT ABOUT OVER THERE?

This is probably the most common form of story development, and the one most commonly abused. The principle behind it is to ask: Is a news event a one-off or part of a pattern? On its own, the news event would not merit a feature, but if it is part of a pattern, then it will. For example, when news broke that New South Wales police were investigating a scam in which thieves were able to withdraw electronically more than $1 million from around 100 bank customers, Cameron

Stewart, a senior journalist at *The Australian*, decided to see whether Internet credit card fraud was widespread.[10] It appeared the cyberburglars had paid bank insiders for confidential customer information so they could hack into the popular Bpay bill payment system. Stewart found that until the Bpay scam Internet fraud had been thought of as rare in Australia. He reported a number of other cases, but did not say there was an epidemic of Internet fraud, which is what can happen with extrapolation.

All too often journalists discover a second instance of an event and suddenly, to them, a crime wave is sweeping the city. Stewart did learn it was difficult to quantify the level of Internet fraud because banks were reluctant to provide details. Why? Because the banks bear the cost of money stolen from customers' accounts unless the customer has carelessly disclosed their password, and because banks have a strong interest in ensuring customers believe in the security of the banking system. This information actually made Stewart's story more disturbing than an easily refuted beat-up about a cybercrime wave.

A second form of extrapolation is to ask how a news event or issue is dealt with elsewhere. That is, look at how one news river compares with another. Natasha Bita injected useful information into the sharp and emotional debate about asylum seekers by comparing Australia's treatment of them with that of France, Britain, Germany and the Netherlands. In her news feature, Bita asked how two boys who had escaped from the Woomera detention centre and urgently requested asylum at the British consulate would have fared elsewhere. She found, for instance, that few countries in Europe put unaccompanied children seeking asylum under lock and key. If the boys had arrived in Britain, they probably would have been able to live with their parents in a council flat.[11]

SYNTHESIS: CONNECTING THE DOTS

Newspapers are unable to distinguish between a bicycle accident and the collapse of civilisation.

George Bernard Shaw

Journalists become practised at focusing their energy on a news event, writing a story then moving on to the next one. The nature of the work does not encourage them to look for connections between events, which means they are missing a powerful tool in their kitbag. At the simplest level, a feature can be created by finding a common element. For instance, the Australian movie magazine, *Empire*, ran a piece across four pages about character actors whose names (John C. Reilly, John Malkovich, Anne Archer, John Rhys-Davies) may not be familiar but whose characters are: Reilly is best known for playing a porn legend in *Boogie Nights*, Malkovich for a series of psychos in *Con Air* and *In the Line of Fire*, etc.[12] Individually, the actors may not have had the following to carry a feature, but collectively they merited the piece.

The *Herald Sun* has also drawn together some seemingly odd bed-fellows, such as in the lead story of its arts and entertainment section one weekend that picked out various comedians (Grahame Bond, Vince Sorrenti and Max Walker, among others) who all had one thing in common—they trained as architects before going on stage.[13] It was a light story made diverting by the common background.

The common element may be a class of people, but may also be a common location or cause or even a common idea. In a magazine feature Kellie Fuller wrote up seven failed projects around Australia, including the Very Fast Train, the second Sydney airport and the Multi-function Polis.[14] All had received publicity over the years, but projects like these are large, complex and, until they are completed, abstract. Readers resist abstractions, but they love lists and a list of seven screw-ups is easier to digest.

Synthesis is less often used for news features but D.D. McNicoll showed quick judgement for a piece published at the end of a week in which three rescue attempts took place—one in Western Australia's Great Sandy Desert for Alaskan fireman Robert Bogucki, one in the New South Wales high country for four Sydney snowboarders and one in Turkey for victims of an earthquake.[15] McNicoll connected these three unrelated rescue attempts by asking the question: How do rescue authorities decide when to call off a search?

FINDING SOMETHING NEW ABOUT AN OLD SUBJECT

This is easier said than done but can make for surprisingly interesting features. The idea behind this strategy is take something everyone is familiar with, and find something new. It works best on mundane topics, which looks like a paradox, given that journalists are preoccupied with finding what's new and different. But that is the strength of the strategy; it finds new material in a place no one, amid information overload, had given a moment's thought to. Cynthia King's article discussed above has an element of this strategy but before her piece (and probably since) vibrators were hidden, literally and journalistically. A better example is a piece written by Gavin du Venage, which took the famous song 'The lion sleeps tonight', sung by baby boomers when they were growing up and by their children after its inclusion in the hit film, *The Lion King*, and told the sad story of how its creator, a Zulu villager, received a pittance for the song.[16] Solomon Linda wrote 'Mbube' (the lion) in 1939 and received ten shillings from a South African music company, Gallo, which pocketed the royalties when the song sold over 100 000 copies. In a costly error of judgement, Gallo failed to copyright the song and it was later picked by a trio of songwriters who retitled it and added the lyric, 'In the jungle, the mighty jungle, the lion sleeps tonight'. The song became a hit, recorded by 170 artists and used in several films. It has made pots of money for almost everyone but Solomon Linda, who died penniless. The piece was aptly headlined 'The lion weeps tonight'.

This strategy applies to major news events such as September 11 or the second Gulf War in 2003, where it is as if the media opened a fire hydrant full bore, plastering its audience against the wall. Readers are soaked wet with information but are still thirsty for knowledge. They need help in understanding the meaning and context of the event and they need to be given more incisive information. Specialist magazines come into their own here; for instance, during the recent Gulf War *New Scientist* reported how coalition troops fired thousands of shells tipped with depleted uranium and discussed how scientists still do not fully understand the long-term health effects of depleted uranium.[17]

LOCALISATION—THINKING SMALL

Comedian John Clarke once said that sometimes the best way to see something was not to get a wide-angle view of the planet from a camera placed on Mars but to observe very closely the head of a pin. So common are road deaths that they are confined to a paragraph or two in the briefs column, unless there is something out of the ordinary about them, either in the people involved (i.e., someone prominent), the number of deaths or the nature of the crash itself. Readers barely notice the briefs. Each death, though, has a profound impact on the victim's family and friends and if told in a feature story this could well move a reader to tears. Andrew Rule wrote one such piece; it opened with a description of two small white crosses planted on the side of a country road to commemorate the deaths of eight-year-old Dan Ferguson and his five-year-old brother Tom.[18]

The boys were in the family car with their father Chris, who was indicating to turn off the Goulburn Valley highway when the second semi-trailer in a three-truck convoy ploughed into the car and sent it careening across the road into the path of another car, the driver of which was killed in the second collision. Passengers in both cars were badly injured. The facts of the crash are painful enough to read, but by the end of the story the Fergusons reminded me of many families I knew; it was hard to contemplate how I would feel if two of my own children were killed in a car smash. The truck driver's genuine anguish over his actions also prompted me to recall moments of carelessness in my driving and wonder how different life could have been if they had caused a crash.

Localising is a strategy that has become more useful the more pervasive the media has become. Barely an evening goes by on network television news without an interview with a grieving relative. Deep, wrenching emotions are snap-frozen into sound bites that make it difficult for viewers to appreciate the weight of what has happened. The problem is not so much that there is more violence and tragedy in the world today, but that we are exposed to so much more about it than were our counterparts 200 years ago. Localisation, then, is predicated on there being a great river of news. By corollary, it should be used sparingly as it suffers from the law of diminishing returns.

If localising restores the emotional content of a common tragedy, it is also useful for making the abstract concrete. Every five years the federal government takes a census. Aside from counting the population, the census provides masses of data about where we live, how much people earn, whether they are religious, how many children we have or whether people are having children at all. It is an issue that affects everyone, but its scale overwhelms readers. Newspapers and magazines always run feature stories about the make up of the nation when the census figures are released, which make interesting reading, but in 2001 there was a story to be told about the actual data collection.

Australian Bureau of Statistics (ABS) officers were trying to enumerate a group lost previously—the homeless. The ABS asked homeless people to help in the count, on the grounds that homeless people are more likely than census collectors to know the whereabouts of other homeless people. Most media outlets reported this news and left the matter there, but Chris Johnston made these ghost statistics real by accompanying a homeless man on his travels for the night and dossing down in the foul-smelling, abandoned office under a freeway that the man used. He wrote: 'Lying down, I remember someone I met on the streets saying that when you're homeless, living rough or in a bad squat, you don't really sleep, you only half-sleep. True. There's noise and discomfort and fear.'[19]

SHIFTING YOUR VANTAGE POINT ON AN ISSUE

The feature writer can zoom in close on an issue or event; equally, perhaps even more, effective is to move the camera elsewhere to get a different perspective. Two pieces illustrate the principle. The first was about professional autograph collectors. Journalist Michael Gross surmised that when people think about autographs, they think about the most prized autographs. Maybe they think about the people whose autographs they'd like and occasionally they might think about how tedious it must be to sign autographs every time you step out in public. Rarely do they think about professional autograph collectors or about the trade in autographs that can apparently earn the top collectors six-figure annual incomes. [20]

By shifting his journalistic camera, Gross offered a fresh view of a subject spun dry by publicity agents. He reported how the autograph hunters had learnt the paparazzi's tricks, such as memorising Hollywood film stars' licence plates in case of chance sightings, and he gave them a twist befitting their peculiar sub-culture. For a client who wanted a photograph of Robin Givens (the former model and ex-wife of boxer Mike Tyson), one collector conned her into signing a topless shot by using a black felt pen to draw a bikini top on her image that could be rubbed off later. The article examined the symbiotic relationship between collectors and film stars. The stars disdain the collectors as parasites yet still crave their attention; the collectors emphasise their professionalism yet display 'a measure of starstruck, decidedly unbusinesslike anxiety about what stars think of them'.

The second example looked at the issue of disabled children from the perspective of their siblings. Susan Skelly's piece enabled readers to see the complexity of a difficult issue by showing its impact on others; approaching an issue tangentially can, at times, enable readers to feel it more acutely. One interviewee, Nance Haxton, recalled how she enjoyed writing at school but was unable to write an essay on her favourite holiday place. Her family could not go away on holiday because her autistic older brother, Ashley, needed constant care and supervision. Nor did she ever go out with both parents simultaneously, and rarely even with one. She once went out with her father, and photos were taken to mark the occasion. 'I was 13, we went to the theatre. It was such a big deal,' she told Skelly.[21]

PROJECTION: LOOKING AHEAD

Where synthesis requires the journalist to draw links between things, projection asks them to look ahead, an acquired habit for journalists focused on daily news gathering. Journalists can project in two ways. First, by rolling out the thread of implication. In early 2001 the big insurance company HIH spectacularly collapsed with multi-billion dollar losses. There was, quite rightly, heavy media attention on the collapse at the time but then the story went quiet. Most journalists noted the date of the royal commission into the debacle, scheduled to begin in mid-2002. By August 2001, though, Peter Hunt of *The Weekly Times* was reporting the fallout on various community groups, sporting clubs and individuals, such as spraying contractors, many of whose insurance premiums were doubling; one was rising by as much as 1000 per cent. Hunt was one of the first to highlight the insurance premium issue which by 2002, when his story was highly commended in the feature writing category of the Quills awards, had been spotlighted in media around the nation.

Second, journalists can look ahead to a scheduled event and ask what implications it might have for the present. In 1999 governments, businesses and airlines were transfixed by the Y2K bug that, it was feared, could melt down computer systems when 31 December clicked over to 1 January 2000. That very little did happen—you're probably struggling to remember what the problem was in the first place—does not diminish the importance of Y2K as a news issue in 1999. For months you could not open the newspaper without reading a computer geek's predictions of a technological Armageddon. During the year, Michelle Gunn turned her attention to the vexed question of the New Year's Eve party of the millennium, asking who would babysit for the nation's families when fevered demand was already pushing sitter rates up to anywhere between $50 and $200 an hour. It is easy to smile now, but at the time it was a smart piece of forward thinking by Gunn. Her piece also illustrates how lateral thinking is value free; it can be applied to all stories great and small.[22]

IF THE MEDIA RUNS IN A PACK, WHY NOT BE A LONE WOLF?

We have to keep the press entertained and on the go. The best junkets are the ones where the press thinks it's a weekend not about the movie but about them.

Billy Crystal, playing a veteran publicist in *America's Sweethearts*

It is a staple of media commentary that journalists exhibit herd behaviour. In 2002, Canberra press gallery heavyweight Laurie Oakes revealed an extra-marital affair between former Labor politicians Cheryl Kernot and Gareth Evans, and everyone else rushed into print. Journalists hate being accused of herd behaviour even as they unwittingly enact the accusation: 'We're not a pack,' they bleat in unison. Leaving aside dark theories about journalists conspiring on how stories might or might not be run, the swift-running river of news imposes a measure of pack behaviour. News issues arise and are replaced by a new story, normally within a week. The enterprising feature writer has plenty of tasty morsels to pick over after the media herd has thundered on. If an issue captivated attention for a week, chances are there is something about it that can be resurrected six months or a year later.

One of the best examples of this was written by Cameron Stewart after the 2000 Olympics, at which every Australian gold medal was greeted by speculation that the winners would be swimming in endorsement and sponsorship dollars. Stewart decided to test this claim and contacted 119 of the 154 Australian medallists. [23] He found just over half had no sponsorship deal at all. The vagaries of post-Olympic wealth were highlighted by the wildly different circumstances of two members of the women's water polo team, which won against the Americans, the first Olympic gold medal in this event. The goalkeeper, Liz Weekes, quickly picked up three sponsors plus pictorial spreads in various magazines while her teammate, Yvette Higgins, who threw the winning goal with barely a second left to play, could not score even one sponsor. Both women were healthy, attractive and articulate. Weekes was blonde, Higgins brunette—did that have anything to do with it?

If the news media is unable or unwilling to concentrate on an issue for more than a week or so, it also struggles to deal with issues that contain more than one story. Again, while the media pack savages its prey, the lone wolf can chase others before they run away. Murray Mottram did just this when he followed up questions raised by ABC TV's *Four Corners* about the Liberal Party's long-running campaign to discredit former Labor Prime Minister Paul Keating over his piggery investment. John Seyffer, a shadowy figure working in the backrooms of the Liberal Party, was alleged to have paid a man named Greg Malouf $18 000 to obtain bank documents that appeared to incriminate Keating. Mottram chose not to focus on Seyffer but on the problems Malouf and a number of other small business people had had dealing with the Commonwealth Bank, whose lending policies had altered sharply since it was privatised in the early 1990s. A federal parliamentary committee investigation had found the bank had poor lending practices and withheld important information from customers but had not acted unlawfully. It was a complicated story involving people no one had heard of, but Mottram suggested the problems affected others on top of those he selected for his story. He also showed Malouf et al. had received no recourse despite being thousands of dollars out of pocket over problems not of their making.[24]

Story ideas, then, can range from the bleeding obvious—how is the airline industry faring post September 11—to the highly unlikely. One of the neatest examples of the latter was published in *The Australian's Review of Books* (now defunct). David Brearley wrote about the booming trade in association copies; that is, books personally inscribed by the author for friends and family. 'Writers hate finding their books sold second-hand; how much worse, then, to find personalised examples of their work flogged off by friends—liquidated, as it were, by those whose respect they value the highest.' He cited the example of the late Raymond Carver, doyen of the dirty realism genre of American writing, whose children flogged off their inscribed copies. 'For Chris and her dreams, with love, as always Dad (RC) 4-26-79.' On the title page, beneath his name, the author added a playful scribble: 'Chris Carver's father.' The bookseller's catalogue priced the book at US$2000. Association copies is an arcane subject that seems entirely unpromising as feature fare, but Brearley winkled out a fresh, if disillusioning, story.[25]

There is a limit to how much juice can be squeezed from the orange, though, a point wryly made in a cartoon in *The New Yorker*[26] showing a man at home watching yet another spin-off of the TV series *Law & Order*. 'In the criminal-justice system, the courtrooms are cleaned every night by members of the cleaning crew. These are their stories.' I can wait.

DISCUSSION QUESTIONS AND EXERCISES

1. Find examples from newspapers and magazines of the different methods of generating story ideas. That is, try and deduce the source of the story idea. What proportion of stories seem to derive from ideas and what proportion from set-piece events, such as the release of a new film or the handing down of the budget?
2. Drawing on the news of the day and using the methods of idea generating outlined in this chapter, come up with three story ideas.

5 SPEND HALF AN HOUR PLANNING NOW, SAVE HALF A DAY LATER

A foreign correspondent is someone who flies around from hotel to hotel and who thinks that the most important thing about any story is the fact that he has arrived to cover it.

Tom Stoppard

CHAPTER SUMMARY

The importance of spending time planning a story is emphasised. Four questions are posed that journalists should answer about their prospective feature: 'Why does the story need to be written now?', 'Who is the audience for this story?', 'What is the story about, in a nutshell?', and 'What are the key questions that need answering in the story?' Six categories of potential questions to ask for any feature are expanded upon.

There is a story about Prime Minister John Howard's first federal election campaign as opposition leader. The conservative side of politics was mired in factional brawling, and when the then prime minister, Bob Hawke, announced the election in 1987 Howard immediately began telling Liberal Party campaign staffers, 'We're going to hit the ground running.' It became almost a mantra as he dashed around the hustings, addressing the party faithful and smacking his fist into his palm: 'We're going to hit the ground running.' But, as veteran commentator Alan Ramsey asked: 'In what direction?'

Precisely. Journalists routinely have lots of stories but little time to write them. They too are tempted to hit the ground running, firing off phone calls to contacts and churning through websites, but they would be equally well advised to heed Ramsey's question. Howard lost that election, though obviously for reasons more complicated than suggested by this anecdote. Journalists feel the pressure to produce, but there is a pragmatic reason for planning a feature story: spend half an hour planning today and you will save half a day later. Or more. You will also produce stronger features.

A few minutes thought helps sharpen the idea and its story potential. If the story has been assigned by an editor, it is important to ensure you are clear about what they are after. The breezy briefing Jon Casimir received for his piece about Kylie Minogue is not typical of newsrooms but not atypical either. It is in the journalist's and the editor's interests to outline and agree on the story idea to be pursued. Poor communication between editors and journalists is a major source of wasted energy and aggravation in newsrooms. Editors should write detailed briefs or, if the brief is delivered verbally, the journalist should send the editor an email confirming the story idea.[1] For freelancers, verifying a brief is doubly important as they work outside the newsroom and probably do not know the commissioning editor personally. Whether the story is assigned or is the journalist's idea, you need to ask yourself the following questions, and you need to inform your thinking by doing preliminary research:

1. Why does the story need to be written now?
2. Who is the audience for this story?
3. What is the story about—in a nutshell?
4. What are the key questions that need answering in the story?

WHY DOES THIS STORY NEED TO BE WRITTEN NOW?

The word journalism derives from the French word *jour* meaning 'diurnal', or 'of the day'. Most journalism is about what is on society's mind at any given moment. The journalist's task is to identify what is on society's mind, or to find fresh and compelling ways of piquing society's interest. *The New Yorker* once ran a lengthy story about the packaged ice cube business—a subject about which I know little and care less—that was nonetheless a fascinating read.[2] The level of work and skill required to bring off such a piece, though, is the journalistic equivalent of a triple backward somersault in the pike position with double twist.

Asking why a story needs to be written *now* focuses the journalistic mind. An allied question is even more blunt: who cares if this story is not published? If you cannot provide a good answer, you need to ask whether the story is worth doing at all. Implicit in satisfactorily answering these questions is a sense of the story's context, or where the story is up to now. A feature about genetic engineering today would ask different questions to one written a decade ago, or even last year. This may seem obvious but it is easy to confuse a keen interest in a subject (i.e., genetic engineering) with an awareness of what is happening in that subject right now.

WHO IS THE AUDIENCE FOR THIS STORY?

It should be obvious the editors of *Practical Parenting* magazine would be unmoved by a proposed story about a hot new surfing talent—unless the waxhead was, say, a single mum (or dad) juggling the twin demands of parenthood and the pro surfing circuit. It is essential for freelancers to study the market before pitching their stories; likewise it is essential for staff journalists to think about who reads their newspaper or magazine, and in what frame of mind. Readers of *The Financial Review* expect solid information and analysis; whether it is attractively presented is of secondary importance. *Marie Claire* readers luxuriate in the glossy ads and fashion spreads that seem to melt into each other, but the magazine also runs lengthy features each issue about serious topics, such as the international child slavery trade, problems faced by women in the military or whether China is executing its criminals for their organs.

Readers are not one-dimensional; after all, we are all readers. A reader may turn to the news pages for information and to a lifestyle supplement for specific information about, say, homes and housing, and to the entertainment pages to find out which movie is worth seeing. It is also possible to come up with a legitimate story idea for the wrong publication. A human interest feature on an ageing woman whose arthritis has forced the end of her long career as a piano teacher would work well in the woman's local paper but would not be strong enough to interest the features editor of a metropolitan daily. Readers, then, read different publications to meet different needs, and readers' tastes differ. Even so, there are various elements that the majority of readers like and dislike.

WHAT READERS LIKE

Themselves

People find themselves endlessly fascinating—that's enough about you, let's talk about me for a while. Newspapers and magazines obviously are not going to publish stories about each individual reader. The idea is to make it seem as if an article is about them or their situation. An advertising copywriter once said he could guarantee I would read his next ad. Yeah, right, I hate ads. On a piece of paper he wrote a single line: 'This ad is about you.' Point taken. This is why newspapers report how the federal budget will affect various groups of people, whether two-income families, pensioners or childless couples, even if such groupings never quite match the particulars of readers' individual lives.

Cute furry animals

Everybody is a sucker for animal stories. Lassie was just about the most popular show on television when I was growing up (we always used to go 'aah' at the moment in the credits when Lassie held up her paw). Many journalists forget this when they begin covering the big grown-up world of elections and scandals and disasters. I know I did. Over the years I've written dozens of articles about freedom of information (FOI) laws and received barely a phone call, let alone a letter to the editor. Yet the national media lapped up the story of how a farmer, struck unconscious by a falling branch, was saved after the family's pet kangaroo, LuLu, alerted the farmer's wife with her yapping.[3] FOI is certainly important, but it is an abstract issue that means little to most readers.

Other people

It may be a truism to say people are interested in other people, but it remains true. Readers are interested in people because at some level they put themselves in the other person's shoes. They are particularly interested in other people when those other people are active or players in the story. That is, they are 'are either pressing the buttons and pulling the levers, or those getting ground up in the gears'.[4] An example of the former is David Leser's 1998 profile of talkback radio king Alan Jones; an example of the latter is Solomon Linda, the Zulu villager whose folk song was ripped off. If it is important to put people in feature stories, it is equally important to get people at the ground level of the story's action. Journalists writing stories about, say, the homeless find it easy to talk to the social workers but hard to approach homeless people themselves. A social worker can provide valuable information and help arrange contacts but they are on the first floor rather than the ground level of the story's action. The social worker—and the journalist—are likely to go home to a comfortable bed each night; the homeless person is not, which is why it is important for journalists to talk to them direct.

Facts

Facts are as important in features as in straight news. More of them are needed in features than in news because feature stories are longer. They must be relevant facts; I could list 25 facts about how I wrote this sentence but do you need to know any of them? Here are some facts that propelled an article by Bruce Montgomery about Australian scientist Frank Fenner, a world authority on smallpox. In 1964, according to official documents, the US army's Special Operations Division used specially designed suitcases to spray a strain of bacteria, *Bacillus subtilis*, on unsuspecting Washington travellers. It was supposed to be a harmless experiment but the bacillus was later found to have caused respiratory infection, blood poisoning and food poisoning. In other words, wrote Montgomery, 'it was a deliberate act of bioterrorism on the US population by the very organisation charged with defending it'.[5] These were shocking and relevant facts.

Stories

The value of storytelling is central to this book. Stories inform, entertain and move readers. Above all, stories draw readers in. What reader doesn't like the feeling of wanting to read on to find out what happens in the end? Before the Harry Potter phenomenon, who would have predicted that millions of children around the world would churn through 636 pages of *Harry Potter and the Goblet of Fire*? Such is the power of a good story. Few features have the storytelling possibilities of a Harry Potter, but the more journalists tap these possibilities the more they give readers what they want.

A personal voice

Just as people are interested in other people, so readers like to hear a personal voice in stories. That is why columnists are popular. A distinctive personal voice is anathema to daily news reporting, which is written in the newspaper's institutional voice. Columns are included in this book, but the tone of the vast bulk of features moves awkwardly between the institutional and the personal. It would be easy to say all features should carry a strong personal voice because that is what readers like, but too often inexperienced feature writers mistake rampant egotism for a strong personal voice. The question of when to put yourself into the story is vexed and will be dealt with in chapter 11. The point to grasp here is that readers like to hear a personal voice in a feature, if only to guide them through a complicated issue. They don't much like the institutional voice; it reminds them of a ruling from the tax office.

Sex and violence

Sex and violence are surrogates for the two core human experiences—life and death. Commerce on the Internet has been with us for just under a decade and the first, and still one of the few, groups of people to turn a dollar from it were the pornographers. We all also knew how the story told in James Cameron's *Titanic* was going to end but that did not stop it from becoming the most-watched movie of all time. What was it about? Sex amid violent death. You cannot open a daily newspaper without reading numerous stories on these topics.

WHAT READERS DISLIKE
Numbers

Numbers are essential in many stories, but should be used sparingly and precisely. Numbers are the ultimate abstraction. An act of translation is required to understand numbers. Not only is it easy to lose things in the translation, it takes effort, which makes numbers unpopular with readers, except in sport (Australians love a good stat) and business (numbers equals money). That is why, by analogy, no matter how good the foreign language films are on SBS, only a minority of people can be bothered reading the subtitles. Consider this paragraph from a feature in *The Canberra Times* about autism:

> Brien said the results [of a survey about the needs of families with an autistic child] showed 87 per cent of respondents wanted to access an autism-specific centre in 2003, 64 per cent wanted full-time placement, 72 per cent wanted specific courses such as on social skills, and 79 per cent needed assistance with the development of individual education plans for their children.[6]

The next paragraph had a further five numbers, by which time I was dazed and confused. Which leads me to readers' next pet hate.

Confusion

Few people enjoy feeling confused, particularly when they are short of time and are looking to be informed or entertained. Again, a minority of readers enjoy puzzling over James Joyce's novel *Ulysses*, but only a minority. A reader will read over one confusing sentence, and maybe plough through a second but not a third. They simply stop and turn to the comics. That is why clarity is a prized journalistic quality. It is embedded in a core tenet of news writing: prefer the active to the passive voice because the active voice makes it is easier to work out who is doing what to whom.

Experts

Readers, and journalists for that matter, feel ambivalent about experts. They like them because experts guide their understanding of an issue; they dislike them because by definition experts are distant from the ground level of a story's action. An expert on autism, to pick up the previous example, can provide context but they cannot give the reader a sense of how it feels to be autistic or to bring up an autistic child. Because experts do not have a direct stake in an issue, their comments can drift into windy pontificating, or into whining as they protect their academic patch. Experts may disregard the newspaper or magazine's audience, and bamboozle them with arcane language, or they may have too much regard for their public profile, becoming what is known in the industry as a dial-a-quote. Good experts, then, are like good columnists: valuable but rare.

Sex and violence

Readers may want to read about sex and violence, but may not want to admit it. Readers seemed endlessly fascinated with scandals surrounding Prince Charles and Princess Diana, but in the outcry that followed Diana's death in 1997 were quick to blame the media and slow to reflect on their own role in the princess' sad demise. Certain Christians may say they do not want to read about sex and violence at all, then manfully ignore the increasing number of allegations—and convictions—for child sexual abuse among clergymen. The news media, for its part, likes to say the amount of sex and violence it publishes reflects public taste—as if the relationship between media and audience was a simple mirror. If that were true, the style and content of the media would not change over time. If that were true, the media would never run editorials or campaigns seeking to influence public perceptions. The relationship between the media and its audience is a good deal more complex than either party likes to admit, and the coverage of sex and violence is as good an example of this complexity as any.

WHAT IS THE STORY ABOUT—IN A NUTSHELL?

You cannot, of course, know exactly what your feature story is before you have written it. You cannot even know for sure if there is a story to be written. You may begin research and watch a promising idea wither under scrutiny. Every journalist runs into dead ends. It is nothing to be ashamed of, but it is a perennial source of anxiety. It spurs some to work harder and others to prefabricate their stories like pieces of Lego. Sometimes it is an editor who comes up with an idea and sends out a journalist to find material to fit. The resulting story usually reinforces viewers' prejudices. The best pieces of journalism travel a long way mentally (and often as not, physically) from original idea to finished story. The deeper a journalist digs into an issue or event or person, the more likely it is they will come up with something they did not anticipate. That is not bad. Discovering something new is one of the great pleasures and satisfactions of journalism. If a journalist always found what they were looking for then either they are god—or they think they are.

At this early stage, though, you need to mark out the territory you are going to chart. One of the most common mistakes journalists make is to try and cover too much. They think because they are released from the stricture of a 600-word news story, they will be able to cut swathes through vast topics. They won't. The average feature is still only 1500 to 2000 words, which is shorter than an undergraduate essay, let alone a thesis. Even authors of full-length books need to carefully define the boundaries of their topic. Setting these boundaries is a deceptively difficult but vital piece of work that will give you a sense of what you are investigating. Any curious journalist wants to know all they can about an issue; that is good, as curiosity is journalism's lifeblood. Curiosity must be harnessed, though, to a limited space within a specified time, which means you need to focus on the material which is of most relevance and interest to your readers. Think of Fiona Hudson's story on bush tracks; the strongest material was about the actual making of the track, the weakest was about the apparent controversy surrounding it. Trying to include many aspects of an issue means superficial coverage; focusing on one or two aspects gives you a greater chance of digging deeper and providing the reader with fresh information.

Write down what you think your story is about at this point. William Blundell's term for this is theme statement.[7] If you cannot describe the story idea in a paragraph or two then it is not sufficiently focused. For instance, in the past couple of years many Australian academics have noticed how much paid work students are doing outside their university work. Students may be working 20 hours a week; some may even be combining full-time work with full-time study. It is a serious issue that places great strain on students, and threatens to undermine the benefits of university study. That is a story idea—in three sentences. Notice how the story is confined to one particular aspect of student life. There are many other issues about students, universities and the workforce that are worth a feature but this story idea is not about, say, the impact of the creeping privatisation of Australian universities, or the value of online teaching.

You may well be worried that by planning a story you are predetermining its outcome. Not so. Setting the boundaries helps you ask the right questions. If you find information that takes the story in a different direction or quashes a hypothesis you had, then change direction. Go where the story takes you. Think of story planning as a rudder that enables you to set a course and to change tack with the wind.

WHAT ARE THE KEY QUESTIONS THAT NEED ANSWERING IN THE STORY?

Journalists begin with Rudyard Kipling's famous six serving men—who, what, where, when, why and how. A news story rarely deals with why; feature stories often do. Why is Kylie successful, for instance. Feature writers need Kipling's six serving men as much as news journalists but because features provide context and analysis, they need to look at the background or history of an issue or event and how they develop over time. What follows is a list of types of questions that will help you map your research.[8]

BACKGROUND QUESTIONS
- What is the history of the event or issue you're writing about?
- Is the history central or peripheral to the event or issue?
- Does the event or issue you are writing about represent a continuation of its history or a change from it?

SCOPE QUESTIONS
- How big is the event or issue?
- How widespread is the event or issue—international, national, local?

- Are there hot spots that epitomise the issue?
- Is the issue rising or falling?
- How many different ways is the issue likely to manifest itself?
- Do other issues or events bear on the one you're writing about?
- Do these other issues heighten its importance or diminish it?

WHY QUESTIONS
- Economic: Is money involved in the event or issue? Can you follow the money trail?
- Political: What role does politics play, whether party political or small 'p' political?
- Legal: Are changes in laws, regulations or taxes affecting the issue or event?
- Psychological: How important are emotional or psychological forces in the event or issue?

IMPACT QUESTIONS
- Who or what is likely to be helped by the event or issue you're writing about? (Quantify the scope of the help.)
- Who or what is likely to be hurt by the event or issue? (Again, quantify the scope.)
- What is the emotional response of those helped or hurt?

REACTION QUESTIONS
- Who is screaming the loudest about the event or issue?
- What are they saying and, more important, what are they doing?
- What impact is this effort having?

LOOKING AHEAD QUESTIONS
- What is likely to happen in the future to the event or issue you're writing about?
- What are various people, whether observers or those involved, saying will happen in the future?

This list looks daunting, but it isn't. Think of it this way: you are writing about an issue or event and you need to get some idea of how big it is, the background, why whatever is happening is happening now, what impact it is having, what people are doing about it and what's likely to happen in the future. This is the range of possible questions. It is important to realise you do not need to answer all the questions for each and every feature.

The focus of a story will generally fall into one or two of the six categories, with less detailed material required in other categories, or maybe none at all. Take AIDS as an example. In the early 1980s it was a new and alarming issue widely covered in the media. By the mid to late 1980s journalists were writing features about people dying of AIDS and how the effects of the disease were most keenly felt in the gay community. The importance of practising safe sex was heavily promoted and this, along with other measures such as retroviral drugs to combat the disease, led to a drop in the number of people becoming HIV positive. The public health campaigns have been so effective in Australia that recently health officials have begun worrying that people are becoming blasé about AIDS and less concerned about practising safe sex.

These are the main developments and counter-developments over the past two decades but there are many more minor developments which have all been written up in newspapers and magazines. In the early 1980s features about AIDS focused on its *scope*. Soon they began dealing with the *reasons* for the epidemic, including the nasty idea propagated by various Christian fundamentalists that AIDS was God's way of punishing homosexuals. No one writes about the reasons for AIDS anymore, but that debate raged for a couple of years. Then stories focused on the *impact* on the gay community, and on the reaction by public health officials.

Journalists, unlike historians, are rarely interested in history for its own sake, though over time most come to appreciate its importance. You need to look at background that is relevant to the issue or event you are writing about. The amount of background needed varies. Anyone writing about the 1999 film *The Insider*, starring Russell Crowe as the tobacco scientist turned whistleblower, had to provide background on the tobacco industry's decades of denial and duplicity over the dangerous effects of smoking. Reading Fiona Hudson's feature on bush tracks, I couldn't help reflecting on the hardiness and determination of early white explorers in Australia. Some information on them could have added texture to the piece. Sometimes journalists add historical material as a kind of garnish; in a piece about the multi-billion dollar racehorse breeding industry, Garry Linnell reported that the entire thoroughbred industry could be traced back to three stallions and 45 royally bred mares imported into England between 1689 and 1730.[9]

The importance of quantifying an event or issue in concrete terms seems obvious but far too many journalists rely on unsubstantiated assertions. Until the advent of the computerised Booktrack system in 2001, for instance, barely a weekend went by without an article about a 'bestselling' author, but rarely were actual sales figures provided, or sourced, or set in context. Such information comes under scope questions. Note too that scope questions are not simply about size, but about the intensity of an event or issue, its location, and whether it is waxing or waning. Asking why something is happening may well not lead to clear-cut answers but the question needs to be asked and journalists need to be open to a range of potential explanations. Even in seemingly dry business stories, psychological forces may be important, as was evident in the meltdown between one-time friends and business associates Brad Cooper and Rodney Adler, who fell out as their roles in the collapse of the HIH insurance company were revealed.

Scouting around for who or what is being helped or hurt by an event or issue has the twin benefit of putting you in contact with the people or institutions likely to be qualified to comment on your issue, and of deepening readers' understanding by showing them the impact of the event or issue. For instance, some years ago I wanted to write a piece about the Holocaust but wondered how to write something new about such a widely documented subject. I knew the Jewish Holocaust Centre was about to mark its 10th anniversary but that was only a flimsy news peg. I also knew the guides were all Holocaust survivors, which was more interesting. Making preliminary inquiries, I learnt that the great majority of the thousands of visitors were schoolchildren, not adults, so I decided to investigate the impact the survivors' testimony had had on the students. I had never seen that written about before, whereas I had seen countless interviews with Holocaust survivors.

Reaction questions are for stories that are already well developed as they depend on the impact of an event or issue being felt. It is always preferable to find out what people do about something as distinct from what they say they will do. Looking ahead questions are, of course, suggestive rather than definitive, but they can be instructive. For example, while writing this chapter the career of John Elliott, long-time football club president, former entrepreneurial giant and one-time aspiring prime minister, was imploding. What would Elliott do if he lost the Carlton presidency and his business fortune? How would he be remembered? These were questions worth asking.

Setting out the questions 'Why does the story needed to be written now?', 'What is the story about in a nutshell?', 'What are the key questions that need answering?', and 'Who is the audience for this story?' provides a readymade brief for an editor, though you should summarise answers to the final question in your brief. Editors do not need to know every rabbit burrow you plan to chase down; they do need to know the key questions you will be asking. They also appreciate journalists who keep in touch during the research, particularly if the journalist strikes snags that could affect deadlines.

The next question is how will you get the story? Journalists have three main methods of gathering information, and these are covered in the next three chapters.

DISCUSSION QUESTIONS AND EXERCISES

1. Do you agree with the list of readers' likes and dislikes? Are there others you would include? Draw on the newspapers and magazines you have been collecting for earlier exercises to find examples of things readers like and dislike.
2. For the feature you are working on, answer the three questions listed in the chapter: 'Why does the story need to be written now?', 'Who is the audience for this story', and 'What is the story about, in a nutshell?'
3. Following the model of the six potential groups of questions, draw up a plan of the questions you want to answer in the feature.

THIS MAN RAPED TWO LITTLE GIRLS . . .

by Pamela Bone[10]

. . . His victims were forced to relive what happened to them over and over again. This is called justice.

In the brand new barrister bustling County Court of Victoria, a little girl in a red jumper is answering questions put to her by a defence lawyer. He speaks to her in a voice of exaggerated kindness: "If there's anything you don't understand, just say so, *OK*?"

"Bonnie wanted to go to the toilet. Bonnie, me and Katy all went together. I heard the man say *Come on.* I was in the toilet. Bonnie said, Katy's getting hurt. He was holding her by the neck. I said, get off her. They were in the classroom. The grade two classroom.

"Yes. On the carpet. Katy was crying, she was saying, Peta, get him off me. He was kneeling. Sitting on her feet. She was kicking. I said get off her. We ran as quickly as we could to find someone to tell. Bonnie got the scooter. I went to get Katy. She said she was sick. While we were running she said she was sick. The man ran to the fence and jumped it.

"We ran to some people who were working in the garden. I said would you please ring Dad."

There are two television screens facing the jury. On one, a tape is playing of eight-year-old Peta being questioned by a policewoman the day after Bonnie and Katy were raped, on May 19 last year. On the other screen Peta, who is in a room two floors below the courtroom, can be seen watching this tape. Nine-year-old Peta is watching eight-year-old Peta tell her story. This is the story:

A quiet country town on a Saturday afternoon in autumn. Three little girls, sisters Peta and Bonnie, aged eight and six, and their friend Katy, also six, go for a walk to the local milk bar. They take it in turns to ride Katy's scooter. They buy lollies—Redskins—and an ice-cream. Then they go to the plant nursery, opposite the service station, because they like to look at the flowers. Then they decide to go to Peta and Bonnie's school to play on the monkey bars.

Driving through the town is Andrew Timothy Davies, 33. He is angry, having had a fight with his sister over a disputed washing machine. He drove all the way from Melbourne to get it and she would not give it back. Davies has a history of taking out his anger, or twisted sexuality, or both, on small girls. He has convictions for raping a five-year-old girl in a school toilet, for the attempted abduction of other girls and for loitering outside school and kindergarten toilets. He has served short jail terms for these.

On this day he watches Peta, Bonnie and Katy as they buy their lollies, and watches them again from the service station across the road as they admire the flowers in the nursery. Peta tells the court this, even though this is not part of the Crown case. He was smiling at us, she says—he had a funny smile. He follows them to the school. While Peta is in the toilet he drags Bonnie and Katy into the classroom, which is open because the school cleaner is somewhere on the school grounds.

A doctor who examined Katy on that night described to the court "bleeding, bruising, acute tearing, lacerations externally and internally and swelling; evidence of penetrative trauma consistent with digital penetration of significant force".

One sick man, three traumatised children, parents blaming themselves—but who would not think it safe to let three children walk to the shops in a quiet country town?—one wigged and gowned judge, prosecuting and defence counsel, instructing solicitors, judge's associate, court tipstaff, and 12 men and women representing the collective wisdom of the community.

There are eight men and four women on this jury. In rape trials, defence counsel often use their right to challenge prospective jurors in order to have more men than women. In this case, they challenged several young, professional women and accepted older women who gave their occupations as "home duties". Why? I could have told the defence that the last people they should want judging this case are mothers and grandmothers.

The jury foreman has neat grey hair, a florid face and an air of authority. He is not the sort of person defence counsel usually want. "Generally, the defence will not want anyone who looks like an organiser," a barrister, who doesn't want to be named, told me. Defence and prosecution have the right to challenge six times before they have to show cause, but the defence is much more likely to challenge than the prosecution.

The defendant, Davies, who stands each time the jury enters or leaves the room, is slight, with hair clipped close to his head. He smiles a small, closed-mouth smile often during the trial.

The hours drag on. Peta's answers are polite, careful, calm. Later, her mother tells me that during the week they had to be in Melbourne for the trial Peta insisted on sleeping in the wardrobe of the motel room they were staying in.

How many times has she had to tell this story? To the people whose home the girls ran to after the assaults. To the police who were called immediately. Then again the next day, in the long videotaped interview that has been played to the court today. A week after the attacks she went to Melbourne to look at a video identification line-up, from which she identified Davies as the man in the schoolyard. She told the story again to the committal hearing, in the Melbourne

Magistrates Court last December, and was cross-examined on it. She has probably told it a dozen times, says one of the policemen from the Sexual Crimes Squad.

There was a different defence lawyer at the Magistrates Court. At committal hearings there is no jury to be alienated by the rigorous questioning of children, so defence lawyers are generally much harder on child witnesses than they are during trials, a County Court judge, who also does not want to be named, tells me.

Some cases never proceed past the committal hearing because the children or their parents decide they cannot go on with it.

Identity is the only issue in this trial. There is no question of consent; in law children cannot give consent to sexual intercourse. There is no doubt that sexual penetration took place; there is medical evidence of this. The only thing the jury needs to decide is whether the man who was at that primary school on that day is the same man sitting in the dock.

There is no forensic evidence to help them. Police investigators gathered cigarette butts from the schoolyard and tested them against a DNA sample from Davies' mouth, but they did not match. All the Crown has to rely on are records of some calls made to and from Davies' mobile telephone, which showed him to be in the area at the time of the offences. That, and the eyewitness evidence of three small girls.

Peta, on the television screen, is being cross-examined by counsel for the defence, Mr Benjamin Lindner, who is in the courtroom: How long did it take you to get from the milk bar to the nursery? Two minutes.

How long from the nursery to the school. Six minutes.

What colour was the T-shirt the man was wearing? It was black or dark blue.

Was there any writing on it? No.

You wouldn't say your memory gets better as time passes, would you? No.

In December you said his top was black. In December you said you were not sure if it had writing on it. You've already told us that the description you gave of the man was the best description you can give. Yes.

Was it possible that the man at the milk bar was a different man to the one at the petrol station? Yes.

his question direct: "Why did you say it was him on the video?"

Peta answers. "Because he looked exactly like the person I seen."

The jury is not allowed to know what I and others in the courtroom know: that Davies already has convictions for sexual assaults on children. Justice requires that he is tried for the present charges and no other.

In some limited circumstances, under legislation relating to "similar fact evidence", the jury can be told of the defendant's prior convictions, but the earlier crimes must be of "striking similarity" to the present ones.

The only thing the jury needs to decide is whether the man who was at that primary school on that day is the same man sitting in the dock.

Was it possible that the man (identified by Peta on the videoed identification line-up) was not that man? Was it possible you made an honest mistake and were confused? Yes.

A County Court judge—not the one hearing this case—told me that when giving evidence children are more literally truthful than adults. Where an adult might say, "no it is not possible I made a mistake", a child will agree that it is possible. Anything is possible.

Peta's face is tired, her mouth downturned. I look at the faces of the jurors. What if, after all of this, they don't believe her?

When Mr Lindner has finished, the Crown Prosecutor, Mr Andrew Tinney, gets to his feet. His manner is gentle, but

In this case, the prosecution has apparently decided the earlier offences are not similar enough to risk a conviction being appealed. Many rape convictions are appealed.

I tell myself that just because Davies has done this before does not mean he is guilty this time. But I tell myself it makes it more likely that he is.

Leaving the court one day, I see one of the jurors standing beside me in the rain, waiting for the traffic lights to change. Will I whisper to him "this fellow's a serial rapist", abort the trial if he tells, get myself charged with contempt of court? I look straight ahead, say nothing.

Bonnie, Peta's sister, was six at the time of the assaults. She is now seven. Judge Bill White, in the absence of the jury, is trying to make sure she under-stands what it means to swear an oath. "Do you know what the Bible is?" he asks.

"It's where God helps you," she says piously.

"So, if you made a promise on the Bible to tell the truth and you didn't tell the truth, would that be a good thing or a bad thing?"

"A bad thing!"

"What is an example of a lie?"

Bonnie doesn't answer. "Well, if I said you came to this court today in a heli-copter, what would that be?"

Bonnie, triumphantly: 'A lie!'

"Yes, well, I propose to have this wit-ness sworn in," the judge says.

The judge tells the jury they are not to draw any inference adverse to the defendant from the fact that the girls are giving evidence from a remote location. In the past the children would have had to be in the courtroom, in front of the man who attacked them. The legislation that allows them to give evidence through a video link is one of a number of measures introduced in recent years to reduce the trauma of child witnesses.

Like Peta, Bonnie gave evidence at the committal hearing six months ago. Like Peta, today she must first watch the video of her younger self giving evidence, so that she can be questioned on it. It is striking how much older she looks now, compared with only a year ago.

On the video, taken the day after the rapes, Bonnie comes into the room with her mother and throws herself on the seat, crying and clutching a large white stuffed toy. She is being inter-viewed by Senior Constable Patricia Allen, from the Benalla Sexual Crimes Unit, who is patient and kind. When six-year-old Bonnie tells "Trish" what the man did to her, the seven-year-old Bonnie on the other television screen puts her hands over her ears and screws her eyes tight.

The answers are all over the place. "Katy said, I don't want to do it. We ran to the house. They rang Dad and he rang the cops. The grade two classroom. I was going to go back and get Katy. Because he dragged us. It hurt. I heard Katy screaming. Katy said, stop it."

Trish: Where? Bonnie: There.

What is it called? A fanny.

Who has fannies? Girls.

What do you do with your fanny? Do wee with it.

What happened when he touched it? It hurt.

It is four o'clock. Bonnie is told she will have to come back the next day. The court is adjourned. "God save the Queen," says the tipstaff, in his long green coat.

The following morning, Bonnie is being questioned by Mr Lindner: When you talked to Trish on May 19 and May 20 you told her he had black hair and black trousers but you didn't say any-thing about his face. Do you agree you didn't see his face clearly? Yes.

Did you see the boy from the school at the milk bar—I withdraw that, I'll start again. So the first time you saw him was at the school? Yes.

What colour top was he wearing? Black.

Are you sure? Yes.

Do you remember at the Melbourne Magistrates Court last December prom-ising to tell the truth, do you remember that? Yes.

Can you remember these questions and answers (reading from the transcript of the committal hearing): "He had black hair. Was it curly? Yes. What was he wearing? A red T-shirt."

Now he asks Bonnie again: Did you answer those questions with those answers? No.

Were you telling the truth to the court then? Yes.

Bonnie rubs her eyes and yawns.

Mr Lindner: You didn't tell Trish anything about the face of the boy at the school. Six days later you picked out a face from the video. The last time you saw him he was jumping the fence. It may have been someone else (on the video)—is that possible? Yes.

At the end of Mr Lindner's cross examination Mr Tinney rises and asks Bonnie: Why did you point out that man on the video?

Bonnie: because it was that man.

Katy has straight, shiny hair, a baby face and a baby voice. She seems younger than Bonnie even though she is slightly older. She is also the one who was most traumatised, physically and emotionally, at the time of the attack.

She was crying when the people in the garden of the house across the road, a retired doctor and his wife, tried to comfort the girls. When Peta and Bonnie's father came to get them she threw herself into the back seat of the car, crying. When she was taken home she ran to the bedroom, crying. When she was questioned by policewoman Trish later that day all she could do was cry. She cried again during the medical examination. The next day, during the videotaped interview, she was still crying, on and off.

On this video Katy is trying to burrow into her father, who is sitting beside her with his hand over his face.

Trish: Can you tell me what telling a lie is? Katy: When you tell a lie you get into trouble.

The questions continue: "He took us into the grade two room, that's what he done. He just dragged us. I told you before. He said a swear-word. It was f———. His voice was funny. Like when your voice goes away. He did it to Bonnie first. I tried to stop him. Bonnie couldn't stand up, her legs were too sore. And that's the end!"

Trish asks Katy how she felt: "Sad . . . Because it was sore . . . That's the end. I'm finished!"

Katy didn't give evidence at the committal hearing, because she was unable to identify anyone from the police video line-up. Today, Mr Lindner asks her: "You didn't point to any face, did you?" "No, because I forgot what he looked like."

"Was it because the man you saw at the . . . primary school wasn't on the video?" Katy: "Yes."

The trial lasts two weeks.

There are long hours of evidence about the reach of signals for mobile telephones. The defence counsel's instructing solicitor appears to be asleep, the judge's associate's eyes are closed, the tipstaff's head droops. But the judge is alert and so are the jury members, listening attentively. The jury is shown a video of a school playground, of monkey bars and slippery slide, the inside of a classroom with its bright children's paintings on the wall and child-height coat hangers.

There is bickering between the prosecution and defence counsel. The judge is testy. The jury is sent out frequently while legal points are argued.

Mr Lindner: "I am astonished by my friend's questions, Your Honour."

Judge White: "Oh, I think we are all past being astonished at this stage, Mr Lindner."

Who cares about the little girls? It is evident that this trial is not about them. It is about criminal justice being done. It's about winning.

I'll tell you who cares. The two detectives from the Melbourne Sexual Crimes Squad, who have been sitting outside the courtroom waiting to give evidence, and who have been with the girls and their families for the past 14 months, and know the impact this crime has had on them. Yes, agrees one, the outcome of the trial does matter a lot to him. "What terrifies me is that this fellow knows he's in there because these little girls identified him. What's he going to do next time?"

Mr Tinney sums up the prosecution case. The jury is shown a video of Peta and Bonnie, separately, pointing to the video identification line-up and saying, "him". Mr Tinney tells the jury that they are entitled to find the accused guilty on Peta's evidence alone. He reminds them that Peta has earlier, unprompted, provided them with a "stunningly important" piece of evidence about the attacker, when she described his teeth.

"Some people just can't help smiling even when they are going to do what he did to these girls . . . and when this man smiled, what a horrible mouthful of teeth he had," Mr Tinney says. The jury is shown a photograph of Davies with his teeth bared.

"Now wasn't the accused terribly unlucky? By an extraordinary coincidence the person Peta picked from the video, from 11 men plucked from the streets of Melbourne, just happened to have been in (the town) at the time of the crimes, just happened to look exactly like the man who attacked them, and just happened to have teeth exactly as described by Peta." Mr Tinney reminds the jury that the standard of proof required, beyond reasonable doubt, is a very high standard but not an impossible one.

Mr Lindner, summing up the defence case, tells the jury their task is of the head, not the heart. He warns that the girls' evidence is "fundamentally unreliable", and of the "grave miscarriages of justice" that have occurred in the past because honest, confident witnesses have identified the wrong person. "You must be satisfied beyond reasonable doubt of the identity of the offender. Your verdict must be unanimous. There are no second chances. You can't come back next week and say, now I have a reasonable doubt."

Judge White tells the jury that the right to trial by jury is one of the most important aspects of our criminal justice system. "I direct you as a matter of law that any sympathy, prejudice, bias you may feel is not to be taken into account," he says. He warns that the history of the law shows that identification evidence should be treated with caution, and that honest, responsible witnesses have made identifications which have later been proved to be wrong.

The jury took three hours to find Davies guilty of two counts of abduction and two of rape. The Department of Public Prosecutions is seeking an indefinite prison sentence for him.

In the days after the attack, some people in the town threw stones at the houses of a couple of men they suspected. No one let their children out. The Sexual Crimes Squad police held a community meeting to calm the town down. One man told Peta and Bonnie's mother something like this was bound to happen because Bonnie was "just too friendly". Others asked what the three girls were doing out on their own anyway.

The girls are going to a different school now. They've been held back a year because their work has suffered. Peta and Bonnie's older sister dropped out of her VCE year. The girls have changed from being happy, outgoing and sociable to "clingy" and withdrawn. They are still having counselling. Their mother told me she feels like she has been crying for a year.

Justice has been done, but at what cost? A recent study by Queensland University of Technology Professor Christine Eastwood of sexual abuse cases found that only one-third of children interviewed in New South Wales would report sexual abuse again. Two thirds of legal professionals would not want their children to take it to trial. Not one defence lawyer interviewed for this study would want his or her child, if a victim of serious sexual assault, in the system.

Studies in the United States show children involved in lengthy criminal cases are 10 times more likely to remain disturbed than children whose cases are resolved quickly.

Suggestions have been made over the years for a different kind of court to deal with crimes against children, more like a Coroners Court with an investigatory procedure rather than an adversarial one. But as one judge said, while you can put in place measures to make it easier on children, as long as child rape is a crime it will have to be dealt with in the criminal justice system.

Peta is a hero. She went to the door of the classroom and yelled at Davies, and he ran away. Her hours of patient evidence will put him in jail, where he cannot hurt any other children, for a long time.

If it were any other kind of physical attack, these little girls might be flooded with cards and toys and public sympathy. But Peta, Bonnie and Katy are of course made-up names. Because it was a sexual attack the law says they cannot be identified. Is this a reflection of the societal view that a person who has been raped, has been shamed? There is shame involved in this, certainly. But it does not belong to them.

THE STORY BEHIND THE STORY

Pamela Bone

I was interested in writing a feature article on why it is so difficult to get a conviction in rape trials. I contacted the media relations person for the

County Court to try to find out what interesting trials might be coming up. She contacted someone from the Department of Public Prosecutions, who was reluctant to advise on upcoming cases and was anxious to find out whether the journalist concerned was aware of the restrictions on reporting rape trials, such as not revealing the names of victims, etc. He was advised that this journalist had been around the traps for about 20 years, and had spent several of those years covering the County Court and the Supreme Court. In the end, he provided the names of four defendants in rape trials that were about to begin.

I dutifully turned up at the brand new and very luxurious County Court and looked for the names on the list. There was no sign of life at the first courtroom I went to. At the second courtroom I was advised the case was unlikely to proceed that week, so I sat around for a while hoping something would happen. Then our permanent County Court reporter, Jamie Berry, told me of a case going on in which a man was accused of having abducted and raped two small girls in the schoolyard of a country town. I decided to sit in and watch this trial for a while, even though it didn't fit the brief I had set myself (I was looking for a 'he said, she said' dispute between a man and woman).

When I walked into the courtroom a little girl was being cross-examined by a defence barrister. The trial had already been underway for a couple of days and I had missed the opening address of the Crown prosecutor. I was struck by the dignity and thoughfulness with which the little girl answered the questions put to her. It occurred to me that it must have been very hard for her to relive this experience again in such detail. I became so interested in this case I decided I would put the other idea on hold for a while (I still have not got back to it) and instead write about the issue of children giving evidence in court.

Three children gave evidence in this case. The two younger girls, who were now seven, had been raped by the defendant when they were six. The older girl, eight at the time and now nine, was a witness. They gave evidence by 'remote facility', which means they were televised into the court from a room two floors below. First they had to watch a video of themselves giving evidence the day after the attacks. Then they had to be questioned by the prosecutor, then by the defence counsel, then in some cases be re-examined by the prosecutor. Before they were sworn in the judge, in the absence of the jury, had to ascertain whether they were capable of understanding the importance of taking the oath. It appeared to me that one of the younger girls, in particular, did not really understand what it meant to swear an oath, or even really the concept of truth and lies. She seemed just too young for the task.

I became mesmerised by the trial and sat through it almost every minute, even though at times the evidence (about the reach of mobile telephone signals) was extremely boring and I knew it would never become a part of any story I would write. I also wanted to reassure Jamie Berry I was not trying to usurp his role; he would write any news stories about the trial and I would write a feature later about the issues. The trial received widespread publicity but there were no other journalists in the court while the little girls were telling their stories. I was relieved about this, because their evidence was riveting.

Because I have a granddaughter about the same age as the two youngest girls some of the evidence was distressing to listen to. I kept wondering how my little granddaughter would have coped with the court process. I feel strongly that no child of this age should have to go through the ordeal of telling her story over and over again. I was also angry during the trial that the jury was not allowed to know the defendant had several prior convictions for almost identical offences against small girls. I understand accused persons must be tried on the current charges and not earlier ones, but it seems to me that in cases of sexual offences against children there is often a pattern of similar crimes.

At the end of the case I did some research about various measures that have been taken to make it easier on children giving evidence in court. In the past the children would have had to be present in the courtroom, in front of their attacker, and this is still the case in some states. I talked to a County Court judge, who was formerly a prosecutor and did not want to be named, and two barristers, who also wanted to remain anonymous for reasons of professional ethics, for more background information.

I had read earlier about the harmful effects on child victims of sexual assault when they are required to tell the story over and over again. The author of this book, noted American psychologist Martin Seligman, wrote that in such cases the best advice he could give to parents was 'turn the heat right down'. Yet these children had had to tell their stories at least twelve times, according to a policeman from the Sexual Crimes Squad.

I should say that the police officers of the Sexual Crimes Squad were very helpful and seemed genuinely concerned about the welfare of the children and the repercussions on their families. Indeed, it seemed to me the only professionals who really cared about the children were the police. One of them arranged an introduction to the mother of two of the girls, who agreed for me to go to the country town where the family lives to talk to her. She told me the girls were still having counselling because of the attack. My own opinion is that it was probably better for the children to be allowed to simply forget about it. According to Martin Seligman, children are able to get over sexual assault more easily than adults can, if repeated telling of the story does not prevent natural healing from taking place. However, I did not say this to the mother, nor did I include this opinion in the story.

The editor, Michael Gawenda, was very supportive when I told him about the story I was pursuing, and he told me to stay with it for as long as it took. Altogether, including the trial, the interviews and the writing, it took about three weeks. I found it a comparatively easy story to write because it seemed to me logical to structure it around the chronology of the trial. I suppose experience helps, but I also feel one either has an instinctive feeling for how a story should be structured or one does not. I am sometimes asked how I go about writing a story and I find the question very difficult to answer. I just find a place where it seems natural to start and go on from there. Of course it doesn't always flow easily and some-times I revise it many times until I feel it is right. Knowing when it is right, or as right as one can make it, is sometimes the most difficult part.

Though this is not my regular practice, at times I did insert editorial comment and information I had obtained through the interviews with lawyers and with the family of the little girls. It is not very common for a journalist to put himself or herself into a story, but I think it can be valid, as long as it does not become self-indulgent. None of us is objective, especially when something as emotive as the sexual abuse of children is involved, and perhaps we should not pretend to be. Of course one would not put oneself into a hard news story.

[6] GATHERING THE RAW MATERIAL

Having interesting things to say and presenting them vividly are both rare skills, and the combination is rarer still. Its value becomes even more apparent in a world where everyone has nothing to say and the ability to say it at great length.

Andrew Brown

CHAPTER SUMMARY

The nature and range of material that journalists need to gather for features is listed—facts, anecdotes, quotes, atmosphere, analysis and telling details—and so are the three groups of people that you need to talk to. Documents are essential for journalists to gather but documents are defined more broadly than paper. The range of potential sources of documents is outlined.

'The journalist with a clear sense of their story idea is ready to go out and get it.' Really? Easier said than done! Journalists may think bureaucrats are bursting to leak them government-toppling documents or that they will conduct electric interviews with celebrities in exotic locations. It is more likely bureaucrats will be zip-lipped for fear of losing their job and the hapless journalist will be shoehorned into a ten-minute slot (18th out of 21 for the day) in a bland, featureless hotel room with a brain-dead actor enthusing unenthusiastically about how great it was to work with Bobby or Steven or Sharon. So let's return to first principles of practice.

Journalists use three main sources for gathering information: documents, interviews and first-hand observation. They use the same sources for news as for features, though features require a greater range and depth of material. Not all features require the same amount of research. Lifestyle pieces do not demand the detailed exacting research of an investigative feature. A textbook approach would deal with these research tools one by one but at times they will be used simultaneously. That is, you may visit a source at home and mid-interview you may be given documents that help explain the issue you are writing about. Whichever tool used there are certain kinds of material that you should always be looking for, which correlate with the list of readers' likes in the previous chapter.

WHAT YOU NEED TO GET FOR THE STORY
FACTS AND FIGURES

Facts remain the bedrock of journalism. Yes, young journalists should be aware of the cultural and psychological baggage they bring to their assignments and, yes, they should be aware that facts sit within ideological frameworks (look no further than the ferocious debate about the historical relations between black and white Australia), but facts are facts. If you are going to write about the Wilsons Prom bush track you need to find out things such as how long it is, how much it will cost and when it will be finished. Facts and figures substantiate assertions, which are as important in features as they are in news. It is one thing to lament the scale of the American prison system, but another to produce statistics confirming the United States has more prisoners per head of population than any country, as *The Economist* did in one feature.[1]

ANECDOTES

Anecdotes are mini-stories that many think are confined to jokes, but like any story they can be sad, funny, awe-inspiring or something else. What they must be, though, is revelatory. For instance, boxing legend Muhammad Ali had the rare quality of simultaneously creating and deflating his own myth. When Ali first registered for the military draft in 1964 he failed an elementary intelligence test, which revealed his IQ as 78. Ali was genuinely embarrassed, but still shot off a one-liner: 'I said I was the greatest, not the smartest.'[2]

QUOTES

Ali's quote is a good one, but most people do not speak in quotes; they push a verbal stew around their plate. Journalists train themselves to hear those moments when people express themselves clearly, even memorably. There are three reasons to use quotes in features. First, to reveal something about a person. Second, because at times it is important to hear what a newsmaker has to say on a key point in the article. Third, to garnish your feature with witty quotations. Adlai Stevenson, one-time American presidential candidate, said this about newspapers: 'An editor is one who separates the wheat from the chaff—and prints the chaff.' If quotes are effective because they report people in their own voice, then reporting dialogue can be doubly effective because it allows readers to hear the actual interplay between people.

ATMOSPHERE

Where hard news zip-locks emotions in journalese, feature stories convey emotions through description, whether of people, events or by quoting dialogue as mentioned above. This is the opening to the piece about the Jewish Holocaust Centre:

> The teenage boy shuffles in his seat before standing up to ask his question: 'Did you get a number tattooed on your arm?' The elderly woman sitting at a desk on a platform in front of him says: 'Of course. Do you want to see it?' Before he or his classmates can answer, Thea Kimla roughly pulls up her jacket and shirt sleeves and waves her arm at them.
>
> Not a movement in the hall. The silence is palpable. But they are not close enough to see her Auschwitz number—79505—or the fading ink-blue triangle that denotes Thea was a political prisoner.
>
> Already she has told these students from St James Catholic secondary college in south-eastern Melbourne that she lost all 39 members of her family in the holocaust.
>
> Now, another student asks bluntly: 'What did it smell like?' She replies, 'Did you ever smell burning meat? I saw thousands of people going to the gas chamber one day in July 1944.'[3]

By dropping the reader straight into the scene at the museum, the effect is disarming, which mirrors the frank yet respectful exchange between the students and the survivor.

ANALYSIS

Features need analysis or insight as well as facts and feelings, though not as much in straightforward features like Fiona Hudson's bush track piece as in more complex pieces like Jon Casimir's story about Kylie Minogue. Remember the strength of the latter piece was Casimir's dissection of the Kylie phenomenon. A journalist does not have to do all the analysis; it is common for them to draw on the expertise of others, particularly for complex, controversial subjects such as crime rates. Peter Ellingsen quoted five different criminologists in a feature asking why politicians and the news media continue behaving as if crime rates are rising when they have stabilised or fallen in most western countries in the past decade.[4]

TELLING DETAILS

Details are everywhere, but few tell you much. Feature writers, like novelists, prize details embedded in the grain of life because they lodge deep in the reader's consciousness. It is one thing to write, for instance, that coal mining is a dangerous job, but bald statements slide by readers. George Orwell, when researching his journalistic account of life in the northern English town of Wigan, found miners' pay cheques carried a stamp marked 'Death Stoppage', meaning a shilling had been deducted to contribute to a fund for fellow miners' widows. Orwell commented: 'The significant detail here is the rubber stamp. The rate of accidents is so high, compared with that in other trades, that casualties are taken for granted almost as they would be in a minor war.'[5]

WHO YOU NEED TO TALK TO

PEOPLE—SHAKERS AND MOVERS

Journalism routinely intersects with the machinery of society, institutions such as the parliament, government, police force, public service, courts and hospitals, or organisations such as sporting clubs, peak bodies, trade unions, churches, arts companies, businesses and the voluntary sector. Representatives need to be interviewed and reported, as Ellingsen did when he quoted Paul Mullet from the Victorian Police Association, Supreme Court Judge Bernard Teague and Police Minister Andre Haermeyer.

PEOPLE—THE SHAKEN AND MOVED

Shakers and movers are voices of authority, those who wield power, make decisions, lobby for policy changes. It is equally important to include the voices of those who bear the brunt of institutional power and policy. To continue with the Ellingsen example, his piece includes an interview with the mother of a young man shot dead in a random altercation at the end of a long, alcohol-fuelled night. While the police minister explains policy, Heather McDonald paces her kitchen clutching court documents that record the conviction of her son's murderer but give her no relief from the grief she still feels five years later.

PEOPLE—EXPERTS AND OBSERVERS

Shakers and movers know a lot about their area but they represent a particular body and they may need to toe a party line. That is why you need other, independent experts, usually academics but perhaps members of private think tanks or even individual experts affiliated with no one in the story. Ian Jones, for instance, is a retired television director and the author of the most respected biography to date of Ned Kelly. He is routinely quoted whenever a new Ned story breaks.

GATHERING THE MATERIAL IN DOCUMENTS

Your story plan has helped identify the relevant questions and the list above identifies the kind of material you'll need. Where to get it? Let's begin with documents, which in this context means not just paper, but radio programs, films and Internet sites, among others. It is tempting just to jump on the Net, tap in, say, crime rates, and scroll through the hits. Resist this temptation. The Internet is a wonderful tool because it has made freely available masses of information that journalists can download onto their desktops. This is a benefit that cannot be gainsaid. The Internet is not, however, the journalistic nirvana some early cyber-gurus proclaimed it. If it was, the media would be overflowing with dazzingly researched stories, wouldn't it? Just why it isn't brings us back to the problem of information overload.

You may find a hundred documents on crime rates, but will you have the time to read them all, not to mention verify the information? Imagine trying to find a shell at the beach. The Internet will hoover up lots of shells and dump them at your feet, but it won't sort them unless you ask it to and it might have broken some along the way. Wouldn't it be smarter to identify the kind of shell you want first, and whether it is even likely to be found at this beach? As with planning a story idea, it is better to spend a few minutes thinking about from whom or where you are most likely to find what you are looking for.

Belinda Weaver is a long-time librarian who writes a weekly Web advice column for *The Courier-Mail*. She says pre-Internet research methods were successful and have not been made redundant by the new technology.

If someone asks me for, say, information on genetically-modified food, I think CSIRO. The Federal Government would also have information. Female circumcision—that's a human rights issue—what about trying Amnesty International . . .? Digital TV and datacasting—I'd try the Australian Broadcasting Authority and also the government for latest news, press releases and so on. Tourism numbers—the ABS (Australian Bureau of Statistics), obviously. Reconciliation—I'd try ATSIC (Aboriginal and Torres Strait Islander Commission) and the Council for Aboriginal Reconciliation. The latest on Kosovo? I'd look at BBC news archives, online Balkan newspapers and possibly the UN Commissioner for Refugees.[6]

THE CLIPPINGS FILE, REFERENCE MATERIAL

Journalists have access to their newspaper's or magazine's clippings file, although these vary in range and quality depending on the news organisation. Freelancers commissioned for a story have access to these clippings files too. Editorial libraries are not open to the public, though some will compile customised files for a fee. Some search engines have specialist (human) researchers who will find information, also for a fee. Many university libraries now have access to searchable databases of newspapers and magazines as well as academic journals. These are free for students but typically go back only a decade or so. Whatever the case, it is important to find out what has been published in the media on your topic. Begin your own clippings file on issues that particularly interest you. Over the years you will pick up relevant information from a wide range of sources, not all of which will be contained in the standard databases.

Newsrooms and university libraries have reference material but it is worth gathering your own collection for easy desktop access. This type of material is not confined to dictionaries and style guides, important though they are, but includes reference works on the vast range of subjects covered by the news media. On the Internet, you can tap into the Librarians' Index at <http://lii.org/> or the Virtual Library at <http://vlib.org/Overview.html>.

PUBLIC RECORDS

Organisations and peak bodies

There is almost always an organisation (often several organisations) representing or investigating the issue you are writing about. Many of these have comprehensive and regularly updated websites. Their specialist knowledge is valuable to journalists; their bias can be a problem. For instance, the National Association of Forest Industries and the Australian Conservation Foundation both know a lot about the woodchipping industry, but they see it from sharply different perspectives. You will need to establish whether the organisation is independent and neutral or is a peak body representing a particular interest or group. The Healthy Weight Task Force, a fine sounding name, was revealed on ABC television's *Media Watch* in 2002 as a front organisation for pharmaceutical companies.

You can find organisations listed in the phone directory; alternatively, search a site such as <http://groups.google.com/> on the Google search engine for a directory of groups and organisations. As with news, in features you need to report both sides of an issue, or more precisely all sides, as most issues are more complicated than the simple binary opposites formula suggests.

Organisations and peak bodies are usually contacted for comment to feed into the feature but they can provide pivotal material. For instance, in researching a biography of Australian children's author Paul Jennings, I could not find data in the publishing industry to enable me to compare Jennings' remarkable popularity with earlier authors. The most reliable information came from the Australian Publishers Association (APA), which released an annual list of bestselling books drawn from sales figures supplied by its members, including all the major publishing houses. The APA list began only in 1983 and early on there were questions about whether the list was comprehensive, but from the early 1990s APA data was accepted as the best available.

The APA's annual bestseller list received moderate newspaper coverage each year but nothing had been written tracking the nation's bestselling authors over time. The data was readily available, so I did the analysis and was able to write a feature naming the bestselling authors of the decade in various categories (fiction, autobiography, etc.). Because no one had pulled the figures together before I was able to sell the piece to four different metropolitan newspapers.

Parliament

Parliaments generate and store massive amounts of information. Parliamentary debates are recorded in Hansard. Politicians have to register their pecuniary interests with the parliament, and political parties must register the amount and source of any campaign donations. Government departments and agencies table annual reports. Much of this information is only casually scrutinised by the news media. In their rush to cover today's news, journalists can miss potential stories buried in, say, ombudsmen's reports. These can be followed up and developed, as often happens with journalists working on Sunday newspapers. But not often enough, according to Jack Waterford, editor in chief of *The Canberra Times*.

The truth is that many journalists do not read much. And they look for shortcuts—preferring, for example, to look at nothing much more than the press statement or the executive summary. It is unlikely that you will find the 'real dirt' in such places. In many cases, however, the more detailed material will be quite frank—concerned even to put onto the public record, discreetly, information an agency does not want to be accused of covering up.[7]

Parliaments also have a committee system. Ministers will refer a matter to the relevant committee, which will investigate and report to the parliament. The children overboard hearings were a well-known recent example. Aside from the daily headlines they prompt, committees gather much information useful to a feature journalist. So does the parliamentary library. Those journalists who tap into this resource, such as Tim Colebatch, economics editor of *The Age*, are rewarded with background material for features or sometimes news stories.

Courts, inquiries, royal commissions

Courts, inquiries and royal commissions also generate a lot of information. News organisations routinely cover the courts, but again there are so many cases that news reports are necessarily limited to the most important and the most obviously sensational. This still leaves much fertile ground, as Pamela Bone's story, reproduced at the end of chapter five, about the man accused, and later convicted, of raping two young girls shows. The case was widely covered but not in great depth. It is not always possible to sit through a case, as Bone did; you can get a transcript from the court reporting service but the cost is prohibitive. Better to develop a relationship with the lawyers in the case and see if you can borrow or photocopy their transcript.

Other court documents, such as judgements and affidavits, are available either at the court or sometimes online. The website <www.austlii.edu.au> is produced by the Australian Legal Information Institute, and it provides an archive of legislation and judgements in most jurisdictions, including the judgements of some non-court bodies, such as the Press Council. Judicial inquiries and royal commissions provide similar opportunities for feature material because of the amount of information available and the necessity for daily news to cover only a fraction of it. Reporters covering inquiries and royal commissions soon amass far more information than is needed for daily news stories, which can be used profitably either in end-of-week news features, or to break new ground.

For the inquest into the Queen Street killer mentioned earlier, police gathered a mass of evidence. Much of it, like Vitkovic's diary of his final days, had been reported, but some of it, such as Vitkovic's earlier diaries, had not. Movie posters from his bedroom and police photos were included in the police brief. One photo was of the murder weapon, which a terrified employee had hidden in a staff fridge amid beer cans after it was seized from Vitkovic. This material, and more, was available on request but for whatever reason none of the other journalists looked at it. It provided valuable information for the story and illustrations for the magazine layout.

Business information

It is important to become familiar with sources of business information for two reasons: first, because the rise of popular business magazines such as *Business Review Weekly* and *Personal Investor* means more journalists cover business and, second, because so much of society revolves around the economy. In July 2001, Messenger Newspapers in Adelaide broke a story about a $15 million property development crash by searching bankruptcy records and court files.[8] Belinda Weaver asserts many bankrupt people defy the law by opening bank accounts or taking on company directorships even though the public record of their bankruptcy is available online in the National Personal Bankruptcy database.[9] Information about incorporated associations and businesses is held by state governments, usually the department responsible for fair trading or consumer affairs. Information about companies, whether private or public, is held by the Australian Stock Exchange, which runs regular seminars open to the public about understanding finance. The

Australian Securities and Investment Commission regulates companies in Australia and, for a fee, you can find out who is running a company. The commission's website (at <http://www.asic.gov.au/>) and its consumer site (at <www.fido.asic.gov.au>) contain much useful information about companies, including scams, company reporting requirements and media releases.

Freedom of Information

All states and territories as well as the Commonwealth have freedom of information (FOI) laws, the core of which is a legally enforceable right for anyone to gain access to documents held by government agencies. Some documents are exempt from release. Many journalists are cynical about FOI, with some cause. Despite its title, FOI costs money, is time consuming and too many documents are exempt. It is also true that too few journalists have used the acts intelligently or consistently. FOI has great potential for journalists, particularly those working on features and investigations where timeliness is not as pressing an issue. The acts can be used either to gain access to documents that provide context for a feature or, more powerfully, to enable you to set a news agenda by disclosing fresh documentary evidence on an issue. Whatever its problems, that is FOI's prime benefit for journalists: it provides documents. Bureaucracies run on paper, though, and when using FOI, and indeed the other public records listed above, it is essential you devise a method of organising and filing documents or you will be overrun.

Anne Davies of *The Sydney Morning Herald* has shown good lateral thinking skills in her use of FOI. On 5 August 2000 Davies wrote a story about talkback king Alan Jones' political influence. The Australian Broadcasting Authority's inquiry into the 1999 cash for comment scandal had focused on whether Jones' on-air editorial opinion could be bought by his sponsors. Davies turned the issue around and focused on how Jones wielded his political influence off-air. She sought and gained access to 148 letters Jones had sent to politicians, including the Prime Minister, John Howard, the New South Wales Premier, Bob Carr, and several state ministers, which offered a fascinating insight into the way Jones relentlessly lobbies politicians on behalf of friends, associates, himself and even some of the 'battlers' who devotedly listen to his program. The flamboyant, voluble letters, sometimes threatening on-air repercussions, were quoted extensively: 'I am sick and tired of defending the police force when it's peopled by yahoos like this . . . Over to you.

I look forward to your response.' The various ministers responded promptly, sometimes adding personal notes. 'Alan, welcome back to the airwaves. I hope you had a good break,' wrote New South Wales Transport Minister Carl Scully.[10]

Historical records

Remembering Graham Perkin's definition of an important news story (it has its roots in the past and a stake in the future), historical records can enrich a feature. You should become familiar with the sources of historical information before using them because there is so much material it is easy to drown in it. The majority of government records, such as federal and state cabinet documents, are available after 30 years. The National Library of Australia has a register of archives and manuscripts that as of June 2001 held 40 000 records.[11] The library also has an extensive and wide-ranging oral history collection of interviews, from prominent people such as former Prime Minister John Gorton to ordinary Australians talking about their lives and experiences. The library bought 177 boxes of material from Lindy Chamberlain for a reported $100 000. These revealed not only how many Australians felt compelled to write to Lindy over her trial for the murder of her daughter Azaria, but that the vast majority believed in her innocence, contrary to contemporary media reports.[12]

Books and documentaries

Books, documentaries and movies contain vast quanties of information but in a more palatable form than a parliamentary committee report. There are three reasons for using these sources. First, for ideas. (In *Newjack*, the American journalist Ted Conover wrote a remarkable account of his year working undercover as a prison guard in the notorious Sing Sing gaol. Could the same be done in Australia?) Second, for information and explanations. (Conover's book contains a wealth of information about the US prison system, both factual and from his rare insider perspective, as well as a devastating critique of its failings.[13]) Third, for quotes with which to garnish your feature.

As with organisations, there is almost always a book or documentary about your feature topic; commonly, there are several, which is not surprising given there are at least 4000 books published each year in Australia alone. There are many good new and secondhand bookshops in Australia. You can also check overseas bookshops on the

Internet to see what is coming up. Online retailers such as Amazon.com alert their customers to new books in their areas of interest.

The ABC and SBS are the primary sources of documentaries on free-to-air television (especially with their continuing series *The Big Picture* and *The Cutting Edge*) and the primary pay-TV provider, Foxtel, has three documentary channels. Most are familiar with ABC's *Four Corners* program but don't overlook its equivalent on Radio National, *Background Briefing*.

A journalist whose work exemplifies the value of documents is Mark Aarons. His 1986 five-part ABC radio series on *Background Briefing* about Nazi war criminals finding sanctuary in Australia after World War II prodded the Hawke Labor government to appoint retired senior public servant Andrew Menzies to inquire into the allegations. How did these men find safe haven in Australia? Was it lax immigration screening procedures or did the Allied intelligence agencies, then swiftly switching their attention to the Cold War, turn a blind eye to the war criminals in the belief they could be useful in the fight against communism, as Aarons controversially asserted?

Menzies' report confirmed Nazi war criminals had indeed entered Australia and recommended the setting up of a Special Investigations Unit (SIU) to gather evidence against any major war criminals still living in Australia. He did not find evidence of a conspiracy within the Allied intelligence agencies to use war criminals. Aarons expanded his radio series into a book, *Sanctuary*, for which he made extensive use of the Australian Archives Act and the US Freedom of Information Act. Then he watched in dismay as the task of bringing people to trial for events that occurred half a world away, half a century earlier, proved too difficult. A court of law proved incompatible with finding historical truth. The SIU was disbanded by the Keating Labor government in the mid-1990s.

In 2001 Aarons updated and expanded *Sanctuary*, retitling it *War Criminals Welcome*. He has continued to apply for declassified documents under both the US and Australian FOI and archives acts, with startling results. For instance, investigating a Belorussion mass killer, who had been used by both American and Australian intelligence agencies, Aarons applied for Nikolai Alferchik's ASIO file in 1993. Seven years—yes, seven years—later he was given access to 67 pages of a 190-page file. Most pages were in any case innocuous—magazine articles and insignificant ASIO letters. Any intelligence reports or memos released were heavily censored. Cannily, Aarons had already sought and gained access under the US FOI and archives acts to declassified documents that outlined Alferchik's work with US intelligence agencies. He commented on the US material: 'It does not withhold either the actual intelligence the files contained or the secret codes, which are virtually identical to those routinely withheld by ASIO. Even the names of career US agents are released, as well as the identity of paid sub-agents and sources.'

Through document after document, Aarons relentlessly built his case that ASIO knowingly used Nazi war criminals and collaborators as intelligence sources in the post-war period. This conclusion was buttressed by devastating interview material from Bob Greenwood, QC, the former head of the Special Investigations Unit, who publicly confirmed for the first time his support for Aarons' thesis. Greenwood, who died in 2001, had seen the original ASIO documents and lamented that ASIO officers resisted his investigation of some alleged war criminals who had been ASIO sources. In his conclusion Aarons' findings made a mockery of Menzies' report.

For more detail on the craft of locating and using documentary material, I recommend the Australian text, *Journalism: Investigation and Research*, edited by Stephen Tanner. Primarily concerned with investigative journalism, Tanner's text includes much useful material about the research process. There are individual chapters on using the Internet, computer databases, basic public records, historical records, Freedom of Information legislation, and on understanding financial statements and opinion polls. English freelance journalist and editor David Spark's exhaustive *A Journalist's Guide to Sources* (1996) is Anglocentric, naturally enough, but provides vast information about where to find organisations, who to look for and how to find them.

DISCUSSION QUESTIONS AND EXERCISES

1. Obtain a copy of the most recent annual report of a federal or state government ombudsman. Read it cover to cover and list three potential feature stories. Go back and compare your ideas with those that were actually covered by the news media on the report's release.
2. Go to the ABC's website and look at the transcripts of *Background Briefing* programs for the past year. Summarise any that deal with

the topic you are writing about. If none do, then look at the range of issues tackled by the program and the way they do it.

3. Working from the list above of potential documentary sources, note down potential leads for your feature and follow them up.

THE SUBTLE AND SLIPPERY ART OF INTERVIEWING

At Wimbledon one year an American magazine journalist asked Pete Sampras the following question: 'Pete, do you think that like, being the best in the world kind of like means that you give it your best or like being the best in the world has its own imperatives, like, or do you just think, hey, I'm the best in the world?' To which Sampras replied: 'No.'

Lynne Truss, 'On the Terraces' in Stephen Glover's *Secrets of the Press* (1999)

CHAPTER SUMMARY

Interviewing is one of the most satisfying elements of journalism, and one of the most complicated, never more so than in feature stories where journalists spend longer with their subjects. Various strategies to persuade people to talk and gain their trust are outlined, as are two guiding principles of good interviewing. The different types of questions and ways of listening are also discussed.

I f there is one thing that consistently alarms inexperienced journalists it is interviewing. Doubly alarming, if you want to be a journalist you can't get away from interviews. Interestingly, interviewing may be pervasive in today's media but the first interview as we think of them today took place only 140 years ago.[1] Before that, the act of interviewing was foreign to journalists. In 1819 John Tyas of *The Times* in London witnessed soldiers bloodily quashing a public meeting supporting parliamentary reform. Hundreds were wounded and up to a dozen killed at St Peter's Field in Manchester. Tyas witnessed the historic event standing on a wagon alongside the reform supporters' leader, Henry Hunt. He was at pains to reassure readers that not only did he not interview Hunt, but 'nor would he have thought of addressing him upon this occasion.'[2] Imagine a journalist today attending a demonstration against a World Trade Organisation meeting and not interviewing any of the protest leaders.

Interviewing, then, is at its heart a presumptuous, impolite activity. On behalf of your readers you are required to ask just about any person any question at any time. It is easy to see how abnormal interviewing is in the early responses to it. In 1892 the English man of letters, Rudyard Kipling, described the interview as an immoral, cowardly, vile crime. 'No respectable man would ask it, much less give it.'[3] The good news is that interviewing can be more fun and more satisfying professionally than just about any other aspect of journalism. The bad news is that interviewing for features throws up thornier, more complicated issues.

INTERVIEWING STRATEGIES

Talk to a range of journalists or read interviewing textbooks and it seems the rules of interviewing are written in water. One book will tell you it is a cardinal rule to be prepared before the interview, another will counsel you not to prepare so as to have an open mind when you meet the interviewee. Ask precise questions to find out exactly what you want to know, some say. Others value discursive, open-ended questions. Some journalists favour using tape recorders, others swear by pen and paper. Always stay on the record in an interview versus going off the record if you cannot get the information on the record. And so on. All this advice, and more, is sensible even if it seems contradictory. It depends on the kind of interview you are doing. There is a world of difference between what you might call routine information extraction ('When did the fire start, and where?'), a combative political interview and a gently probing interview for a profile. There is also a difference in how you treat an image-conscious celebrity and an ordinary person caught up in a news event.

The reason interviewing is so elusive a topic is that you are dealing with people, and you are dealing with them under pressure—for them and for you—which can magnify the smallest impediments. When I was writing a story about twentysomethings still living at home, I interviewed a 20-year-old daughter in her family home and found it hard to develop a rapport because we were sitting on opposite sides of the lounge room. The interview felt like an audience when it needed to feel like a conversation.

There appear to be two guiding principles underlying successful interviews.

LISTEN TO THE SUBJECT

Sounds like a no-brainer, but it is alarming how frequently journalists don't listen to the interviewee and garble what they say, or more importantly, what they mean. More on this later.

BE FLEXIBLE IN YOUR APPROACH

Be attuned to the way the interview is going. You may have prepared thoroughly for a particular line of questioning, but if the interviewee has much more interesting things to say on another topic go with that.

There is another conundrum about interviewing, and it has received comparatively little attention in textbooks. Is an interview business or is it personal? Is it a commercial transaction or a personal relationship? What if it is both? The interview has been defined as a 'face-to-face meeting for the purpose of a formal conference, between a representative of the press and someone from whom he wishes to obtain statements for publication', and 'the art of extracting personal statements for publication'.[4] Leaving aside the crusty, sexist language, these definitions connote both a formal, professional relationship and, in the words 'art' and 'personal,' something more personal.

It is easy to see the routine information-driven interview as first and foremost a professional transaction. You need information and the firefighter, say, needs to let the public know about the bushfire. What if you want to interview someone who has lost a relative in that bushfire? If you shoot questions at them like a census collector how well will they respond? And what if you do a feature on a hospital's burns unit, as several journalists did after the 2002 bombings in Bali left several people severely burnt? To successfully interview staff and patients you need to build trust and rapport, which takes time and skills other than the orderly asking of questions.

Many journalists set out with strong convictions about not getting close to the people they interview for fear of clouding their professional judgement, which is fair enough as some journalists become so close to their sources they don't write the stories that need to be written because they don't want to hurt the source. The issue is more complicated than that, but the point here is that much journalism is about people and nobody ever gave a good interview to an automaton. You need to develop rapport and trust with all interviewees and that requires giving something of yourself. It also requires you to be clear about professional and personal boundaries. It is possible to draw up a list of dos and don'ts (yes, it is okay to have coffee with an interviewee; no, you shouldn't sleep with them), but it is more useful to delineate the issues that consistently arise. The first, and most common, is that inexperienced journalists are overwhelmed by the prospect of talking to someone famous, as Lynn Barber, a well-known English interviewer, explains:

> They are flattered that a famous person is apparently confiding in them (even telling them things off the record!); they respond to the famous one's kindness with genuine enthusiasm; they find themselves agreeing fervently with everything the famous one says. And then they go back

to the office, out of the famous one's orbit, and listen to the tape and decide they don't like the famous one after all, and, because they are rather annoyed with themselves for being 'taken in', write a particularly bitchy piece.[5]

The problem is aggravated if you are interviewing someone you admire. It is easy to think, 'Well anyone can see this person is a genius; I couldn't possibly criticise them.' You could and if need be, should. Veteran American interviewer John Brady says journalists who become fans return to the newsroom 'glassy-eyed and unreliable, or bitter at the discovery that their gods often have feet of interviewing clay'.[6] The key advice here is to ask your heroes the same tough questions you ask your villains. It is hard to put into practice, but an important habit to aspire to, as Sarah Macdonald did when she worked on ABC's Triple J network. She said the best audience response she received was when she pushed federal Green MP, Bob Brown, sometimes known as Saint Bob. How did she do it?

> I pissed him off a bit. When he gets fired up he's great but when he thinks he's preaching to the converted he's boring. When I interview him I try to think like a young Liberal would think. I respond the way they would respond. If I were interviewing (Prime Minister) John Howard I'd think like a young greenie and ask those questions. I try to approach it from every point of view and not give anyone a free ride. That's just boring.[7]

The second issue that regularly arises was articulated most powerfully by American journalist Janet Malcolm in the opening sentences of her book *The Journalist and the Murderer*:

> Every journalist who is not too stupid or too full of himself to notice what is going on knows that what he does is morally indefensible. He is a kind of confidence man, preying on people's vanity, ignorance, or loneliness, gaining their trust and betraying them without remorse.[8]

Like many a journalist before and since, Malcolm's lead is aimed at grabbing attention. It certainly aroused the ire of other journalists, who preferred to denounce her rather than reflect on her assertions, the implications of which were teased out in her account of an action brought by a convicted murderer, Jeffrey Macdonald, against a journalist, Joe McGinniss, for breach of contract.

Even the most ethical journalists struggle with the shift in role from being a sympathetic, charming listener in an interview to a dispassionate, tough-minded writer sitting at the keyboard. You can feel as if you are 'seducing' then 'betraying' the subject, particularly in profiles where you get closer to the person. It is probably more important to be aware of this shift in attitude than to actually change it, because part of the dilemma is inherent in the job.

Interviewers and interviewees have different purposes. The interviewer's first duty is to their reader, while interviewees are, understandably, concerned about themselves. For a feature, journalists may interview a dozen people with widely differing views on a topic, and they need to weigh them up. Invariably, their features will make some people unhappy, especially if they are writing about a controversial topic. One reason for journalists' poor public image, though, is that they present themselves as the subject's best friend, then shaft them in print. That is what McGinniss was accused of doing to Macdonald; it is a sobering thought that the jury sympathised with a man convicted of murdering his wife and two small children over an award-winning journalist![9]

What journalists should do is be as honest with interviewees as possible and, simultaneously, engage them and gain their trust. For instance, you are writing a feature about abortion and need to interview a Right to Life leader. You may believe in the right to abortion, but you can say to the interviewee it is important for the story that you present a range of views as fully as possible. Most people respond well to an appeal to their sense of fairness and accuracy. Some journalists use this as a ploy, but it is better for you and for the story if you really do want a broad range of views and you are genuinely curious about why someone believes abortion is a crime. Genuine curiosity, to rephrase Goethe, has a power and magic of its own. The award-winning ABC TV investigative journalist, Chris Masters, has written:

> People do not tell all on the first visit. It stands to reason they need to develop some degree of trust before they part with important information . . . It might take five visits or fifteen . . . This is probably the hardest work of all. People are not likely to trust you unless they sense you have a sincere interest in them, as well as their story.

There is no point in feigning an interest. The worst 'investigative' reporters are the ones who come on like wall-cladding salesmen. I have watched them work and listened later to them puzzling over why they get little cooperation.[10]

Masters is writing about investigative journalism where the stakes are highest, but journalists commonly find it difficult persuading people to be interviewed.

The challenge of persuading an ordinary person caught up in a news event differs from persuading a celebrity or politician to be interviewed. The former group are likely to be accessible but uninterested in publicity and, quite possibly, hostile towards the media. The latter are also likely to be hostile but, in addition, guarded by minders. The key is to distinguish yourself from the pack. With ordinary people, you need to alleviate their anxiety and likely ignorance about media practice and convince them of your commitment to fairness and accuracy. I have found it effective to talk to prospective interviewees about the way the media works, what I'm looking for and explaining where the piece will be published and in what context. It can be useful to set out the ground rules; what does 'off the record' mean? Is it different from speaking for background information, etc.? Many practitioners treat this as secret journos' business, but aside from it being good professional practice to be clear about such matters, the information lets interviewees feel more comfortable about the process, and a comfortable inteviewee is more likely to be cooperative.

How else can you separate yourself from the pack? Send a couple of samples of your work to the prospective interviewee. Offer to meet busy interviewees anywhere at any time. John Brady once scored an interview with writer Jessica Mitford, who did not have a spare half hour in her touring schedule, by offering to drive her to the airport. He asked questions while she spoke into his cassette recorder. It was hardly ideal, but better than no interview.[11] Capture the interviewee's imagination by finding out something interesting about them and using that as bait. This requires extra preparation as Gideon Haigh, a journalist who writes mainly about cricket and business, attests. Haigh once lured touring English batsman Graham Gooch with the irresistible morsel: 'Do you realise that you have made more runs in test cricket over the age of 30 than any other player? Do you mind if I come around so we can talk about how you've achieved that?'

Gooch had been entirely uninterested in an interview until that point. He had not been aware of the abstruse statistic Haigh had dug up, but he had given a lot of thought to how to keep playing successfully into his thirties because his career had begun slowly and he had always felt he had ground to catch up.[12]

The message is twofold: first, the thrill of being interviewed palls once you've been asked the same questions a hundred times; second, most successful people are passionate about what they do and your job is to find a way to let them express that passion. That may be interesting enough in itself; at the least you've got them talking. Occasionally, you need to do something outlandish to jump-start a jaded interviewee. Assigned to interview Hollywood star Tommy Lee Jones, a notoriously reluctant interviewee, about a wan sequel in the *Batman* series, film writer Jim Schembri walked into the room and before sitting said, 'You know the best thing you've ever done on the screen?' Jones looked up. 'It was that 1977 made-for-TV mini-series, *The Amazing Howard Hughes.*' He then proceeded to re-enact a scene where Jones as Hughes threw a hammer across a room at a steam-powered car. Schembri is no actor but he got Jones' attention. He kept it by asking questions about films Jones himself had directed, questions no other interviewer thought to ask him.[13]

Aside from the longstanding difficulties of people being busy or reluctant to speak publicly, there is the problem of public relations officers or spin doctors whose job it is to guard access to newsmakers and to either snuff out, sideline or spin news in favour of their client. Public relations, like journalism, has a history. The first firms dedicated to public relations were set up in the United States early in the 20th century.[14] Many early press agents, as they were called, had been journalists, a trend that has continued despite the establishment of public relations courses in universities. Public relations has grown increasingly sophisticated in recent years; it has also simply grown. According to figures supplied by their peak bodies, there are almost as many PR officers working in Australia as there are journalists. A good PR officer can provide useful information as well as access to newsmakers, but you must never forget that a PR officer is paid to present their client in the best possible light. Journalists, however clumsily, however imperfectly, pursue truth.[15]

The problem facing many journalists, whether writing news or features, is gaining access to newsmakers, and gaining it free of the interference of PRs. Several strategies can be used. First, follow the example of the great American journalist, I.F. Stone, who thought access to newsmakers was overrated anyway because it was too easy for the journalist to be flattered into docility by, say, a president asking their opinion on foreign affairs. Stone, whose eponymous weekly newsheet was published between 1953 and 1971, worked by the credo: every government is run by liars and nothing they say should be believed— until proven to the contrary. Stone pored over the public records and broke numerous stories simply by pointing to inconsistencies in governments' published positions.[16] Few journalists have Stone's prodigious energy and most remain reliant to at least some degree on newsmakers, but it is still worth following the spirit of his strategy.

Second, journalists need to work hard to cultivate a broad range of sources. If PRs control access to, say, politicians, then develop contacts in the public service. This is not easy as government departments have their own spin doctors and most public servants are reluctant to speak out, but those at middle and senior levels know a good deal about how policies are developed. A good way to meet such people is on neutral turf at conferences and seminars. A couple of years ago I attended a conference about freedom of information legislation and saw how after the speeches various journalists and FOI officers got together over coffee and began talking about their problems using and administering the legislation. From such meetings contacts can be developed and story leads followed up.

Third, bypass the spinmeisters by focusing on features about the lives and struggles of ordinary people. This is not a new idea, but the trend towards writing about ordinary people accelerated in the 1990s, especially in the United States where some of the best work was collected by Walt Harrington in an anthology entitled (somewhat confusingly) *Intimate Journalism: The Art and Craft of Reporting Everyday Life* (1997). In it Susan Orlean wrote a story headlined, 'The American man at age 10'. Originally asked to profile Macauley Culkin of *Home Alone* fame, Orlean found the prospect of yet another glossy celebrity profile less interesting than trying to understand what goes on inside the head of the average kid. There is not as much journalism of this kind in Australia, but it appears to be slowly developing. Over three days in March 2002, Misha Ketchell of *The Age* chronicled the putting together of a secondary school's annual musical, complete with pre-production jitters and backstage romances. There was nothing special about the production, yet the piece reads like a short story.

Finally, write about the very problem that is preventing you getting an interesting story to your readers. Spin doctors prefer to remain in the shadows, so spotlight them. Nowhere have they been better skewered than in a Tad Friend piece in *The New Yorker*. Friend decoded Hollywood publicist-speak:

> A journalist who calls a publicist hoping for five minutes of a star's time quickly learns that "she's spending time with her family/shooting in Europe/scouting in Japan" all mean the same thing: she was just chatting on the cell phone for an hour with me, but she sure doesn't want to talk to you. "He's transitioning" means he got fired, and "He's suffering from exhaustion" means he was found wandering naked in the street, waving a gun. Likewise, "It's in turnaround" means a project is dead; "It's a work in progress" or "They're doing a few pickup shots" or "The print isn't finished but you can see the script" means the movie is a disaster; and "The film is not for everybody" means it's not for anybody.[17]

Of course, publicists tell outright lies too and ask lawyers to write journalists threatening letters even if a story is true. As one Hollywood director told Friend: 'Publicists are the death of interesting journalism about entertainment.' Almost as bad, journalists and their editors are complicit in the recycling of fairytales through celebrity interviews.

FRAMING THE QUESTIONS AND HEARING THE ANSWERS

Rock journalism is people who can't write interviewing people who can't talk for people who can't read.

Frank Zappa

Many journalists find this element of technique difficult. Again, much depends on whether you are interviewing an ordinary person or a media-savvy politician or celebrity. For the former you may well be able to develop a rapport and find your curiosity carries the interview along without any great effort being required to structure it. An interview with a politician is a verbal martial art, in which government ministers hold at least a second dan black belt. That said, there are various types of questions, each with their own strengths and weaknesses.[18]

OPEN-ENDED QUESTIONS

Tell me your life story is an extreme example of an open-ended question. A more focused one might be: tell me about your love of mountain climbing. The advantages of open-ended questions are threefold: they are not threatening to the interviewee; they allow the interviewee to do most of the talking, which is the purpose of most interviews; they allow the interviewee to voluntarily reveal information unanticipated by the journalist. The disadvantages are twofold: they can overwhelm interviewees, especially those unused to ordering their thoughts or to whom the focus of the interview is a difficult or traumatic experience; they can hand over to the subject too much power in the interview.

CLOSED QUESTIONS

Journalists needing unvarnished facts ask closed questions, such as how many cars were in the collision, and was anyone injured? The advantages of closed questions are twofold: they enable the journalist to get specific information without waiting for the interviewee to volunteer it; they discourage rambling. The disadvantages are several: closed questions inhibit efforts to build rapport; they can leave interviewees feeling as though they have been interrogated; they discourage explaining the complexities of an issue, among others.

DIRECT AND INDIRECT QUESTIONS

Blunt questions are remembered. 'Mr Hawke, could I ask you whether you feel a little embarrassed tonight at the blood that's on your hands?' Richard Carleton famously asked Bob Hawke in 1983, hours after he had won a caucus ballot over Bill Hayden to head the Labor Party. More recently, Heather Ewart asked failed entrepreneur John Elliott if he had a drinking problem just days before Elliott was forced to stand down as president of the Carlton football club. Blunt questions may be necessary, in major stories and with resistant interviewees, to blast out admissions. Journalists habitually ask direct questions; many are not as blunt as the two examples just given, but the effect of direct question after direct question can be intimidating. That can work against you in many interviews for features, especially if you are writing about a difficult subject like, say, euthanasia.

DUMB QUESTIONS

The dumb question is trickier to identify than it looks. Most journalists, if they were honest, would admit that all too often the most obvious question about a story is the one they failed to ask. This happens because you are so busy gathering information and trying to understand the ins and outs of an issue you overlook the first question someone who knows nothing about the story (i.e., the reader) will ask. Researching a profile of Australian author Paul Jennings, I heard in detail the story of how the difficulties Jennings had helping his 11-year-old son learn to read had prompted him to begin writing his own children's stories, thus launching his highly successful career. I had almost finished writing the piece when a colleague asked, 'Can the kid read now?' I'd been so focused on Jennings' career I'd forgotten to ask. This can happen to the most experienced journalists.

John Hersey's account of the dropping of the first atomic bomb, at Hiroshima in 1945, was voted the best piece of American journalism of the 20th century, yet when he first submitted it he had failed to answer an obvious question: what exactly did the 100 000 victims die of?[19] The dumb question, then, may simply be the most obvious one. It may also be the one that most people are too polite to ask, exemplified by Carleton and Ewart's questions above.

The 'how do you feel' question is maligned as dumb and tasteless. Relatives of those who died in the Bali bombings should not be asked how they feel. How do you think they feel? Fair enough too, but isn't that what readers really do want to know? They don't want to hear the relatives' views on the falling stock market. The trick is in how you ask these questions. Rather than shove a microphone under someone's nose and ask how do you feel, journalists may need to approach the topic more gently, asking the relative to describe what happened and then ask questions like, 'And how did you respond to that?' or 'I imagine that would have been very difficult to deal with' or 'What would you like me to write about your feelings on these events?'

As this suggests and as mentioned earlier, it is as important to listen to people's answers as to ask strong questions. American journalism educators George Killenberg and Rob Anderson say listening is less a technique than an attitude. The worst journalists assume interviews fulfil a simple, predetermined purpose, but 'assumption is the enemy of listening. Effective listeners let themselves be surprised. In fact, they invite it, for surprise is a sign of learning. And what, if not learning, is the reporter's primary motivation?'[20] They outline three kinds of listening:

INFORMATIONAL LISTENING: 'WHAT HAPPENED?'

This is listening to gather information and facts and to report as accurately as possible. It is useful, especially when dealing with complicated topics, to play back to the interviewee what you've heard. 'Can I check that I've understood what you are saying about changes to the pest control legislation?'

DISCRIMINATIVE LISTENING: 'WHAT'S DIFFERENT?'

After gathering basic information, journalists need to be what Killenberg and Anderson call 'sensitive sceptics'. That is, a sifter and sorter of information, views, differing perceptions and logic. Five witnesses to a car accident will have five different versions. Interview half a dozen experts about, say, the nature/nurture debate and you'll get half a dozen perspectives. Interview a politician and you'll need to be checking mentally against what they said six months ago on the same issue. You also need to be ready for various fallacies of reasoning, such as argument *ad hominem*, where the interviewee attacks a person rather than their position.

PERSONALITY LISTENING: 'WHO ARE YOU?'

For interview pieces and profiles, you need to listen for what kind of person the interviewee is. Print journalists are word people and it shocks them to learn that only about one-third of the meaning of a social interaction derives from words. Most of the meaning we glean from a conversation—or interview—comes from what psychologists call nonverbal communication. Just how journalists can observe and report this form of communication will be discussed in the next chapter.

Rolling Stone: "Okay, you and Madonna—the truth!"
Warren Beatty: "Art is truth."
RS: "That's all? You want to go with that?"
Beatty: "Okay by me."
RS: "Describe the qualities she possesses that convinced you to cast her as the sexpot temptress Breathless Mahoney in Dick Tracy. How does she qualify?"
Beatty: "Madonna is (21-second pause) simultaneously touching and more fun than a barrel of monkeys. (11 seconds) She's funny, and she's (21 seconds) gifted in so many areas and has the kind of energy in a performer that can't help but make you engaged."

RS: "You mean sexual energy?"

Beatty: (47-second pause) "Um, she has it all."

RS: "Do you think that your reluctance to give personal interviews has inflated your personal mythology?"

Beatty: "I can't accept your flattering premise of me. To do so is unattractive or self-serving. It's hard to misquote someone who doesn't say anything. There's almost nothing that hasn't been said about me."

Rolling Stone interview with actor Warren Beatty, conducted by Bill Zehme in 1990

DISCUSSION QUESTIONS AND EXERCISES

1. Do you agree with Janet Malcolm's famous assertion that interviewing is morally indefensible because journalists 'seduce' then 'betray' the subjects of their stories?
2. For your feature, identify the people you want to interview, whether observers, the shakers and movers or the shaken and moved, and list the key questions you want answered. These will primarily come from the story plan you have made.
3. Group exercise: give a published news story to someone who plays the role of a person who is central to the news story. Give another person a bare outline of the news story but not the story itself. The latter interviews the former and gathers information contained in the story, within a time limit. Roles can be interchanged and others given an opportunity to interview or be interviewed.
4. Group exercise: divide into groups of three. One person interviews another about themself while the third observes. Each person plays each role. The aim is to find out something about the interviewee that the others don't know. In other words, the interview needs to go beyond the standard where were you born and which school did you go to. Then write a 200-word pen portrait of the interviewee which can be read out loud and discussed. Note how you feel as the interviewee, especially talking about yourself.

SEEING THINGS FOR YOURSELF

*Now she leant towards Harry and said, 'So, Harry . . . what made
you decide to enter the Triwizard Tournament?'*

*'Er—' said Harry again, but he was distracted by the quill. Even
though he wasn't speaking, it was dashing across the parchment
and in its wake he could make out a fresh sentence:*

> *An ugly scar, souvenir of a tragic past, disfigures the
> otherwise charming face of Harry Potter, whose eyes—*

'Ignore the quill, Harry,' said Rita Skeeter firmly.

**Rita Skeeter, journalist with *The Daily Prophet*, in J.K. Rowling's
Harry Potter and the Goblet of Fire, uses a Quick-Quotes Quill,
saving herself the trouble of taking notes—or
listening to what is being said.**

CHAPTER SUMMARY

The importance of witnessing events first-hand is stated. Not all feature stories need first-hand observation, but it should always be considered as it adds greatly to the atmosphere and authenticity of the story. Four principles of gathering material first-hand are outlined and discussed.

The value of being an eyewitness to events is unarguable. Perhaps the most important example in Australian journalism is Wilfred Burchett's account of the destruction caused by the dropping of the first atomic bomb on Hiroshima in 1945. Until Burchett journeyed to Japan all the world knew was that the bomb had been dropped. He saw with his own eyes a city that looked as though 'a monster steam roller had passed over and squashed it out of existence' and people suffering from what he described as 'the atomic plague', which was later identified as radiation sickness. If being an eyewitness is so valuable why do journalists spend so much time in the office?

Much journalism, such as reporting the latest employment statistics, does not require journalists to leave the office. That is the simple reason. Less straightforward is the nexus between masses of information available to the desk-bound journalist, either by telephone, email or the Internet, the increasing amount of space to fill in newspapers and magazines and the number of journalists to fill it. Pressure of time is an occupational hazard for journalists, and getting out of the office eats into precious time. You need to fight for this time because it can make the difference between space-fillers and journalism that sticks. Paul Toohey of *The Australian* has been journalist of the year and won the 2002 magazine feature writing Walkley Award because in covering indigenous issues he regularly travels thousands of kilometres to see what life is like for Aborigines in remote communities.

THREE REASONS WHY OBSERVING EVENTS FIRST-HAND CAN IMPROVE YOUR FEATURES

IT CAN MAKE A SLIGHT PIECE PUBLISHABLE

In the mid-1990s *Gladiators*, a TV show imported from America, enjoyed a brief flowering of fame. No doubt you've forgotten it, and rightly so, but at one point it was the number one ranked program in Australia. I saw an ad asking for potential challengers and wrote a light piece about the tryouts at Festival Hall. The event itself carried no news weight, but the people who showed up (bodybuilders, aerobics queens, stubby-shorted labourers) and the glitzy-tacky atmosphere at the tryouts did. Everyone, whether the potential challengers, the supervisors or the spectators (yes, there were nearly 150 of them), seemed totally oblivious to the absurdity of the tryouts, let alone a show in which garishly costumed muscle men and women bopped each other over the head with foam-covered sticks. Only by turning up on the day and observing could such a piece be written.[1]

IT GIVES A FEATURE DRAMA AND ATMOSPHERE

If observing and describing events can make a lycra-thin piece work, they can help make a solid feature sing. Craig McGregor made his name as an innovative feature writer for Fairfax publications in the 1970s and 1980s. In 1977 McGregor profiled Bob Hawke, then leader of the ACTU, later to become prime minister, for *The National Times*. He tagged along with Hawke for several days, watching him at work, at home, in press conferences, noting everything he said and did, his dress, mannerisms and interaction with others, whether friends, enemies or strangers. Here is a typical passage, where Hawke bumps into Ron Barassi, the famous AFL coach, at Melbourne's genteel old Windsor Hotel:

> Barassi comes up, hits Hawke on the shoulder, and they stand laughing and shouting at each other. 'G'day fuckface', says Hawke.
>
> But before Barassi can say anything in reply, an elegantly dressed woman in huge, fashionable sunglasses whom I had noticed walking into the lift walks out of the lift again, throws her arms around Hawke, and gives him a warm, sensuous kiss. "I adore you," she says. "I just couldn't believe it was *you*." The Great Barassi backs off enviously. "By Christ," says Hawke, "there's some bloody hope for Australia when

women prefer politicians to footballers!" Barassi himself is a strong, handsome man with a rake's moustache. It's an instructive comparison of the power of sex appeal, and the sex appeal of power.[2]

This vivid, earthy description has lengthened the feature's shelf life. I have shown it to several classes and most students find it fascinating even though it was written before they were born.

YOU PICK UP MATERIAL YOU WOULD OTHERWISE HAVE MISSED
In the mid-1990s I did an interview piece with Joyce Brown, former coach of Australia's world champion netball team and then enjoying success as a member of the ABC's football commentary team. At my suggestion we watched an AFL match between Carlton and Essendon. I knew she was a keen student of sport but nothing prepared me for the experience of how she watched the game. She provided an urgent running commentary on the coaches.

> 'What's David (Parkin) doing? The players are still going through their warm-up and he's gone straight to the coach's box. Is it a good idea to leave your players so early?'
>
> The excited buzz from the rest of the nearly 90,000 spectators builds in anticipation but Brown has eyes only for Kevin Sheedy. 'He's still out on the field. He can't leave his players! You see how he's going over to young players like Matthew Lloyd. They haven't played many games this year. Maybe by patting them and touching them he's trying to reassure them. Why is he still out there? Is he a bit nervous? Maybe he's trying to put psychological pressure on Parkin.'[3]

Not only did her stream of words open my eyes to their behaviour but to hers. You don't get this kind of material if you are not there.

GATHERING MATERIAL FIRST–HAND
The next question is how do you go about gathering all this seemingly unwieldy first-hand material? Think about it while reading the following passage from Michael Frayn's wonderful comic novel *The Tin Men*. One of the characters is himself writing a novel entitled *No Particle Forgot*, which begins like this:

There was a cry from the terrace. Shielding his eyes against the hard, almost tangible glare of the noonday Mediterranean sun, Rick looked up.

Rick Roe was tall. But his shoulders were broad, so that the first impression was that of a man of average build standing some way off. Some might have called him handsome, but Rick did not think of himself as being so. His features were almost classically even, but the mouth had a certain humorous twist which made the statuesque proportions of the face seem gratefully human. The mouth, in fact, was interesting. The regular teeth stood out very white amid his deep tan, while the lips were firm but somehow sensuous, belying the almost ascetic nose. The eyes were blue—like aquamarines nestling among the jeweller's crumpled chamois leather as he narrowed his gaze against the hard, almost tangible noonday glare. The eyebrows were russet thickets—slightly raised, as if surprised and perhaps a little scandalised to find themselves sitting on top of a pair of aquamarines. The hair was russet, too—cut *en brosse*, and there were fine russet hairs gleaming along the forearm raised to ward off the hard, almost tangible noonday glare . . .

Rick could feel the roughness of his fingers against his deeply sunburnt brow as he gazed. His fingers were long—surprisingly long and fine for such a well-built man. The nails were cut square, and shone like the mother-of-pearl Rick saw when he was skin-diving off the end of the Island.

The fingers grew from strong, well-formed hands, with russet hair on the back of them, and the hands were attached to the muscular arms by broad, sinewy wrists. There were four fingers and a thumb on each hand . . .[4]

And so it goes on, until two pages later we learn that the cry from the terrace was 'Lunch-time!' It should be clear what is wrong with *No Particle Forgot*—nothing indeed has been forgotten. So much space has been devoted to description that the action of the novel proceeds at glacial pace. It is an example of what not to do. What, then, do you do?

TAKE IT ALL IN

When you go out on a story you need to begin by observing and noting everything. Yes, this contradicts the previous paragraph but that is the difficulty; you won't know the telling details until you've taken in a mass of humdrum detail. If you are interviewing someone at their home, for example, your work starts the moment you arrive in their suburb. You note the weather, the house, the garden, the furnishings, the artwork, the books (or absence of them), the home entertainment system, the noticeboard in the kitchen, and so on. You note how people look, what they wear, how they carry themselves, their gestures, their speech, their laugh (or absence of it), whether they look you in the eye, etc.

Remember, only around one-third of communication is verbal. Use all five of your senses. It sounds unexceptional but Gary Tippet, an award-winning journalist, distinguishes between gathering material for daily news stories, where listening and seeing are paramount, and feature writing, where the journalist should notice taste, feel and smell.[5] Cal Fussman, a survivor of the September 11 terrorist attack on the World Trade Center buildings, said six months later that what haunted him still was the smell. 'I had vaporised people packed up my nose, in my mouth and ears. For weeks, I was picking stuff out of my ears.'[6] Describing the smell of dead people makes dramatic reading because it is such an intimate detail; for the same reason the decision whether to include such details needs to be weighed carefully so you find the balance between providing what the reader needs to know and treating people with respect. In the story about the Holocaust centre, for instance, it was important to record the Auschwitz number on the volunteer guide's arm, but I needed to approach Thea Kimla carefully for that information.

The need to notice everything sounds exhausting, which it can be, but it is also exhilarating. You become like an overseas traveller who sees everything afresh, enjoying the constant pleasure of discovery. As Tom Wolfe, the American journalist and novelist, with typical gusto put it: 'You feel as if you've put your whole central nervous system on red alert and turned it into a receiving set with your head panning the molten tableau like a radar dish, with you saying, "Come in, world," since you only want . . . all of it.'[7]

THROW LOTS OF IT OUT

If you are noticing anything and everything, you will soon have an overwhelming amount of material. Inevitably there will be wastage; journalists almost always gather far more than ends up in print. The good journalist must cultivate an innocent eye, but must not be innocent.[8] Even as you are soaking up all the material around you, you are squeezing out the excess water, or at least some of it. You are guided by your story plan, your sense of what the story is, but as mentioned earlier the plan is only a plan. There is a continual flow back and forth between the story plan and what you are finding; each informs and shapes the other.

Just how much you absorb and how much you discard is influenced by the amount of time you have. If you have only one chance to interview a person in their home or to watch an event, you need to notice and retain as much as possible. If you have time for more visits, you can gather more detail and can check things you are unsure about. Apart from developing photographic recall, you can help your memory by examining the many shots taken by the newspaper's or magazine's photographer or, if you are freelancing, by taking your own camera as John Bryson did for his account of the Azaria Chamberlain case. You can use a tape recorder not only to record the interview, but to pick up the tone of people's voices, when they paused, background noise and dialogue that happens too quickly for all but the fastest note-takers.

American journalist Walt Harrington accompanied detectives during an investigation for a story, noting at one point that a detective knocked on a door nine times. How could he possibly have known it was exactly nine knocks? He tape recorded the scene.[9] If you are observing events you may also want to record your own observations and thoughts as they occur to you. You may feel like a ponce but when information and impressions are flying at you from everywhere, it is hard to hold it all. Alternatively, after leaving an interview, pull over and jot down impressions, details, atmosphere, etc. Do it quickly or you'll soon forget.

In March 1999 I bumped into Alan Jones at Michael Kroger's wedding in Melbourne. It was the first time we'd seen each other since our interview and he seemed genuinely pleased to see me. We shook hands, and it was then that I realised he wasn't sure who I was. 'Do you remember me?' I asked.

'Yes, you're the gardening writer aren't you?' (I should have quit there and then.)

'No,' I said, 'I'm David Leser and I wrote a . . .'

'OH, DON'T REMIND ME,' he said, his voice turning to cold fury and his finger beginning to point in my direction. 'YOU TOLD LIES ABOUT ME . . .'

'Alan, I never . . . '

'DON'T YOU INTERRUPT ME. YOU TOLD LIES. I HAVE PEOPLE WHO WOULD HAVE TESTIFIED IN COURT ABOUT YOU . . . YOU LIED.'

For 15 seconds or so, Jones maintained this harangue—much to the incredulity of our fellow guests—and then turned on his heels. I never got the chance to respond—to tell him there had been no such lies—but, perhaps, that is as it should be. Everyone, radio demagogues included, deserves a right of reply.

David Leser

DON'T CENSOR YOURSELF

Pressure of time can close journalists' eyes and ears. As Harrington, who has run advanced feature writing seminars at *The Washington Post*, says:

> . . . we must not become too obsessed with asking ourselves, "What's the story here?"—and thus fall victim to the reporter's paranoia that we've got to produce something out of this mess and we better figure it out fast. That undermines our ability to grasp the story, because it means we'll inevitably fall back on well-worn themes and observations—interpretive cliches—and not give ourselves the time or frame of mind to see anything beyond that.[10]

Keeping your eyes and ears open means you will observe a great deal, some of which will be odd, contradictory or embarrassing. Many journalists unconsciously 'censor' such material. One of Helen Garner's strengths as a journalist is that she doesn't. In a memorable moment in *The First Stone*, her account of the Ormond College case, she observed the 'strange reflex of helpfulness' that prompted the wife of Alan Gregory to look around her for a chair when, from the witness box, one of the young women who had accused her husband of sexual harassment asked for a seat.[11]

LOOKING FOR TELLING DETAILS

Now you can see the dilemma faced by Hugh Rowe, the aspiring novelist in Michael Frayn's *The Tin Men*. How do you sift the telling from the mundane detail? Two guidelines help:

Relevance to the story

In the story about the former netball coach, Joyce Brown, I could have included lots of detail about the Melbourne Cricket Ground, about the crowd there that day, and about the football match, but most of it was irrelevant to the story. Essentially, the story was about the way a netball coach watched a football match. When I met Brown that day I certainly noticed how she was dressed, how she interacted with other commentators, whether spectators recognised and talked to her, etc. That provided moderately interesting material, but it was when we sat down in the crowd and she began commenting on what the coaches were doing that the story came alive. I focused on that and much of the other material melted into the background.

Uniqueness to the story

Find the details that are unique to the story; that is, details embedded in the fine grain of life. Telling details are the opposite of clichés, which slide by our consciousness precisely because they are generalised. Good journalism always conveys what John Carey calls 'unusual or indecorous or incidental images that imprint themselves scaldingly on the mind's eye'.[12] As an example, for years Barry Humphries, creator of housewife megastar Dame Edna Everage, has presented himself as an erudite dandy. When he released the second volume of his autobiography, accompanied by a well-oiled publicity tour, Caroline Overington showed that behind the poise and patter, decades of solo shows were finally exacting a toll:

> He is now almost 70 years old. The stage make-up is no longer thick enough to cover the liver spots on the backs of his hands. He gets tired more easily (he was still asleep at 10am one morning, when an *Age* photographer called at his hotel in New York, as previously arranged, to take his picture).[13]

Overington attests to Humphries' continued ability to make performing look easy but,

> Only later, when Humphries had cold-creamed Edna's face off his own, and come up the stairs, with a cold, pale hand shaking a bit as it clung to the balustrade, did it become clear how much the performance takes out of him.

That we all age is a cliché, but Overington took the reader inside the specific particulars of Humphries' life and art through acutely observed and sympathetically reported details. She tied together the make-up (a lifelong tool of the trade) with his liver spots, provided evidence of his frailty (needing to sleep in) and neatly juxtaposed his seemingly effortless performance with the effort needed for the seemingly simple task of climbing stairs.

DISCUSSION QUESTIONS AND EXERCISES

1. Go to a public place, such as a shopping mall, or a public event, such as a football match and write a 1000-word colour or slice-of-life story about what you observe. Be descriptive and aim to convey the atmosphere of the place or event and how people interact.
2. For your feature, decide whether it will benefit from first-hand observation. Assuming it does, gather the material. Write a 200-word pen portrait of the key person in your story and a 300-word description of a central location or event in the story.

THE PASSION OF JOHN MARSDEN

by David Brearley[14]

Tomorrow is judgment day in John Marsden's bitter defamation battle. **David Brearley** spent two years following the court spectacle, and wonders if victory will mean much at all.

The pot-smoking poofter keeps his Order of Australia in a display cabinet on the bathroom wall. He packs his house with trophies, even here, but it's the ducks that catch your eye. A ratbag army of ducks is camped around his spa, tin ducks and rubber ducks and 100 other ducks of uncertain provenance, and real live ducks scutter about the lush green acreage outside. "Duck-duck-duck-duck," he calls in his big gruff voice, but the inscrutable little birds pay him no mind.

The ducks seem to be totems of one sort or another, and their owner waddles when he walks. His legs are still coming to terms with the extra weight that bunches about his middle these days, giving him a profile and the gait of a Telly-tubby. He once quipped that "rich, generous and emancipated personalities" shared a "well-rounded silhouette", but that was in 1992, when his belly was still flat enough for mirth, and all else in life was perfect.

In 1992, John Marsden was president of the NSW Law Society, proud leader of 11,500 solicitors. He sat on the state's police and anti-discrimination boards while resting between presidencies of the Council for Civil Liberties, and his tiny legal practice at Campbelltown in Sydney's south-west had spawned a chain employing 140 professionals. The trophies were piling up fast, and—a nice little sweetener—his old mate John Fahey was premier.

The two men studied for the priesthood together, then Marsden employed Fahey as his articled clerk. Later, he used to babysit the Fahey children.

But that was then, and these days he's not welcome in the house—

broadcasts—*Today Tonight* in March 1995 and *Witness* in May 1996—which imputed that Marsden paid boys for sex. These were the years of Justice James Wood's royal commission into the NSW Police Service, when ranking MPs were using parliament to name alleged paedophiles, and any whisper of the subject could find a captive audience.

Marsden sued and was found to have been defamed—four days was all it took—but the sewers erupted when he pressed his case for damages. Seven defended its broadcasts as truth, producing 11 young men, ex-rent boys mostly, to amplify its original slurs from the witness box. From February 2000, the court became a forum for talk of riding crops, anal relaxants,

If the original slurs hurt, then the law's remedy has proved 10 times worse

Mrs Fahey won't have it.

These days, he is the pot-smoking poofter.

Of all the vile and hateful epithets slung at him in recent years, amid all the noise about nipple torture and whips and weeping boys, it is these three words that really bring up the veins in Marsden's neck.

They were first uttered in the NSW Supreme Court in April 10 last year by Robin Small, a crusty Kings Cross copper of the old school who would almost certainly be played by Bill Hunter, should anyone choose to make a miniseries of that absurd melodrama, Marsden v Amalgamated Television Services Pty Ltd.

The case concerns two Seven network

golden showers and worse. Two brothers described a druggy threesome, with Marsden on hands and knees begging for the whip. Another man claimed he was buggered and belted at 15, but never paid.

Marsden was always the plaintiff, but Seven's aggressive conduct of the case effectively made him the defendant.

In this context, Superintendent Small was a fringe witness at best, a bit player called in to spice up Seven's case on credit and credibility, which is what lawyers call a smear campaign. Small told the story of a failed drugs raid on Marsden's house, offered nothing on underage sex, and added with something like pride: "[Marsden] was known in the police force as a pot-smoking poofter."

That Marsden is in fact a gay male who enjoys cannabis gives rise to a profound question. "Does it mean," he asked the judge at the business end of proceedings last November, "that because I am a pot-smoking poofter then I am entitled to less damages?"

While Justice David Levine has spent a clear-headed summer applying the strictures of law to this abstruse conundrum, Marsden has been seething. He quotes Small's words obsessively, spits them out, as if they were the worst thing anyone ever said about him. He repeats them incredulously, as if they were untrue.

"Pot-smoking" demeans Marsden because it negates his thoughtful position on drugs issues. He was a director for several years at Odyssey House, a rehabilitation centre for addicts, and has delivered lengthy speeches here and overseas on the case for decriminalisation.

"Poofter" is a story in itself, a semantic nightmare. Gay men will apply it to each other, but rarely with any affection; it's not like queen, or even bugger, in that respect. On the tongues of straights it is loaded with latent violence. Poofter is the preferred usage among poofter-bashers. Of all the terms for male homosexual, only faggot can match its offensive punch.

Put the words together and Marsden seethes. He is of the suburbs, and he hears in their rugged poetry the authentic voice of middle-Australian bigotry—the voice of conventional wisdom.

Small's words remind Marsden that gay men still live in a hostile world. But it's worse than that, more personal. Pot-smoking poofter insults his ego, for it is the antithesis of everything he believes himself to be.

Since 1993, John Marsden AM, LLM etc, has furnished Who's Who with a remarkably eclectic list of his recreations: "Art, ballet, reading and rugby league". Throw in the CV and you have the raw stuff of Renaissance Man—a man for all seasons; a man of substance, at the very least. It's an image he strives to reinforce.

He dresses for the boardroom, in sober suits with the obvious flourishes: lapel pins, matching ties and handkerchiefs. His haircut is a schoolboy's bowl, but it's a thick growth that looks suitably severe when he slicks it back. He drinks Johnnie Walker Blue Label neat, makes his own sambuca, and keeps a magnificent table.

People find him charming or rudely engaging. He is a tireless gossip, generous and young at heart, with an easy body language. He loves company and keeps a colourful entourage, and there's always a factotum nearby.

Much was made during the trial of his art collection, and he likes it that way. Star billing went to an explicit erotic lithograph by Brett Whiteley, but Marsden surprised the courtroom one day by appearing with two small James Gleeson oils wrapped in newspaper. His stated reason for this unsolicited exhibition was to resolve any confusion between the Whiteley and the Gleesons, which also depict the male member. In fact there never was any confusion: Marsden was simply playing show-and-tell.

The art is just one part of the trophy collection. Marsden is a keen observer of his own press, prized examples of which hang framed in his home. These share wall space with caricatures of himself, photographs of important house guests and lovers (including some of Seven's witnesses in their glorious prime), and certificates for everything from bungy jumping to membership of the Gay and Lesbian Mardi Gras Hall of Fame.

Pride of place goes to a copy of Martin Luther King's "I have a dream" speech. Marsden is a dreamer himself, a card-carrying idealist. He loves a good quote and litters his speeches with a typically impressive selection: King, and Oscar Wilde of course, but also Cicero, the Oracle of Delphi, Shakespeare, Jerome K. Jerome and—a personal touch—one Joseph Choate, a 19th-century American jurist who celebrated the legal profession

is gay. There is nothing camp about him. He can be the most dreadful ham in court, but you won't catch him mincing this side of six whiskies, and even then it's low-level stuff. He's nobody's dandy.

His sexuality was hard won. Late adolescence was a commotion of anguish and fear—active ingredient: Catholic guilt—and the middle years seem to have been a succession of comings-out. He sometimes gives the date as 1992, his annus mirabilis, when he slipped the word "we" into a public statement on the HIV epidemic. Yet he nominates 1984 as the year he first took an active position on gay rights. He told his parents in 1972, before a political enemy could beat him to it. And then there was 1960, when Marsden, the blushing but (he says)

"Does it mean that because I am a pot-smoking poofter then I am entitled to less damages?"

in lofty prose.

This, then, is Art Marsden, rounded and refined, if not quite the aesthete he suspects himself of being. You could fairly say he has more style than class.

The flip side is Footy Marsden, a role he plays with comparative ease. Footy Marsden is your basic have-a-go Aussie, loud, reckless, reared in the old man's pub. He's the sort of bloke who yells at boxers, but rugby league is his passion, and he workshops the weekend's results with Les Murphy, the youngest of Anita Cobby's killers, who calls him from jail on Sunday evenings.

Marsden is a man's man—the father of a young adult, for what it's worth—with the important qualification that he

brilliant novitiate, fessed up to Cardinal Gilroy at Springwood seminary. He was a teenager at the time and it's still one of his favourite yarns.

He is almost 60 now and he has had many lovers: 100 was the figure he offered the court, but that seems modest. Promiscuous is a label he will not deny, but predatory he will not accept. There were men he loved for years on end, and fast times in between.

He does beats and he fancies rough trade, manly men with hairy chests, truck drivers and such, but only those with their own teeth. Muscle Marys need not apply.

Finally, he is a top, meaning he likes to be the dominant party in any sexual arrangement, within limits. Seven says his tastes run to whips and other nasties; Marsden counters that he has a reputation in gay circles for "lollipop sex", meaning no kinky stuff.

That such details are now a matter of public record is the price he has agreed to pay, and not unwillingly, for his battle has become a quest.

Messianic passions were stirring within him by 1997, if not before, when he posed for photographer C. Moore Hardy. The crucifixion concept was Hardy's alone, but it must have piqued something deep inside Marsden, whose Christianity and civil liberties background commit him to a creed of fearless passive resistance. The true enemy of

he wears only a rag about his loins. His wrists are strapped high and behind, the better to display a superb upper-body musculature, and his skin is flawless, save for the wounds of the arrows, which are no less obscene for being neat. Trussed and pierced, he averts his gaze to heaven, a model of constancy.

This loaded image, a favourite with artists since the Renaissance, exercises a powerful grip on the collective gay unconscious today. The Beautiful Saint embodies the righteousness of the cause, the cruelty of the persecution and the nobility of the suffering.

The martyr figure is a carefully nurtured motif in gay culture. Harvey Milk, San Francisco's first openly gay elected

> There is nothing camp about him. He can be the most dreadful ham in court, but you won't catch him mincing this side of six whiskies, and even then it's low-level stuff. He's nobody's dandy

injustice, he told the judge last year, was the man who put his principles above his person, whatever the cost.

Lately, martyrdom has become his preferred disposition. Marsden sees himself in the tradition of Saint Sebastian, a man who suffered greatly that other men might suffer less, and one of the most enduring figures in all of gay culture.

While the case for Sebastian's homosexuality is circumstantial at best, he enjoys a stellar afterlife as homoerotic pin-up boy. He is commonly pictured not at the moment of his death—he was bashed and dumped in a sewer in about AD300—but during an earlier ordeal at the hands of Roman archers. Invariably

official, murdered in 1978, is enshrined in biography, documentary and opera. More recently, Matthew Shepard, the angelic University of Wyoming student killed in a horrendous gay bashing in 1998, has been immortalised by Tectonic Theater in *The Laramie Project*. But it is an earlier Tectonic production, *Gross Indecency: The Three Trials of Oscar Wilde*, that best maps out Marsden's route to martyrdom.

Marsden laughs off the analogy, but the parallels between his pursuit of Seven and Wilde's prosecution of the Marquess of Queensberry 100 years earlier are beyond uncanny. Each case began with a sexual slur against a prominent gay man. Each slur resulted in a civil suit for defamation. Each suit turned on the evidence of rent-boys whose calumnies fuelled the fires of common prurience.

That Wilde's suit eventually found its way to the criminal courts is a matter of legal interest only. His action and Marsden's are identical in spirit: moral convictions, unfashionable ones at that, tested in the hostile world of the courts; designs for martyrdom, in other words.

Wilde succeeded, partly because the judgment went against him, partly, too, because he conducted his great self-destruction with such bravura. Adopting the name Sebastian for an alias, he composed The Ballad of Reading Gaol, turning his incarceration into a potent symbol.

But Marsden is no Oscar Wilde. He cannot match the Irishman for intellect or social graces, let alone rhetoric. His final submission last November was shambolic—emotional, rambling, occasionally incoherent: "I suppose, Your Honour, in summary, you look at a young man growing up at the plaintiff's age where his life, up until 1984, was one of illegality because of the way he was born, and it was difficult and encouraged people to live double lives and remain in the closet, as people say.

"Then in [19]84, the law changed but the stress (sic) for the gay man was only short-lived because, by late '84, early '85, the AIDS virus hit and one became on a rollercoaster as to whether one was going to die or not, and one was rushing off for tests.

"And as things started to pull out of that, in '93 and '94, Your Honour, I was suddenly hit with [Seven's defamation]."

This is the Passion of John Marsden: outlawed by birth, hunted by nature, hounded by men. Injury piles upon injustice in an epic continuum of suffering, with Seven squarely implicated. But is it enough?

Edward Gibbon in Decline And Fall [of the Roman Empire] reasoned that vanity was the seed of all martyrdom, and Marsden is a candidate on that score. Conversely, a certain humility is required to wear the martyr's robes with any style, and humility is one quality Marsden does not claim to possess. His temper is altogether wrong, too angry, and too flighty.

Broadcaster Phillip Adams testified to Marsden's "preposterous candour", and it's true that he has the boastful sexuality common to many gay men. He imagines, for example, that his pillow talk is tremendously thrilling to straight people.

A part of him is hurting, no doubt, but there's another part that's not entirely uncomfortable with the notoriety.

Saint Sebastian or pot-smoking poofter? Reputation is the prize here, and tomorrow's Supreme Court judgment will not be the final word on the matter. There is simply too much Marsden in the public arena these days for one man's findings to tell the story.

Ultimately, it is homosexuals who will weigh Marsden's claim on martyrdom and determine his place in the greater public narrative. He has other constituencies, of course—the legal profession, politics, the western suburbs—but these are hardly points of popular interest. It was as a proud gay man that he was defamed and as a proud gay man that he hit back. It is therefore as a proud gay man that he will be judged, in time.

But gays and lesbians are as fractious as the next demographic, maybe more so, and they do not speak with one voice on the delicate subject of Marsden. When the Mardi Gras potentates inducted him into their Hall of Fame last year, 200 people gave him a standing ovation, but 200 more stayed in their seats.

Some say Marsden walks on water, others think he's a sham, and these views can be held quite discrete from opinions on the truth or otherwise of Seven's broadcasts. Put another way, two men who believe precisely the same things

Marsden claims is beyond the comprehension of straight people, creates a pool of residual sympathy for him within the gay and lesbian community.

Still, many ask why he sued in the first place, knowing the dirt such a tacky case was always going to generate. People feel exposed, invaded.

Today Tonight and *Witness* said some creepy things about Marsden, but it was not until he sued that the shit really rained down. If the original slurs hurt, then the law's remedy has proved 10 times worse. Because whatever reputa-

Marsden sees himself in the tradition of **Saint Sebastian,** a man who suffered greatly that other men may **suffer less,** and one of the most enduring figures in all of gay culture

about Marsden's private life are likely to adopt radically opposed positions on the man himself.

Where straights reduce their thinking on Marsden to a simple question—*Did he do those things?*—older gays in particular bring some seriously heavy baggage to the reckoning. *Did he do those things?* is only part of a highly complex equation.

These men were born outside the law. They remember a time when Mardi Gras was a protest and all High Court judges were straight, and they reckon they know a witch-hunt when they see one. Moreover, they understand the legal subtext to Marsden's prosecution—the NSW consent laws that say girls may sleep with other girls at 16, while boys must be 18 before they sleep with men.

This rich layer of context, which

tion Marsden had on May 8, 1996, the day after the second Seven broadcast, he has 10 times that reputation now.

Jeff Shaw, who was NSW attorney-general during most of this business, spoke about the futility of defamation actions at a Law Society function last year. His advice to the slandered: turn the other cheek. "Surely a decorous silence is preferable to a media hell," Shaw said in a speech that covered some celebrated cases: the Andrew Ettingshausen penis photograph, Abbott and Costello v Bob Ellis and, of course, always Oscar Wilde.

Shaw never once mentioned the society's illustrious former president, but clearly had Marsden in mind when he asked: "Why bother? Why take your life in your two hands like water, then make a fist and lose it all?"

Why bother?

Marsden might be asking himself this very question today, sitting out there with his ducks and his fine art, sweating on a verdict. His name has taken a thrashing, yet his case never really became the catalyst it might have been.

Her Majesty's courts proved an unwilling forum for a civil liberties debate.

Or was it simply that the man in the middle lacked the substance—the gravitas—to elevate this whole sordid business above the level of lewd curiosity?

Why the ducks, I asked him once, fancying there were too many of the critters to satisfy a mere affectation. The answer didn't amount to much, at first.

It turns out somebody gave him a pair, then somebody else did the same, and so the joke went until the ducks were legion. "So there's nothing to it," he said flatly. But then, in a very Marsden moment, his eyes creased at the corners and a broad smile crossed his face. "Except that duck rhymes with . . ."

BATTLE OVER THE TRUTH

JOHN MARSDEN
Born January 3, 1942
Educated St Joseph's College, Hunters Hill; De La Salle College, Armidale; Sydney University. Seminarian, solicitor, networker. Former president of the NSW Law Society and Council for Civil Liberties, sat on the NSW Police Board, NSW Anti-Discrimination Board. Multiple memberships and affiliations. Stood for parliament as Liberal Party candidate, maintains powerful contacts across the political spectrum. Order of Australia since 1994.

November 1995: Deirdre Grusovin names Marsden as a pederast in NSW parliament.
March 1995: Channel Seven's current affairs program *Today Tonight* implies Marsden paid boys for sex.
May 1996: *Witness* on Channel Seven repeats the implications.
August 1996: Wood royal commission into NSW Police Service investigates Marsden. He is cleared.
February 1999: Supreme Court jury finds Seven defamed Marsden.
November 1999: Damages hearing begins, at which Seven defends its broadcasts as truth.
February 2000: Truth witnesses testify against Marsden.
May 2000: Marsden testifies.
June 2000: Marsden calls Anita Cobby killer Les Murphy to testify.
November 2000: Hearing finishes after 214 days.
June 27, 2001: Judgment day.

THE STORY BEHIND THE STORY

David Brearley

The Marsden case dragged on for years and every lurid story it produced made an even greater mockery of the defamation laws at its core. It began in the mid-1990s when Channel Seven broadcast two current affairs items about John Marsden, an openly gay Sydney solicitor with strong political connections, alleging that he paid boys for sex. Marsden sued Seven, which presented a defence of truth and called a number of middle-aged men to the witness stand, where they told outrageous stories about encounters they claimed to have had with Marsden many years prior. These stories came unstuck under cross-examination, but not before they had received the sort of publicity that will ensure Marsden's name is forever linked with paedophilia. As a man of the law, he cannot claim to have taken that risk blindly.

I reported the case daily, placing the latest evidence in the context of evidence already heard. It was sensational material at least two days out of five so there was no problem getting a run, but public interest in cases of this size and complexity can dry up very quickly without regular features to sustain it. Another consideration, peculiar to a national publication, was to create broader interest in what was essentially a very Sydney story.

During one of the duller sections of the hearings, I wrote a feature comparing Marsden's defamation action with two others: the first, brought by Oscar Wilde about 100 years earlier, was remarkably similar in subject matter and dramatis personae; the second, brought by the Reverend Samuel Marsden, the so-called Flogging Parson of Parramatta, involved a historical figure with whom Marsden could actually claim an ancestral link. The piece was conceived as an idle diversion but some telling comparisons emerged and the overall effect, I hope, was to bring some richness to readers' appreciation of the daily news stories.

When the case went into Christmas recess, I wrote a series of features about the role of psychiatrists in Australian courts. The idea for these came from one of Marsden's witnesses, a psychiatrist who made a goose of himself by admitting he had tailored his medico-legal report at the request of Marsden's lawyers. That sort of behaviour turned out to be endemic in Australia's courts.

Other features were written to mark key junctures in the trial. 'The Passion of John Marsden', published the day before the judgment, was the last of these but the first to focus hard on Marsden himself. It made sense to finish with an intimate profile, because the case had been all about the man and his reputation.

Research took the obvious forms. There was no substitute for sitting in court day after day, hearing what Marsden had to say about himself and what others had to say about him and what he had to say about them in return. This material was colourful and voluminous and needed to be treated respectfully, with the judgment yet to be tabled.

Outside court, although Marsden would not give me a formal interview, he was talking to me all the time, which was helpful some of the time. I read a book of speeches he had made as president of the NSW Law Society. This sort of material was valuable, but only when approached with appropriate scepticism. Meanwhile, I spoke to several people I trusted who had known Marsden or been in a position to observe him at different points in his extraordinary life. I monitored coverage of the trial in the gay press, where the legal battle was merely the starting point for a wider story. I read widely and historically, a habit every journalist should cultivate. The idea is to over-research: the more you know about your subject, the more options you have when you come to write it.

I avoided reading an earlier Marsden profile by Frank Robson in the *Good Weekend*. This was because Robson is a very powerful writer and I didn't want his Marsden in my head when I came to write my own.

My decision to present Marsden impressionistically gave me freedom, but also imposed certain obligations. Impressions owe a continuing and absolute duty of truth to facts. So when I write, for example, that Marsden is 'the sort of bloke who yells at boxers', it means that I have in fact been at a fight and heard him do it and that I think the image works best in the abstract. When I write that he suspects himself of being 'an aesthete', then I have satisfied myself that this is true but have decided not to burden the story with the various cross-referenced observations which led me to that conclusion. When I write that he considers himself a martyr, it is based on dozens of things he's said off the record, plus the photograph he posed for and what I learned from interviewing the photographer, plus a hazy knowledge of the Saint Sebastian story and its iconography within gay circles.

I had about two weeks of pure writing time, most of it spent on structure and shape. The story needed a lot of background to sustain its real-time focus, but the background needed to be worked in as quickly and seamlessly as possible. It grew to more than 5000 words and benefited from some very good editing (the Sebastian stuff, for example, was cut by about 500 words). The published version comes in at about 3500. By the end of the two weeks and a dozen or so drafts, I knew the piece well enough to write the entire thing out from memory, word for word.

Marsden was a challenge to write because he polarised views so strongly. This was one of the reasons why interviews with third parties were only marginally useful. I lost a friend over the story, someone with a distant interest in the proceedings and a great hatred of Marsden. She thought my story was too favourable; I actually felt it was the story of a shallow man. Probably, the story's real triumph was to set out the lunacy in the libel laws—a man had to destroy his reputation in order to protect it—and to do so without being pulled up by the judge for contempt.

FINDING THE RIGHT
STRUCTURE FOR THE STORY

The art of writing consists of applying the seat of the pants to the seat of the chair.

Mark Twain

CHAPTER SUMMARY

As the research phase ends, journalists need to go through the mass of gathered material, discarding whatever is irrelevant to the feature story's theme and marshalling the relevant. Journalists need to mull over the material—if they have time—to find the story structure best suited to the material. Five broad story structures are discussed.

Most journalists enjoy researching feature stories. They meet interesting and famous people, they learn new things, they get out of the office. A tight deadline will lasso some to their desk but others baulk at the task of writing; just a couple more interviews, they rationalise. True, exceptional journalism relies on making that extra call, but equally true, journalists need to learn when they have enough material and how to give themselves enough time to do it justice.

The popular historian Barbara Tuchman used to tell a salutary story of meeting a woman in the Washington archives in the late 1970s who had been studying US–Moroccan relations since the 1930s. Now in her seventies, the woman had recently suffered a heart attack. 'Would she ever leave off her research in time to write that definitive history and tell the world what she knew?' Tuchman wondered.[1] Editors are unlikely to leave you mouldering in archives, but how do you know when to stop researching, how do you organise the material you have gathered and how do you ensure you are ruthless about jettisoning dead wood?

David Brearley emphasises the need to over-research to give you more writing options, and Gideon Haigh says he always gathers three times as much as he needs.[2] Both Brearley and Haigh are perfectionists but if you have only enough material to fill your designated word limit chances are the piece will feel thin. Of course, you might be the sort of person who writes as they research. Kimina Lyall says if she has to write a feature quickly she may type the most relevant paragraphs from an interview immediately afterwards, to alleviate the anxiety she feels writing features against tight deadlines. More commonly, there will come a point when you feel you have enough material and you need or, better still, you feel an urge to begin writing.

In any case, the line between researching and writing is not necessarily so clear cut. You may well need to do more research once you have written a draft, and you should have been thinking about how you will write the story as you did the research, partly because the continual interplay between gathering and thinking about material drives the story along and partly because it is an efficient use of time. Before outlining what I do at this stage in the process, it is important to emphasise that different people work in different ways and that what suits one person will not suit another. William Blundell, for instance, sets out an exhaustive system of indexing all his material that I have tried and found too complex and time-consuming.[3]

SIFTING AND SORTING THE RAW MATERIAL

So much of journalists' energy goes into quickly understanding complicated issues that they struggle to keep perspective on what all their raw material means. If you've done your reporting and research work properly, inevitably there will be a lot of material to process. This is the time to sit down and go through it all, with a highlighter pen and a clean notepad. The benefit is twofold: first, by reading through everything it reminds you of interesting things you may have forgotten; second, it helps clarify exactly what you think the story is. As you go, look out for the following.

FACTS AND FIGURES

Highlight the facts and figures most relevant to your story. When you are writing, stopping to scrabble through 30 pages of notes to find that knock-'em-dead statistic is annoying, and breaks whatever flow you had going.

QUOTES

Again, a lot of sifting is needed here, as most people ramble. Glean factual material from quotes and list it. Find the most memorable quotes and those that illuminate the main people you are writing about.

On your notepad it is enough to write 'great quote from so and so', and write a key word or two to jog your memory.

THE CREAMY STUFF
The creamy stuff, as Tom Wolfe calls it, is the anecdotes, the telling details, the dramatic scenes.

LEADS AND CLOSES
The lead and close of a feature are important, and often hard to find, so keep an eye out particularly for potential leads and closes.

THEMES AND ARGUMENTS
As you read, note the themes that emerge and the various strands of arguments about the themes.

DEAD WOOD
Looking for material to include in the story means, by definition, sloughing off anything that is irrelevant to the theme of the story, or relevant but not particularly interesting or incisive. This work is equally important, perhaps more important, given the amount of information journalists gather and the deadline pressure they work under.

You may choose to categorise your notes in different ways, according to the complexity of the feature and the amount of time you have. You may be doing a straightforward piece with fewer than, say, half a dozen interviewees, and only a handful of documents, and the material may be fresh in your mind because the whole job needs to be turned around in a couple of days. For such stories, it is probably enough to make a list of your interviewees and the documents and to summarise the strongest quotes, facts, etc. under each person's name. Most likely, the feature will be more complex and will be competing with several other stories for your attention. In these cases, it is preferable not to list the material under different sources' names but instead under the six categories of questions listed in chapter five, on planning. That is, under background questions, scope questions, why questions, impact questions, reaction questions and looking ahead questions. Blundell spent years trying to nut out the reason certain features worked while others failed. He found almost invariably that where a journalist had organised their material into these six groupings the piece worked, and that the most common flaw was poorly organised material.[4]

FLESHING OUT THE STRUCTURE

Next, let your mind roam for a while. It is a good time to talk to the editor about the story, which in all likelihood has moved on from the original idea. They may well have suggestions for structuring the story, but even if they do not, or if they do not have time to talk, let the raw material wander around in your head and see what story shapes come up. People feel they are doing nothing unless they are hammering away at the keyboard, but this stage is about learning to use both sides of the brain, as has been advocated by writing coaches such as Blundell and Pulitzer Prize-winning journalist Jon Franklin.[5]

The left side of the brain is logical, orderly and moves in straight lines. It is the left side you use to read through your notes and organise your material. The right side of the brain is intuitive, emotional and creative. When people say, 'this idea just popped into my head' they are describing the right side of their brain at work. Many think journalism is simply about objective facts soberly reported, which aligns it with left brain activity. I don't accept simple notions of objectivity—to say a journalist is biased is simply to state they are a human being—but in straight news reporting the emphasis is on gathering and reporting factual information as quickly as possible. It is no insult to say that in a literary sense straight news reporting is formulaic. The need for speed dictates a formula that once learnt is never forgotten. News desks cannot afford journalists suffering writer's block, a very real problem that afflicts novelists and poets. Writer's block, in fact, is about the right side of the brain. Ideas may pop into the writer's head, but they may remain unpopped. If you are tired or gazing longingly out the window at sunshine you can still cudgel the left side of your brain into working, however resentful it might be.

A successful feature needs well organised material, but it also should be shaped into an engaging story, with a strong lead and lively writing. Sometimes the words flow, sometimes they don't. The feature writer's problem is that they need both sides of the brain, and they need them now. One side will play ball, the other is as likely to take its bat and ball and go home. What to do? Begin by working in an orderly logical way and give the right side of your brain room to work. The worst that can happen is you write a clear but dull feature. At least the job will be done and on time—two professional virtues. If you refuse to write until inspiration strikes, you may end up rushing the piece, risking factual errors and structural flaws, and you may miss the deadline altogether—two professional vices. You will be pleasantly surprised to see how well the right side of your brain works if you give it space and if you become more alert to what it is trying to tell you.

Some years ago I was working on a feature for a television magazine about the rise of football shows, such as *The Footy Show* on Channel Nine and *Talking Footy* on Seven. After doing the research—reading about earlier programs, interviewing producers and hosts, sitting in on the taping of shows—I sat down to write and struggled with various story structures. It was a weekend and my children wanted to go to the park. Getting nowhere, I decided to take a break. As I was pushing my daughter on the swing this phrase began going through my mind: 'Yabba, yabba, yabba, yabba, yabba, yabba, yabba, yabba, yabba, McFeast!' At first I dismissed it, but it wouldn't go away. Hmm, what's this about? I knew yabba, yabba was part of the opening credits for another TV program, Elle McFeast's chat show about the weird and wonderful world of Canberra politics. Suddenly, a light went on in my head. I connected the yabba, yabba, yabba with the most striking thing I had seen in my research on the football shows. The moment Bruce McAvaney, Mike Sheahan and Malcolm Blight met at Channel Seven's studios to tape the program they began talking about footy, and they did not stop—not even during the ad breaks—until they bid each other farewell after a post-taping drink. The right side of my brain was helping me find a way to structure the story around their non-stop chatter, which would be interspersed throughout. This is how the story began:

'G'day Malcolm. Welcome to the commentary box,' says Mike Sheahan.
'Whaddya mean?' replies Malcolm Blight.
'Well,' says Sheahan, 'I saw that Shawie (Robert Shaw, the Adelaide Crows coach) had a go at you after what you said during the call (on Channel Seven's broadcast) on Saturday night. There's something on AAP (the wire service, Australian Associated Press) about it.'
Blight is bemused. 'Yeah? Really? But that was just a couple of coaching decisions that I really couldn't see the point of, and I said so during the call.'

That's how it starts the moment Sheahan claps eyes on Blight in the makeup room at Channel Seven's studios in Dorcas Street, South Melbourne. Sheahan is a respected football writer and winner of the AFL's sports media award for the past five years, while Blight was a freakishly gifted player in the seventies, Geelong's coach until the end of last season and now a commentator. Together they join host Bruce McAvaney for their late Monday night program *Talking Footy*.

They don't even stop to draw breath. Within the next five minutes in the makeup room, Blight and Sheahan have chewed over Blight's column in that morning's newspaper about the late E.J. Whitten, whether they were going to the funeral—they were—and Carlton's steamroller win on Saturday over North Melbourne at Optus Oval, with special attention paid to Carlton ruckman Justin Madden's skilled palming at the centre bounces.

Don't worry about going into the studio, boys; set up the cameras in here. There is a footy show rolling before our very eyes![6]

From there it went on to discuss other football shows like *4 Quarters*, also on Seven, and Channel Nine's *The Footy Show* before closing the story by returning to the *Talking Footy* panel:

As McAvaney throws to a commercial break during the shooting of *Talking Footy*, going out on highlights of the goals of the round, the three of them, plus studio guest, umpire John Russo, watch the monitor screen with rapt attention, pleasure radiating from their faces as another miraculous snap scores from the boundary line. Even off air, McAvaney can't resist calling the action. 'That was a nice throw by Dear wasn't it?' he says of a dubious handpass by the Hawthorn player. 'Quick hands as they say,' replies Russo, noticing how the umpire had been caught on Dear's blind side.

Sheahan turns to McAvaney and they yack at each other non-stop throughout the break while Blight, ever the student of the game, turns to Russo and says, 'John, that was really interesting what you said before about that decision. I was just wondering . . .'

There are many more story structures available in features than in straight news. The sheer volume of media circulating today means readers are familiar with, even tired of, many of these structures, however. There are three ways of piercing this media ennui: first, ensure the structure is not imposed on the story but arises from its content; second, drill down deep into the subject to excavate fresh material; finally, acknowledge the reader's media literacy and play with it. The last option is an advanced strategy, but is worth keeping in mind for future reference.

There are elements common to all feature structures, and they derive from the iron law of the yawning reader, or the Scheherazade principle. *The Thousand and One Arabian Nights* is a collection of centuries-old stories (Sinbad the Sailor is the best known) that sit within a larger story, of a king who killed each of his wives the morning after their wedding night until he married Scheherazade, who saved her skin by telling him a fresh story each night. Your livelihood rather than your life is at stake when you write a feature, but you get the idea. The Scheherazade principle is that readers have always been easily bored; what is different today is the sheer volume of media and entertainment competing for their attention.

What all feature structures include, then, is:

A GOTCHA LEAD
Whatever work layout, pictures and headlines do for the story, you still need to get the reader's attention, whether by enticing them, intriguing them or alarming them.

THE BILLBOARD PARAGRAPH
Soon after you've got the reader's attention, you need to tell them why the story is worth reading. What is the main issue your story is exploring? Note this is different from what your story might conclude about the issue. This section may be as brief as a sentence. More likely it is a paragraph, and it may require a couple. If it is much longer than that, though, it becomes the story itself rather than the reason why the story is worth reading. This section flows from the question you posed in the planning stage: 'What is my story about, in a nutshell?'

EVIDENCE TO BACK UP THE REASON WHY READERS SHOULD READ THE STORY
Okay, you have the reader's attention and you have made them a promise (this story is important because it is about, say, the growing threat of bioterrorism). Now, fulfil that promise. Show the reader how the threat of bioterrorism is growing, where and why now. This section forms the bulk of the story.

A MEMORABLE ENDING

If the reader is still with you, send them on their way with a strong ending that imprints the story on their mind. An ending that dribbles away is not only irritating but threatens to undo the earlier good work.

This is a useful guide that can help you keep in mind how readers read, but it does not flesh out a structure for an individual story. As mentioned above, the evidence makes up most of the story's length. How do you structure that into something more appetising than a big glob of information? You can talk to editors and colleagues for suggestions and they may well be useful, but these discussions can also curdle into procrastination. At some point it is up to you—yes, as the advertisement says, just do it.

Here are the most common feature structures: keep in mind that an individual feature may draw on elements of more than one of these common structures, and that this is by no means an exhaustive list.

THE STATE OF PLAY, OR ROUND-UP

Most commonly used for news features, the state of play or round-up is a meat-and-two-veg story structure aimed at clearly setting out an issue. They are a staple of weekend newspapers and news magazines. For example, *The Weekend Australian Financial Review* ran an article spread over two full pages comparing public and private sector executive salaries that typified the newspaper's dry, information-dense news features.[7] The precede—'Public sector executives are paid a fraction of their private sector peers. The result is a looming brain drain, and a shortage in public sector expertise'—gave a fair summary of the piece to come, which began:

> Been keeping an eye on the bonuses paid to your company's most senior executives? How much did they get last year—$80,000, $800,000, $8 million?
>
> Spare a thought for the public sector, where in many cases the only bonus senior executives of billion-dollar businesses can hope for is the warm inner glow that comes from the knowledge of a job done well.

After two more paragraphs journalists Michael Cave and Annabel Hepworth set out their reason for writing the piece:

> In an era when corporate leaders in this country are earning seven-digit salaries, the growing disparity between public and private sector remuneration is like the punch-line to a bad joke. Disturbingly, it could be that one about paying peanuts and getting monkeys.

You and I might not be earning millions like private sector CEOs or hundreds of thousands like senior bureaucrats, but the article is well pitched at the newspaper's business readership, as it goes on in the next two paragraphs to justify the piece. In paragraphs nine to fifteen Cave and Hepworth set out in detail the scope of the problem, comparing public and private sector salaries: Reserve Bank Governor Ian Macfarlane, the man responsible for the stability of the nation's economy, earns $500 000 while the head of one of the major banks, Frank Cicutto, earns nearly six times that amount. Paragraphs sixteen to eighteen start to outline reasons for the disparity, while paragraphs nineteen to 21 ask what impact such disparities will have on future recruitment. The following ten paragraphs begin to wander, providing more information on the scope of the salary disparity problem and the difference between the public sector and government-owned business enterprises. The next eleven paragraphs—32 to 43—provide yet more detail about differing salary levels in different states and introduce a senior public servant who briefly explains that his job satisfaction is not connected purely to his salary. In paragraphs 44 to 55, common salary package elements of the private sector, stock options and bonuses, are discussed. They cannot be translated easily to public sector packages because public servants are paid for by taxpayers and their salaries can become politically sensitive. In the final three paragraphs—56 to 58—Cave and Hepworth return to the issue of job satisfaction and close by suggesting that following the 'Enron-style corporate melt-downs' experienced executives may opt for lower paid but more personally satisfying public sector positions.

It is a long article that begins reasonably well and provides a lot of comparative information about salaries. It succeeds when it follows Blundell's notion of grouping material according to the key questions, but it gradually loses its thread, crisscrossing back and forth between various key questions. Perhaps unknowingly, the article contradicts itself. It asserts that the disparity in public and private sector salaries is a problem, but happily accepts that politicians are smart not to award bonuses for senior public servants. The journalists appear to have spent a lot of energy gathering information, but far less analysing what it means.

In the same period *Reader's Digest* dealt with a similar topic in a similarly structured article.[8] What might surprise many is how effective the piece was for its audience. Headlined 'Piggy banks', the precede read 'These once-revered institutions have fallen out of public favour'. Sandy Guy and David Crofts' article began with three crisp anecdotes showing banks failing their customers, then outlined the reason for reading the piece:

> Stories like these are disturbingly frequent in Australia. In the past decade, banks have shut more than 2100 branches and sacked 55,000 staff. By next month, National Australia Bank will have closed another 56 rural outlets. Says Catherine Wolthuizen, financial services senior policy officer with the Australian Consumers' Association: 'These are deliberate efforts to phase out face-to-face banking.'

The next two paragraphs—six and seven—elaborate on the level of customer dissatisfaction before paragraphs eight to fifteen outline how online banking is supposed to help customers but isn't. Paragraphs sixteen to eighteen step back and remind readers what banks used to be like, before moving smoothly onto paragraphs nineteen to 21, describing an annoying legacy of bank deregulation of the 1980s—mushrooming account fees. Paragraphs 22 to 26 assert that since deregulation the banks have targeted wealthier customers for preferential treatment while poorer customers are charged higher account fees. The next logical question is to ask how customers feel about bank service; this is done in paragraphs 27 and 28. For the next seven paragraphs the banks are given an opportunity to respond to customers' grievances and put their case. Paragraphs 37 to 42 look ahead, asking what reforms are needed to improve bank service. Guy and Crofts close with a summarising quote from Wolthuizen that essentially restates the thrust of the piece. It is true that the article is not as newsy as the 'Public v. private' salaries piece (declining bank service has been an issue for several years) and also true that it did not delve deep into the issue (despite initial resistance customers are slowly embracing online banking), but 'Piggy banks' was clear and easy to read.

TIME LINES

The time line, or 'tick tock' as Michael Keaton calls it in the movie *The Paper*, is simple chronology, usually broken down into a single day. There are two reasons to use chronology: first, because there is not much action in the story and the movement of time will bring out any action there is; second, when there is a lot of action that needs to be described in detail. The latter falls into the next category of story structure, narrative drive, and will be dealt with there. An example of the former is a story I was commissioned to write for the 'Media' section of *The Australian* in 1999.

Section editor Eliot Taylor wanted a piece about the media monitoring company Rehame, which he thought was beginning to influence political decision-making through comprehensive monitoring of talkback radio calls and prompt relaying of results to Canberra. The influence of talkback radio on politics is generally accepted but finding government ministers willing to admit they shifted policy because of talkback callers is hard. None of the politicians—government or opposition, press secretaries, press gallery journalists or other media monitors interviewed thought Rehame was becoming a political player in its own right. What emerged was that the firm's founder, Peter Maher, is a fine self-promotor.

Unable to support the section editor's story idea, but unwilling as a freelance to give up a commission, I decided to focus on a profile of Rehame and Maher since few people know how a media monitoring company works. Few people care perhaps, but those who did were probably readers of the 'Media' section. I felt sure a media monitoring company would have to be an intricate operation and, as discussed in the chapter on story ideas, readers can be pleasantly surprised by new information about something they take for granted. This is how the article began:

> 5.20am: Pitch blackness envelops the first person arriving at Rehame media monitoring company's head office in the inner-city industrial suburb of Port Melbourne. Marnie Fitz unlocks the door of the redbrick building that still carries the barred windows from its previous life as a small factory and walks up a small flight of stairs to start setting the

rows of 24 audio tapes in time for the first news services of the day at 5.30am.[9]

Of itself, the action is nothing special, but it establishes how early media monitors have to start and has an air of routine that actually describes the job, which is contrasted with the radio and TV newsrooms they monitor, where at exactly the same time staff are rushing to put together their shows. There is a pause in the time line to bring in the billboard paragraphs:

> Rehame is actually anything but quiet; the noisy self-promotion of its founder and head, Peter Maher, has forced the company to market leadership in electronic media monitoring in Australia, shading the longer established Media Monitors company.
>
> In the past five years Rehame has trebled its staff to 150 as Maher has fashioned for himself a media guru reputation, appearing on four high profile radio programs each week—John Laws in Sydney, Neil Mitchell in Melbourne, Howard Sattler in Perth and Cathy Van Extel in Canberra.

From there I took the reader back to the time line.

> 8.30am: David Kiefer, one of three sales and information managers in Rehame's Melbourne office, sits at his desk, eyes darting from a radio in front of him, to one on a side desk and up to a TV screen perched in front on a table. He has been at Rehame since its first year in 1985 and while some co-workers gobble bowls of cereal at their work desk, he has neatly set down a glass of water, an apple and a mandarin. As Kiefer looks through summaries of the overnight news, he says it has become second nature for him to listen, watch and read simultaneously. 'Most of the time you are looking out for a particular word or two.'
>
> He does pay attention each morning, though, at 7.07am to the *Rumour File* on Dean Banks and Ross Stevenson's 3AW morning show, a segment where listeners are invited to ring in scuttlebut. 'It is more accurate than you might think, judging by the reaction of some clients. When I call them, there is a minute's silence, or an immediate demand for a transcript.' He keeps two tape recorders on his desk whose tapes he turns over through the day; he uses them to play back radio items to clients over the phone.

The piece alternates between the observed action, low-level though it is, and discussion about media monitoring, where it came from, what Rehame's clients say about it and the difficulties of doing it well. When Peter Maher arrives in the office at 12.40pm the piece pauses to background him and air his views about talkback radio. Along the way the reader learns interesting information. There is a huge volume of media flying around Australia—Rehame monitors up to 12 000 items daily. A big story for Rehame is not necessarily a big story in a newsroom. For Rehame a big story is one that enables them to sell transcripts to many clients. The day I visited the news was dominated by the Balkans war, but David Keifer was much more interested in reports of a request by Kerry Packer's media empire to halt its trading on the stock exchange later that morning. 'Everyone jumps when Packer is doing something.' The story ended with the last of the day's monitoring:

> 10.30pm: The last monitor goes home, half an hour after her two colleagues, leaving only Louise Curham, a film school graduate and sometime director, who spends the next two hours following up the work of various regional monitors and setting up newsline feeds for two companies that are to receive a free two-week trial of the company's products.
>
> 12.40am: Curham takes down the day's audio cassettes to the studio, brings up the next day's tapes and puts them in the tape decks in readiness for tomorrow. She picks up her handbag, turns off the lights and goes outside to her 1970 Valiant station-wagon (ideal for carrying film gear), pausing only to notice that it is not only dark but unseasonally cold.

The story ends, then, as it began, in darkness and routine; media monitoring is hardly glamorous. It was a bread-and-butter story made moderately readable through observing Rehame's operation first-hand and using the time line structure. I could perhaps have focused the story on Peter Maher but I felt his views on talkback radio were simplistic and as this was a feature, not an opinion piece, I would have been giving him yet another platform to air his admiration for Alan Jones and John Laws, who soon after became mired in the cash for comment scandal. I was not convinced a more critical feature would be run uncut. As it was, the most critical line in the story about Rehame was cut, and it was scarcely earth-shattering. The paragraph read:

'Others say the quality of Rehame's monitoring has improved dramatically after shaky beginnings. Once a federal political party was sent a list of media mentions—for state politicians.' The second sentence was cut.

The charm of a time line structure lies in its unfolding of fresh, close-up detail. Times lines are over-used though because they are such a simple story structure to write. Too often journalists reach for it when with a bit more thought they could have found a fresher structure. I've been guilty of it myself. Too often too, journalists have not been sufficiently observant and have only the most mundane details to report.

NARRATIVE DRIVE

The narratives of journalism, like those of mythology and folklore, derive their power from their firm, undeviating sympathies and antipathies. Cinderella must remain good and the stepsisters bad. 'Second stepsister not so bad after all' is not a good story.

Janet Malcolm

The majority of feature subjects have little real action, so when you find a story that has genuine narrative potential grab it with both hands. Journalists will say of these stories that they almost write themselves. What they mean is that the pressure journalists routinely feel to make bland or complicated material interesting is absent. It is a deceptive remark, though. Good stories don't write themselves; attention has to be paid to what details to include, the tone, varying the pace and so on. A journalist on *The Daily Telegraph* wrote a narrative reconstruction of the chilling gang rapes in Sydney during the 2000 Olympic Games, for which the offenders received record long prison sentences. Cindy Wockner's strong investigative work was blunted by a style that read almost as a parody of a hard-boiled detective novel:

There are condoms scattered in the brown Corona's glovebox, female clothing on the back seat.

There's a man named Sam and a white van that pops up more than once. A $50 note at the Harbour Bridge toll booth and a city so dazzled by the Olympic flame it's taken its eyes off the cockroach corners. We're waiting for Cathy Freeman to breast the line, but three detectives are beginning to connect the dots—starting to understand that there is a group out there preying on teenage girls. Hunting its prey in a pack.[10]

Later we are told 'Constable Tamer Kilani's got a copper's instinct. A gut feeling for no good.' Sometimes less can be more.

Consider how John Hersey handled what remains one of the biggest stories of the 20th century—the dropping of the atomic bomb. Hersey visited Hiroshima nine months afterwards to see how the Japanese were recovering from the bomb. Faced with the appalling scale of destruction and radiation sickness, Hersey resisted what must have been a powerful urge to express his outrage directly and instead wrote in precise, detached prose. The effect is to allow the reader to see even more clearly the horror and tragedy of the bombing.[11]

Sport, crime, disasters and war are subjects with the most potential for narrative drive, but the one that offers an almost textbook example of the gripping narrative comes from Paul Barry's bestselling biography *The Rise and Rise of Kerry Packer*. An experienced, award-winning journalist, Barry opens his biography with a retelling of the 1990 day Packer was happily playing polo at Warwick Farm when he suffered a massive heart attack and was to all intents and purposes dead for nearly eight minutes. The narrative begins slowly with a calm description of the game then, with an almost quizzical air, describes the initial unhurried aid given to Packer. As spectators become aware of the situation, the pace of the narrative quickens. The tone is urgent but by no means gushing with concern. Packer, despite his vast wealth, is not a well-loved man. Packer enjoyed two pieces of fortune on this mild spring day: an off-duty ambulance man happened to be at Warwick Farm; an intensive care ambulance, one of just twelve on duty in Sydney that day, happened to be nearby when the emergency call came through. Amazingly, the overweight, heavy-smoking, chronic heart problem-ridden Packer survived, enriching the Packer legend. But Barry is not done yet; he adds a coda, when Packer returned to Warwick Farm the following weekend where he was besieged by photographers and TV news crews:

> The passenger door opens and Kerry comes almost running out. He looms up to the cameramen with all the subtlety of a nightclub bouncer moving in for the action. 'I'll tell you how I'm feeling. Leave me alone, get out of my way.' A huge face and hand fill the lens and the picture goes spinning.
>
> The television footage is unforgettable. Last time the world saw Kerry Packer he was on a stretcher, huge, pale, unconscious, and

apparently dead or a vegetable, with a forest of tubes protruding out of him: now he's charging out of the television screen like a mad wounded animal. He seems vast, superhuman, angry and unstoppable.[12]

THEMATIC

Rather than structure a story according to its narrative action, you might shape it according to a theme. In contrast to a state of play structure, a thematic structure focuses on one or two elements and uses them as the prism through which to see an issue or person. For instance, in late 2002 Australia was suffering its worst drought in a generation and many feared a terrible summer of bushfires. Such a scenario suggests many potential features. Margaret Simons focused on just one—why do people deliberately light fires?—and poured all her reporting energy into that. The result: a thought-provoking article about a complex issue.[13] Thematic structures are less common than time lines because they rely on the journalist to identify the theme and organise their material accordingly. This takes time, and as we know time is not standard issue equipment in newsrooms.

Thematic structures can work powerfully, as Tom Wolfe showed in much of his journalism (before he became a novelist). The catchphrases Wolfe invented to summarise his story themes—'radical chic', 'the Me decade', 'the right stuff'—have passed into the vernacular. For a profile of historian Geoffrey Blainey, I used a thematic structure that grew out of my surprise at the contrast between Blainey's reputation before and after controversial remarks he made about Asian immigration in 1984. The piece began:

> Visitors driving down the winding highway into Queenstown in Tasmania are confronted by hills stripped of their vegetation. Late last century, to feed the furnaces of the Mount Lyell copper mining company, its workers felled the trees that matted the hills. The mine's sulphurous fumes were so dense they choked new growth and the district's 250cm annual rainfall flushed away the soil, leaving only bare, eerily tinted rock.
>
> To many, these hills bear ugly testimony to the miners' short-sightedness. Not so to Geoffrey Blainey, who made the company the subject of his first book. Even today, to his eye the hills resemble a lunar landscape. 'It really is a spectacular sight on a sunny day,' he says. 'It is

like skinning an animal; you can see all the colours of the bedrock. The light will play on it, all the reds, browns, whites and so forth.'

The vegetation that has been peeping up only spoils the picture for him. 'I can understand the conservationists who say this is a disgrace, but I can support the townspeople who say, 'This is our town and our landscape and we like it.'

The Queenstown hills are also an emblem for Professor Blainey's role in public life. He has made a career out of taking unfashionable stands on highly charged issues. His remarks on Asian immigration, the Greens, mining, the republican movement and, most recently, the Mabo decision, have cleaved the community as have those of no other. He is either revered as a latter-day Tiresias bravely pointing out unpalatable truths, or reviled as the hired gun of the Right, cloaking inflammatory, even racist, remarks under the gown of academia.

Yet to profile Blainey today compared with that of a decade ago is seemingly to write about two different people. To paraphrase Robert Louis Stevenson, this is the strange tale of Dr Blainey and Mr Right.[14]

This seeming split in Professor Blainey's career set up the structure for the rest of the article, which turned first to his successful and well-recognised career as an historian before looking at how he had become a polemicist. The first career was described in detail to remind readers not only of his achievements but his benign public image before signalling the next section of the profile: 'It was at this pinnacle, in the early eighties, that Dr Blainey turned into Mr Right.' The second career was set out and analysed in detail. Blainey denied he had become a hired gun of the Right but by the early 1990s he was in danger of becoming a dial-a-quote. 'Would anyone have said that of Dr Blainey?' The final section of the profile examined how such a quietly spoken, courteous professor got himself into so much trouble. The piece concluded:

> The effect, it seems, of the immigration debate has been to distort Blainey's independent approach into a kind of professional negativism. To lionise or demonise Blainey from a Left–Right ideological perspective is to miss the point that Blainey the great historian has become Blainey the lousy polemicist. It is only his sheer intelligence and flair with words that masks the gap between the two.
>
> Blainey baulks at such a suggestion, saying it is for others to judge.

So, how will historians 100 years hence assess his contribution to public life? Blainey is reluctant to answer but eventually says: 'Some might say I was a fairly original and innovative historian at the time. They might say I write lucidly and have a gift for trying to re-create the past.'

That sounds more like Dr Blainey than Mr Right.

If the strength of the thematic structure is its unifying effect, that is its weakness too; what if important, relevant material is ignored? Certainly, Professor Blainey felt this, saying in a letter to *The Australian* that I had used a 'rather loaded technique' that led to more inaccuracies in a single article about him than he had ever experienced. He declined to cite a single inaccuracy, however.

THE PACKAGE

For at least the last century newspapers and magazines have used a myriad devices to present news and information in interesting and appealing ways, a process accelerated by the Internet. Packaging is not so much a story structure as a content provider's structure. This ghastly term was spawned by the Internet. A newspaper might group several stories on the same topic; none is a feature, but together they add up to a feature package. For instance, in 2002 *The Advertiser* in Adelaide ran a front-page news story about the coming eclipse of the sun that spilled over to page ten where it had a double-page spread comprising two further articles—a full schedule of viewing times, and an illustrated guide to making a pinhole projector. Even standard features are routinely broken up into a main story accompanied by a box summarising the views of experts and another summarising the FAQs (frequently asked questions, an Internet device).

Editors realise there is an appeal in presenting subjects' voices without apparent interference or shaping by the media. Following the abduction and murder of Holly Wells and Jessica Chapman, *The Guardian* in England ran a double-page spread about whether children should be fitted with a microchip tracking device to keep them safe.[15] Apart from a precede, there was no narrative, just the words of seven people presented as speeches with interview questions removed. The seven included an eleven-year-old girl; the designer of the microchip; the chief executive of the National Family and Parenting Institute, and the mother of a fifteen-year-old boy who had been missing since January.

Magazines use package structures routinely. For instance, *Who Weekly*, the Australian edition of the US magazine *People*, ran a cover story headlined 'Hollywood heartache: why stars can't stay married', that filled six pages, only a third of which was narrative text.[16] The rest of the space was taken up by generous photos of various A-list celebrities 'in happier days' accompanied by extended captions outlining the circumstances of their marital collapse. There was also a breakout box on the rash of celebrity couples, such as Angelina Jolie and Billy Bob Thornton, who feel it necessary to tattoo each other's names on their arms or wherever. Sometimes the right packaging can make an otherwise unappealing topic work. In *Men's Health*, an Australian lifestyle magazine for wannabe himbos, Steve Calechman tested the truth or otherwise of 24 pieces of classic parental advice. Number nineteen, for instance, was 'that music is too loud'. The verdict:

> RIGHT: Too many years of being blasted by Ozzy or Led Zeppelin can lead to permanent damage to your cochlear hairs, which, unlike Styx, will not make a comeback. You'll lose the higher-frequency sounds, such as consonants and women's voices. If you don't want to confuse 'Let's go' with 'Let go', sit in a corner of the room where sound is more contained, advises Dr Jo Shapiro, chief of Otolaryngology at Brigham and Women's Hospital in the US.[17]

DISCUSSION QUESTIONS AND EXERCISES

1. Revisit the theme statement for your feature, then sift and sort through your gathered material, discarding anything not relevant to the story theme, and clustering relevant material according to the six types of questions—background, scope, why, impact, reaction and looking ahead questions.
2. As you organise your material, try and identify potential leads and closes, key facts and figures, key quotes and the arguments surrounding the main themes in the story.
3. Mull the material over in your mind and work to find the most suitable structure for your story.

|0] LEADS, CLOSES AND THAT BIG LUMP IN THE MIDDLE

'All right. Personal level. It's not the kind of thing that turns me on.'
　'What do you want, a nude torso in his freezer?'
　'It's not political. It has no ramifications.'
　'You're wrong, Grace.'
　'Could be. Prove it to me.'
　'He's got a man on staff who runs around the country buying this bric-a-brac. That's travel dollars plus the guy's salary.'
　'This sun feels so good.'
　'Obviously taxpayers' money.'
　'You're boring me, Moll.'
　'Sex is boring?'
　'I guess I miss the conspiracy.'
　'Like how?' . . .
　'Conspiracy's our theme. Shit, you know that. Connections, links, secret associations. The whole point behind the series you're doing is that it's a complex and very large business involving not only smut merchants, not only the families, not only the police and the courts, but also highly respectable business elements, mostly real estate interests, in a conscious agreement to break the law.'

Moll Robbins, in Don de Lillo's 1978
novel *Running Dog*, is working on a story about
the erotic art collection of a United States senator,
but Grace Delaney, her editor at an alternative
magazine, is unmoved.

CHAPTER SUMMARY

The four principles of writing strong leads and closes—story relevance, simplicity, intrinsic interest of the material and delivering what you promise—are outlined. The various commonly used types of lead and close are discussed, with numerous examples. The body of the story is discussed and the four principles of organising material are set out.

LEADING THE WAY

Writing a strong lead is important to a feature's success, but don't be enslaved by it. You know from previous chapters that creativity cannot be turned on and off like a tap and you also know the headline, layout and precede do a lot of work in attracting or losing readers before their eyes light upon your beautifully polished lead. If a reader has to wade thigh-deep through a lead, though, chances are they will not read on. If a reader had time for only one paragraph, they could get the gist of a straight news story from the lead. Not so the feature story.

If there is a key paragraph it is the billboard paragraph discussed in the previous chapter. This may well be more than one paragraph and it won't be the lead. The lead for a feature may be one paragraph but it is more likely to be two or three or even four. As noted before, the boundaries between news and features are not set in stone; there is room for wit and style in hard news and not all features have leisurely atmospheric intros. An Associated Press correspondent in Malibu once wrote a smart news lead about a Hollywood star's jailing for his drug problems: 'Actor Robert Downey jnr's next two movies will be out before he is'.[1] For an interview piece with comedian Andrew Denton, Tony Squires nailed his subject in paragraph one:

Andrew Denton has a really attractive brain. If there was a 'Playbrain' magazine, Denton's would be draped seductively across its centrefold. It is lean and athletic, as quick off the mark as any we've seen but big enough to ponder the issues of life, to have a conscience.[2]

There are many more possibilities for leads in features than in hard news, but let's begin by identifying the core principles underlying successful feature leads, bearing in mind that these principles also apply, if a little less critically, to the rest of the story.

RELEVANCE TO THE FEATURE'S THEME

This seems obvious but you would be surprised how many people think writing a feature lead is all about composing a flowery, atmospheric scene-setter that stakes their claim as the next Margaret Atwood. It is actually about picking something attention-grabbing that illustrates the theme of the feature. Most journalists understand this; a more common error is feature leads that are generally but not precisely relevant to the story theme. For instance, a journalism student once submitted the following lead:

> It was the first day of classes at university. All the first years had arrived early in the hope of getting to know the other students before the lectures began. One glance around the room and my blood ran cold. I realised that I was different. I was an Indian in a room filled with local, white Australians. I was the only overseas student in the room.

What feature does this lead suggest? The experience of an overseas student in Australia, I'd say. That is generally what the story was about, but more precisely, as was revealed later, the piece was about how overseas students were becoming a significant part of Australia's higher education system and how universities appeared more interested in revenue-raising than in the quality of teaching for overseas students. Midway through the story the student quoted educational researcher Simon Marginson: 'The general attitude of most universities is, "Put your cheque on the table; and now it is up to you to pass".' The writer needed to choose material to illustrate that particular theme in the lead.

Sometimes the journalist may not have found a strong lead, as in a piece published in *The Advertiser* about BRL Hardy: 'Adelaide was the place for the young—and a century and a half ago that meant young

Thomas Hardy.'[3] Buried in the body of the story was a fact that, in the absence of anything better, would have improved the lead: 'a bottle of Hardy's wine is sold somewhere around the world every third of a second.' That said something about the company's success, which was the theme of the piece timed for its 150th birthday. Recall the profile of Professor Geoffrey Blainey from the previous chapter. The lead described the denuded hills outside Queenstown. On the face of it, this has nothing to do with Blainey, but in the second paragraph the reader learnt that Blainey's first book was about Queenstown and in the third a link was drawn between his idiosyncratic view of the hills and his habit of taking unfashionable stands on highly charged issues: this was the theme of the profile. The lead to the feature and the billboard paragraphs were in harmony, which increased the prospect, never a certainty, of the reader reading on.

SIMPLICITY

Consider the following lead about a new series of the award-winning Australian children's television series, *Round the Twist*:

'Have you ever, ever felt like this, when strange things happen . . .'

If the next words of this ditty roll trippingly off your tongue—'are you going round the twist'—then you are probably a child who owns one of the *Round the Twist* videos whose theme song opens with these lines.

Or maybe you are a twentysomething who saw the first two series when they originally aired in 1990 and 1993, or a parent who has laughed along with your children at the truly bizarre things that befall three kids and their widowed dad living in a lighthouse.

If you knew that it is a common playground chant to rewrite the theme song viz—

'Have you ever, ever felt like this, when strange things happen when you're going to take a piss'—then you must be a hardcore Paul Jennings fan.

What is wrong with this lead? It is complicated. The reader is plunged into minutiae about Paul Jennings with no thought whether they need to or want to. I'm not proud of this lead except for its usefulness as an example of what not to do. I had just finished writing a biography of Jennings and knew so much about his life and work that it just spilled over into this feature about a new series of a TV program adapted from his stories. The problem of over-complicating the lead is common.

A feature lead is harder to write than a straight news lead because it needs to do more work—in only a few more words. As in hard news every word must count. The lead just quoted was a draft. I worked on it, and came up with this:

> When is a Paul Jennings story not a Paul Jennings story? Answer: when a new series of *Round The Twist* is made.
>
> Paul Jennings and *Round The Twist* are almost synonymous but when a third series of the hugely popular children's TV series was announced recently by the Australian Children's Television Foundation (ACTF) Jennings's name was nowhere to be seen. Why?
>
> Answering that question means telling a story almost as surprising as a Jennings tale. It is also a story whose ending is not yet known. Children know Jennings's stories end happily even if they struggle to pick his trademark twist in the tail; the story of Jennings and *Round The Twist* may end happily, but it may not.[4]

This works better, I think. By providing background information, the lead paragraphs assume less knowledge of Paul Jennings. It is reasonable to assume that readers of the television supplement, where this story was published, would have heard of *Round the Twist*, and if they had not, the second paragraph informs them of its popularity. This lead fixes a second problem in the original; it is precisely relevant to the story theme. The original lead pointed to a story theme about the great popularity of the TV series, which was only generally relevant to the actual story. This lead is also in tune with Jennings' style, which only a minority of the supplement's readers would appreciate, but there are internal pointers in paragraph three (his stories are surprising, with a twist at the end) that enable the reader to see this. I still feel the lead is a touch complicated but was not able to simplify it further. Why don't you try?

INTRINSIC INTEREST OF THE MATERIAL

Bear in mind the intrinsic interest of the material for the lead. Sometimes journalists are over-zealous about personalising their stories, forgetting that people spend much of their time engaged in unremarkable activities and that some people, no matter what they are doing, are dull. The following lead was published in the business pages of *The Age*:

> The weather has been very ordinary this month in Paris, where Australian Competition and Consumer chairman Allan Fels and his deputy, Ross Jones, have been attending OECD meetings on international competition law and regulation. Strong winds and rain showers disrupted the French Open, and the days have been chilly, well below 20 degrees.
>
> For Fels and Jones, the weather they experienced while attending the Organisation for Economic Cooperation and Development meetings may have been useful acclimatisation. They returned on Thursday to face a decision that is almost guaranteed to cause a storm of protest and controversy.[5]

This lead is 96 words long, most of them wasted. That two senior public servants have been attending conferences overseas is entirely uninteresting. The link drawn between the weather and the 'chilly reception' they are likely to receive on their return is strained. Note too that the lead tells the reader little about the rest of the story, which was about Fels' looming decision whether to approve a content-sharing arrangement by Foxtel and Optus that the two companies argued was essential for the survival of the struggling pay TV industry. The rest of the article was informative, but if a lead can be cut without affecting the body of the story, that is a signal to rewrite.

DELIVER WHAT YOU PROMISE

This is a magnification of the principle of theme relevance, brought on by the hype swirling around modern media. In Tom Stoppard's play *Rosencrantz and Guildenstern are Dead*, Rosencrantz demonstrates the danger of unfettered free speech by shouting 'Fire!' in a crowded theatre. Similarly, it is not difficult to capture readers' attention if you play dirty. 'Iraq has launched a nuclear attack on Australia' is a lead that would, I imagine, get your attention. Be careful, then, not to overcook the lead. If the rest of the feature does not live up to it, readers will not only stop reading, which is bad enough, they will feel betrayed and come to the next article bristling with suspicion, which does your colleagues no favours.

A *Herald Sun* interview piece with journalist Andrew Morton was pegged to his recently published biography of soccer star David

Beckham and former Spice girl, Victoria 'Posh' Beckham. Morton had become (in)famous and rich for his authorised 'unauthorised' biography of Princess Diana. Headlined 'Tables turn on Diana's tattler', the article's precede read: 'After lifting the lid on Princess Diana's secrets, Andrew Morton found his own life exposed, reports Bruce Wilson.'[6] But the lead took us instead to a sedate interview at Morton's comfortable home in Highgate, north of London. The article took up a full page but it was not until the final four paragraphs that the reader learnt what the precede was hinting at: other London tabloid journalists had revealed Morton had been having an affair. There was one quote from Morton, and that was it. It is possible Wilson had more material, which was cut in production; equally, it is possible the sub-editor ramped up what was otherwise a bland interview piece. In any case, *The Guardian* in London later ran an interview piece with Morton that carried a similar headline–'An author unmasked'–and precede–'Andrew Morton's unauthorised biography on Madonna is being released this week. But how did he feel when his lover dished the dirt on him?' Simon Hattenstone delivered what he promised, devoting much of the article to grilling Morton on why his affairs are not fair game for the media when he has made millions revealing personal foibles despite other people's desperate pleas.

> Morton finds the interrogation painful. I do, too. He also gives me the feeling that he isn't used to it. After all, most of his work is done at a distance from his subjects; he meets his anti-heroes, those who don't want their stories told (Charles) more rarely than he meets his heroes (Diana).[7]

There are five main types of feature leads. They are:
1. Summary lead
2. Suspense lead
3. Descriptive lead
4. Anecdotal lead
5. Surprise lead.

SUMMARY LEAD

A good summary lead is effective–and hard to write. They are effective because they capture a key element of the story in one enticing paragraph, and hard to write for the same reason. Here is one about the state of journalism education in Australia for a piece I was commissioned to write for the 'Media' supplement of *The Australian*:

> Most older journalists reckon the only way to learn the business is through the school of hard knocks, the university of life. Most young people know the surest route into a notoriously competitive industry is through a journalism school. And, chances are, most middle-aged journalists have no idea how many of their colleagues hold journalism degrees.[8]

Does this lead work? Perhaps. On the plus side, it provides a fresh perspective on the topic. The preparation of journalists is rarely written about; when it is, a simplistic debate is set up between the school of hard knocks and theory-laden university courses. This lead immediately takes the story past that. It is crisply written, using colloquial language—'reckon', 'the business', 'chances are', 'no idea'—partly because it mirrors the plain language of journalism and partly because an abstract topic combined with an abstract lead needs help to engage the reader. Grouping the topic into a trio of older, younger and middle-aged journalists also helps because these figures are easily identifiable. On the minus side, at 56 words the lead is long and even for a specialist publication like 'Media' could be too complicated. Perhaps the problem is not so much how the lead is written but that the idea it contains is too complicated for a single paragraph.

This sense may be heightened in the story's next two paragraphs:

> If you find that confusing, consider these apparent contradictions: journalists are deeply unpopular according to public opinion polls, yet journalism courses are among the most popular in any university. At latest count there are 25 journalism courses in Australia but there is little agreement about exactly what should be taught.
>
> Even firm advocates of journalism education concede there is still broad scepticism in the news media industry about what they provide. Finally, it may be a truism that the news media is a powerful institution that plays a vital role in a democratic society, but the average journalist is deeply ambivalent about the value, or even the need, to study what they do and how they do it.

More ideas, more paradoxes. It is fresh information and perspectives for the supplement's readers, but probably far removed from their understanding of the issue. They may have needed simpler material to be drawn into the story.

In any case, here is an example of an unambiguously successful summary lead:

> Nothing, it has been said, is duller than accounting—until someone is defrauded.

I laughed out loud when I read this because it is so true, and because the joke is set up by the highfalutin sounding 'nothing, it has been said'. The headline, 'The accountants' war', sat above a picture of a retired accountant in pale blue shirt and light brown trousers. Not exactly a carnival beckoning you in, but having read the first sentence I had to read on.

> And after every modern financial disaster—the stock-market crash of 1929, the bankruptcy of the Penn Central Railroad in 1970, the savings-and-loan crisis of the eighties, and now the bankruptcy of the Enron Corporation—investors have tended to ask the same question: where were the auditors?[9]

This is detailed information provided by American journalist Jane Mayer and her next paragraph is equally detailed:

> Arthur Levitt, Jr., who was the chairman of the Securities and Exchange Commission under President Bill Clinton, believes that in the years leading up to Enron's collapse the auditors were busy organizing themselves into a lobbying force on Capitol Hill—one that has been singularly effective. Levitt, who issued a series of warnings about the accounting profession in those years, suggests that the aim of the so-called Big Five accounting firms—PricewaterhouseCoopers, Deloitte & Touche, Ernst & Young, K.P.M.G., and Arthur Andersen, Enron's auditor—was to weaken federal oversight, block proposed reform, and overpower the federal regulators who stood in their way. "They waged a war against us, a total war," Levitt said.

The rest of the article substantiated Levitt's thesis. Notice how there is as much information in Mayer's first two paragraphs as in the journalism schools piece, but her witty opening line bought her readers time to contemplate a profession in which they have no interest at all—and alarming information it was too.

SUSPENSE LEAD

Suspense is a stock in trade of any storyteller, but not among journalists hard-wired by years of hard news stories, where the guilty party is named in the first paragraph rather than the last page. Most features do not give opportunities for suspense on the scale of the movie *Scream*—'Pick up the phone Sidney.' Suspense in features is about playing with readers' expectations and withholding information to entice them to keep reading. Eliza Griswold wrote about children hired as assassins in *Marie Claire*:

> Tiny has always been just that. He's 14 years old and about 1.2m tall. His grey Levi's hang off him, despite the belt he wears wrapped around his waist twice. He looks about eight, and no-one would suspect him of inflicting harm. That's one of the reasons Tiny makes an effective assassin.[10]

Griswold's lead builds up a picture of innocence and scruffiness before the sting-in-the-tail final sentence.

American writer Pat Toomay wrote about his brief involvement in the film industry in a story that could have begun any number of ways. He chose this:

> The congratulatory messages started flowing in last summer. Via e-mail, the postal service, the telephone, from friends and acquaintances across the country.
>
> "How wonderful for you!" "You must be thrilled!" "We're so proud of you!"
>
> Even today, I get them. Less frequently, of course, but expressing similar sentiments. Now they're a mere annoyance. In the beginning they were a shock.
>
> The first call came from Ari Susman, a Dallas businessman. "Well, schmuck-o, how does it feel, anyway? To finally hit the big time?"
>
> "What are you talking about?" I wanted to know.
>
> "It's in *Parade* magazine," he said. "An article about the new Oliver Stone movie, *Any Given Sunday*. Why didn't you tell me Oliver Stone was making a movie out of your book?"[11]

Toomay grabs the reader's attention not by talking directly to them but by recounting something interesting happening over here, tacitly inviting the reader to come across and have a look, but not explaining why until the sixth paragraph. Toomay, a retired footballer who had written two books about the destructive culture of the American National Football League, unfolds a tale about being swallowed in the ravenous maw of Hollywood. Just as he is forced to hang around waiting for a brief meeting with bigshot director Stone so he makes the reader wait until near the story's end before playing out the scene.

DESCRIPTIVE LEAD

Describing a scene is the most novelistic way of drawing the reader in, which is why a descriptive lead can be engaging, and why it attracts feature writers with literary talent. It is particularly important that a descriptive lead sticks to the precepts outlined above—relevance to the theme, simplicity, intrinsic interest of the material—because in describing a scene your natural tendency is to try and paint the whole picture. The reader only needs to see that part of the picture relevant to the story theme. You may well find that first up you need to describe the whole scene, then cut away anything irrelevant to the theme of the feature. Be wary of scene-setting leads that evoke the weather in detail, like the one about Allan Fels quoted earlier. They are often no more than window-dressing. 'It was a dark and stormy night' is the hackneyed opening line of a famously awful 19th-century novel by Edward Bulwer-Lytton. To see how weather can be used effectively, read the opening of Charles Dickens' *Bleak House*; the description of a London fog prefigures the interminable gloominess of the legal case, Jarndyce and Jarndyce, at the heart of the novel. Both the profile of Geoffrey Blainey and the piece about the Jewish Holocaust Centre have effective descriptive leads.

ANECDOTAL LEAD

Where a descriptive lead paints a scene, an anecdotal lead tells a mini-story. The two leads may cross over: a descriptive lead may contain a mini-story and an anecdotal lead will of necessity contain description but the emphasis differs for each lead. Here is an anecdotal lead about the stevedoring boss Chris Corrigan, who in 1998 used a secretly trained workforce to break up the Maritime Union of Australia's strangle-hold on the docks:

For a multimillionaire, Chris Corrigan has frugal habits. When staying at his weekend retreat near Goulburn, south-west of Sydney, the Patrick Corporation boss has been known to drive around the countryside with his trailer collecting fallen branches for firewood.

"If there is something lying around the place for free, there is no way Chris is going to pay for it," says a former associate.[12]

The lead is then tied to the billboard paragraph:

And on the latest evidence, Corrigan has not lost his taste for squeezing as much value as possible out of a deal, or for characterising those who stand in the way of his business goals as vested interests.

It is a straightforward and businesslike anecdotal lead, as befitted the publication (*The Financial Review*) and the length (under 1000 words).

Music writer Iain Sheddon used a more elaborate anecdotal lead:

The undisputed masterpiece of rock 'n' roll autobiographies is *The Dirt*, a tome published last year that details explicitly the lives, loves, party drugs and multifarious babes of American rock band Motley Crue.

It's a classic, not least because it documents the band's unparalleled excess without a hint of irony. The protagonists' unflinching honesty, bound in a moral code inherited from Attila the Hun, makes for a riveting read.[13]

Sheddon provides three lengthy quotes from the book, one of which will suffice:

"Instead of drinking and drugs, I'd fuck a lot of groupies. And there were tons of them. I'd go through four or five girls a night. I'd have sex before a show, after a show and sometimes during a show. A few times, when I really needed a distraction, I'd line up half a dozen naked girls on my hotel room floor or facing the wall, then run a sexual obstacle course. But the novelty wore off quickly. Even though I was married to Beth and we had a daughter, our relationship had hardly improved. Besides, her orange [Datsun] 240Z, which I loved so much, had blown up. So it was only a matter of time before our relationship did too."

Anecdotes like these are compelling reading even if their subject matter is repelling. The leisurely pace of the piece suits the Saturday edition of *The Australian* where it appeared.

SURPRISE LEAD

Surprises are fun, as any child will tell you. There are two kinds of surprise lead—the teaser and the shocker. Here is an example of the former.

> One of the most important figures in Australian sport at present is a tall, fair-haired teenager who looks younger than his 18 years. Quick with his hands and boasting a long and impressive record, he recently graduated into the major league. But if you're a sports agent looking for the next big thing, don't get too excited . . . Gavin Massey can't come to the phone right now. He is sitting in a small cell in Goulburn prison.[14]

That is the first surprise. You think you are reading about a budding athlete only to find he is a criminal. Garry Linnell then writes:

> Massey is a thief and heroin addict, and is now serving a three-year stint in the big house for burglary. Along with a fellow addict, Matthew Taylor, Massey still has some pretty hot stuff in his hands. This time it's the reputation of Australian sport.

The reader is still being teased. Over the next six paragraphs Linnell reveals the connection. Massey and Taylor robbed the home of Australian Olympic swimming coach, Gennadi Touretski. Police found Touretski's personal safe dumped in a local pond; inside it, they also found banned performance-enhancing drugs.

And how is this for a shock lead? 'Ian Thorpe is overrated.' What kind of idiot would say that about our beloved Thorpedo? Michael Cowley supplies the answer:

> But before you clog *The Age* switchboard with complaints or fire off abusive e-mails, that is not my judgement of the swimmer who has dominated the world championships. It's a critical assessment of someone far more qualified . . . Ian Thorpe himself.[15]

ORGANISING THE BIG LUMP IN THE MIDDLE

Leads are critical in features, endings important too, but they comprise only a small proportion of the total article. The big lump in the middle is the body of the story where the feature is substantiated. It is common for journalists to spend a lot of energy writing a crackerjack lead and a clear billboard paragraph, then throw the rest of the piece together as if it was straight news. A feature story needs to be told from beginning to end.

It is blindingly obvious that readers do not know what is in the feature before they read it, but many journalists forget exactly that because they struggle to separate what they know about the story (a lot) from what the reader knows (zip). It might help to imagine the reader as a blind, caneless person; it is your job to guide them through your house. You take them gently by the wrist or shirtsleeve—you don't really know them well enough to hold their hand—and lead them into the lounge room, making sure they don't crack their shin on the coffee table. That is the kind of relationship the average feature should develop with the reader: friendly and helpful. By contrast, a tub-thumping columnist develops a different relationship, yanking the reader through the front door without worrying whether they whack their head on the hatstand.

The previous chapter dealt with finding the right structure for the feature, which helps mould the big lump in the middle into a pleasing shape. The principles of organising story material provide the tools to make that happen. These principles do not apply to every single story but they do work often enough to offer guidance.

1. Keep related material together.
2. Let what you have already written suggest what you write next.
3. Try to isolate material from one source in one place.
4. Digress often, but do not digress for long.[16]

It is easiest to understand these principles by seeing them at work in a feature, and David Brearley's piece about the infamous John Marsden defamation case in chapter eight offers a shining example of a well-organised feature. It is also well informed and well written.

The feature ran the day before Justice David Levine handed down his judgement in which he found the Seven Network had failed to prove its allegations and ordered it to pay Marsden nearly $600 000 plus the bulk of Marsden's multi-million dollar costs. He was, however, critical of Marsden, finding he had given police 'false information' in one matter and had probably used notorious killer Les Murphy to intimidate a witness in the case.[17] Brearley covered the case and his feature was a profile of Marsden. After such a long case that produced almost 10 000 pages of transcript, it is easy for a journalist to be overwhelmed with information. Brearley's article showed he was in full command of the case details and was able to stand back from it and offer, not a neutral backgrounder, but an interpretative profile that was both sympathetic and critical.

Brearley opened with a shock lead: 'The pot-smoking poofter keeps his Order of Australia in a display cabinet on the bathroom wall.' In paragraphs three to seven he contrasted Marsden's former position as a successful and politically engaged lawyer with his present predicament, explaining that of all the insults hurled at him during the case, 'pot-smoking poofter' was the one that raised in him the greatest ire. Brearley summarised the background to the case, then outlined how the man who had so insulted him, Superintendent Small, was a fringe witness brought in to further smear Marsden's reputation. From the witness box, Small recounted a failed drugs raid on Marsden's house, offered no new material on underage sex, then added, almost proudly, that Marsden was known in the police force as a pot-smoking poofter.

Brearley spent the next five paragraphs—fourteen to eighteen inclusive—discussing why Small's remarks so wounded Marsden, but at this point the third organisational principle—*try to isolate material from one source in one place*—was illustrated. Superintendent Small probably had a good deal to say about Marsden but Brearley chose to include only that material most relevant to the profile and isolated it in one place. It is not always possible to follow this principle as a source may have important things to say about several aspects of the feature subject and, where they do, they should be quoted accordingly, but the principle is aimed at avoiding what might be termed 'source spaghetti', where masses of sources are quoted throughout a feature. As Blundell puts it: 'Too many stories are cluttered by the inclusion of too many people. The few doing or saying something interesting are burdened by the many who are just beating their gums, and the reader quickly gets confused trying to keep track of everyone.'[18]

The depth of wounds caused by Small's remarks reminded Marsden that gay men still live in a hostile world. 'But it's worse than that, more personal. Pot-smoking poofter insults his ego, for it is the antithesis of everything he believes himself to be.' What is the question that comes to mind here? How does Marsden see himself? That is exactly what Brearley proceeds to outline, thereby illustrating the second organisational principle—*let what you have written suggest what you write next*. This principle aids the flow of a piece; few things satisfy a reader more than the sense that their questions are being answered almost as soon as the thought occurs to them.

The next section of the feature described two strands of Marsden's personality, which Brearley characterised as Art Marsden and Footy Marsden, and it illustrates the first principle—*keep related material together*. Keeping related material together intensifies whatever quality the material has; in this section of the feature, I recall thinking I was learning more about gay male sexual practices than I really wanted to know (earlier paragraphs had referred to anal relaxants and golden showers) which, again illustrating principle two, Brearley answered in the next paragraph: 'That such details are now a matter of public record is the price he has agreed to pay, and not unwillingly, for his battle has become a quest.'

The fourth and final principle—*digress often, but not for too long*—is illustrated in the next section, following the Art Marsden and Footy Marsden section, which is a discussion of the importance of martyrdom in gay culture, taking in Saint Sebastian, Matthew Shepard and, most famously, the playwright Oscar Wilde. Brearley then related his discussion to Marsden's seemingly overt quest for martyrdom.

The gay martydom digression was obviously a digression, and a lengthy one at that, but in a feature a digression is anything that does not move along the action of a story, including explanations, description and analysis. A good quote bejewels a feature but jewellery is decorative, not essential, and so too is a digression. Features need explanations, descriptions and quotes, but once you realise they are digressions from the main story action, and knowing how readers enjoy action, you are compelled to write them economically so they can be read quickly and easily.

ENDINGS

Finishing a feature well is important, but again many journalists struggle with endings because they are superfluous in hard news. The principles outlined in writing leads apply, especially making them relevant to the story's theme, and keeping them simple. The key additional principle is don't save your best material for the ending; that should have been used in the body of the story. If you have a strong anecdote, put it in the lead rather than the close. This is journalism, not a novel, and the task, first and foremost, is to persuade people to read what you have written. The task of the ending is to help the reader remember the story. Paradoxically, just as readers feel let down by unsatisfying endings, so the very fact that a sentence is the final one can lend it significance. In other words, the ending itself will do some work for you. Note 'some work', not all of it. There are four main types of endings:

1. Rounding up and rounding off
2. Circling back
3. Looking ahead
4. Spreading out.

ROUNDING UP AND ROUNDING OFF

A feature can end with a paragraph or two rounding up by summarising and restating the feature's theme. It is acceptable for a school essay to finish by writing 'in conclusion we can see that capital punishment is a bad thing, etc.', but a feature needs to summarise in a more appetising way. A final quote from a key person is a common way of achieving this, as Jane Mayer showed in her piece about the corruption of the accounting profession. The key problem she outlined in the piece was the weakened independence of accounting firms relying on consultancies to big corporations such as Enron for much of their revenue. Arthur Levitt's successor at the Securities and Exchange Commission, Harvey Pitt, rejected Levitt's approach of separating auditing from consulting as a simplistic solution to a complex problem.

> "That's the same argument that the accountants put forward," Levitt said with a sigh. "I didn't accept it then, and I accept it even less today. I have to conclude it's specious. It's very sad. The Administration is missing a glorious opportunity to reform this industry."

Alternatively, a feature may need a line, preferably witty, to round off the piece. Recall, for instance, Jon Casimir's feature about Kylie Minogue discussed in chapter three, which ends with another scribe's description of Kylie's bottom moves as Wiggle One and Wiggle Two. 'And you always thought Wiggle Two was the purple one who sleeps a lot.'

CIRCLING BACK

Returning to the idea or scene in the feature's lead is a way of unifying a piece, as Fiona Hudson did with the distance markers in her feature about the bush track discussed in chapter three, and as Eliza Griswold did in her piece about the fourteen-year-old Colombian assassin, who gets in a car belonging to his boss. 'As the car pulls away, the top of Tiny's head is barely visible through the windscreen.' The circling back ending is commonly used, which has blunted the pleasantly surprising effect it can achieve. It works better when it picks up a motif running through a piece than when it returns to a scene or idea that was used in the lead but which disappeared for the rest of the story.

LOOKING AHEAD

Journalism is preoccupied with the here and now, so a good way to end a feature can be to cast your gaze forward. The profile of Geoffrey Blainey in chapter nine looked ahead, but in a way that also circled back to the theme running through the piece.

SPREADING OUT

By necessity features focus on a particular aspect of an issue or event. At the end of the piece, it can be refreshing to momentarily broaden the focus and give the reader a glimpse of new terrain. The piece about the Jewish Holocaust Centre focused on the unique nature of the museum and on its impact on visitors, mostly schoolchildren. In the final four paragraphs the piece asked questions, such as what would happen when the guides—Holocaust survivors—eventually died, and was there anything to replace the experience of talking to people who were in the camps. The guides mentioned an ambitious project to videotape the testimonies of survivors. The piece concluded:

> What is left unsaid is the knowledge that videotapes can never replicate the experience of speaking face-to-face with a survivor. But perhaps the real test of this vision is what schoolchildren make of their visit. Will it stay with them? Will it influence their behaviour? Most importantly, will it help prevent another Holocaust?

Reflecting on her experience, Julie Fenwick (a secondary student) says: 'History makes such an impact on us. It is not just something that happens and is finished. A lot of people are still racist and anti-Semitic. There are still concentration camps in the world.' If there is something deeply depressing about what she says—for it is surely true—her insight and maturity are also cause for hope.

DISCUSSION QUESTIONS AND EXERCISES

1. Choose two newspaper and two magazine features at random and before reading them cut out their lead paragraphs. From these paragraphs see if you can identify the theme of the story.
2. Taking the two newspaper and two magazines features you have chosen, see if you can rewrite their leads to improve them, and their endings too.
3. Drawing on the principles outlined in the chapter, write your own feature story.

▮▮▮ WORDCRAFT

'Feather-footed through the plashy fen passes the questing vole'
... 'Yes,' said the Managing Editor. 'That must be good style.'

Evelyn Waugh, from *Scoop*

CHAPTER SUMMARY

Advice is offered not so much about grammar but about how to make your prose clearer, cleaner and crisper. This covers nuts and bolts matters such as handling quotes, numbers and attribution, but also more obviously literary matters such as the principles of good description, plus a sampling of rhetorical devices. The question of when journalists should put themselves directly into their features is discussed.

I f you approach this chapter thinking, 'at last he's going to tell me how to write', then either I have failed dismally or you have not been paying attention. Creating a good piece of writing depends on decisions made long before you sit down at the word processor. Finely polished prose is less important to a successful feature than a well-developed story idea, thorough reporting and sound story structure. With these three elements a journeyman writer will produce a better feature than a wordsmith without them. That said, a well-developed story idea, thorough reporting, sound story structure and wordcraft makes for a feature story readers remember.

Wordcraft does not mean grammar and word usage, topics on which there are countless books available and on which I am not expert. I am a professional writer and in the space available it is preferable to refer you to a couple of good grammar books and move on to specific tips to make your prose clearer, cleaner and crisper.

Almost every book about writing mentions Will Strunk's *The Elements of Style*, with good reason; it is a model of brevity and precision about grammar and usage. Strunk was so obsessed with omitting needless words, however, that his explanations are too terse for modern students. A more recent, Australian, text is Mem Fox and Lyn Wilkinson's *English Essentials* (1993), which outlines the principles of grammar and usage in easily digestible prose. The noted essayist E.B. White was a student of Strunk's and he contributed a chapter on style to later editions of *The Elements of Style* that is compulsory reading for any aspiring writer.

Books about writing are, like muesli, good for you but hard to digest in large doses. What follows is drawn from the best of the books I've read, colleagues and my own experience.

WHEN CAN I PUT MYSELF IN THE STORY?

The first of the 21 cautionary hints E.B. White offers writers is to place yourself in the background of the piece. Feature writers sometimes ask, however, is there a time to put yourself in the foreground? They have rejected the hard news model as restrictive; they may have read Hunter S. Thompson's wild gonzo prose or Danny Katz's humorous columns and think feature writing is where they are going to unleash their hidden creativity. A hard lesson for any writer to learn is that the principles of good writing and storytelling are sound and not in need of overhaul. Harder still is the lesson that at the outset writers do not really know much about writing. Hardest of all, learning to write well takes time, is essentially a solo journey and invariably includes numerous crash landings.

You may not like reading that, but even if you agree you will need to make your own mistakes, because good writing is not simply a matter of choosing the right words but of developing a style, and developing a style jogs alongside developing personality. Hence White's advice: 'To achieve style, begin by affecting none—that is, place yourself in the background. A careful and honest writer does not need to worry about style. As he becomes proficient in the use of language, his style will emerge, because he himself will emerge.'[1]

The simple question to ask when considering whether to put yourself in a feature story is: will my presence improve the story? If you cannot answer yes confidently, don't put yourself in. The most important thing is not you but the story. Recall that the story about the Jewish Holocaust Centre focused on the centre's impact on visitors, most of whom were schoolchildren. There was plenty of material from teenagers but not as much from adults. I had visited the centre and felt my experience added another layer to the story's theme.

> I vividly remember looking at a grainy, chilling photograph of a group
> of Jews standing at the foot of a pit that was to be their grave. Behind

them were their executioners. What struck me about these soldiers was their casual air and the utterly vacant look in one man's eyes.

Despite the monstrosity of their actions, these men didn't look like monsters.

They looked like you and me. I thought about whether in their shoes I would have done what they did, and felt sick in my stomach. I then saw photos of naked young girls who were later tortured and killed by the Nazis. Thinking of my own daughter, then not even a year old, tears welled in my eyes.

The visit to the centre was the original impetus for the story, and perhaps I could have written the whole article from my perspective but that would have made it a personal essay. It may have been worth reading, but a core mission of journalism is to explore the world around you and so the piece was broadened to encompass the range of visitors and the centre's survivor guides.

TONE OF VOICE

One of the pleasures of features is that they can be written in tones other than the institutional voice of hard news. The closer a variety of feature is to news—backgrounders, news features—the more its tone resembles the institutional voice, but the institutional voice is a dull companion over 2000 words. At that length, readers welcome conversation, a tone of voice that seems to be speaking to them, and them alone, over a beer, or a caffelatte if that is your poison. The world is full of people and institutions who use specialist language as a way of excluding others from a discussion or, worse, of fudging the truth. For example, American scientists have been engaged in a series of remarkable experiments to find ways of keeping soldiers and pilots awake and alert for up to five days at a time, such as zapping their brains with electromagnetic energy or trying to identify the gene that enables a variety of sparrow to remain awake during its migration season, so they can use it on the hapless grunts. They call this project the 'Extended Performance War Fighter'.[2] During the previous Gulf War, in 1991, military leaders used the term 'collateral damage' when they really meant dead civilians.

Grotesque as these terms seem, the sheer volume of jargon and obfuscating language swirling around affects journalists. In an article about the media landscape, the following appeared: 'After being stuck at penetration levels of around one-fifth of all Australian homes for several years, pay-TV providers are confident the sector will resume growth towards internationally comparable penetration levels this year.' And this: 'Apart from expected trends towards anxiety avoidance, increased security and emotional fulfilment, Euro RSCG Worldwide predicted a further blurring of gender lines as young men explore variety and glamour.'[3] The job of a journalist is not to call a spade an outdoor implement of bucolic intent but a spade—or, if necessary, a bloody shovel.

Recall Jon Casimir's piece about Kylie Minogue, which was not only conversational, but smart and sassy. Or David Brearley's profile of John Marsden, sympathetic to Marsden's plight but also a step removed. There was an impressive worldliness about it too, as when Brearley wrote that Marsden 'can be the most dreadful ham in court, but you won't catch him mincing this side of six whiskies, and even then it's low-level stuff. He's nobody's dandy'. Beware, though, of the siren song of smartarsery. Journalists routinely deal with famous people, on their good days and their bad. Journalists are routinely told lies. Scepticism is their inoculation against the world's chicaneries. Cynicism is the untreated disease. A cynic, Oscar Wilde wrote, 'knows the price of everything and the value of nothing'. Cynics have a limited tone of voice; they can sneer with the best but are incapable of much else, such as the compassion Sebastian Junger, in an article for *Vanity Fair*, showed for young women and teenage girls from Eastern Europe lured to Kosovo by promises of work, then virtually enslaved and forced to work as prostitutes.[4]

The tone of voice in feature stories, then, can range widely, from those already mentioned to irony, outrage, revulsion and more besides. It is important to match the tone with the content. Jon Casimir's smart tone would have been inappropriate for Sebastian Junger's piece, and vice versa.

CAN I EXPRESS AN OPINION IN A FEATURE STORY?

The oft-quoted line in newsrooms, 'comment is free, but facts are sacred', by C.P. Scott of the *Manchester Guardian* early last century, suggests a clear dividing line between fact and opinion. It is not so clear, or more precisely, the amount of opinion embedded in fact is rarely acknowledged. The hard news piece is held up as a totem of fact, but how are decisions made to cover some events and not others? Why is certain information put in the lead? Similar processes of selection occur in feature stories, though the combination of fact, description and analysis inherent in features means at least some of the opinion is easier to spot. It is important for journalists to develop an awareness of their own preconceptions and prejudices. Just as there are some stories for which your background equips you better than the person sitting at the next desk, so there are some that blindside you. As you develop this self-awareness, the most ethical professional course is to practice a little humility in expressing your opinions. You may think the Australian government's policy on asylum seekers is morally bankrupt, but how much do you really know about the worldwide flow of refugees or about the difficulties of stopping people smuggling? When was the last time you were Immigration Minister?

Along with humility, it is safer to find out as much as you can about an issue before venturing an opinion. That way you are less likely to make mistakes; gathering and analysing information also grounds your opinion in honest work. In the profile of Professor Geoffrey Blainey, for instance, the statement 'Blainey the great historian has become Blainey the lousy polemicist' is an opinion, but it comes in the third last paragraph and flows from evidence and argument presented earlier in the profile. Not everyone agreed with this opinion, but they could at least see where it came from.

LINKS

Within the sound structure that helps a story flow are strong links between sections. Like learner drivers, journalists sometimes perform five, even seven, point turns when a three pointer will do. In an interview piece with novelist E. Annie Proulx, the journalist reported an incident where a young Proulx nearly drowned, trapped in an upturned canoe, then began the next paragraph: 'For all her fearlessness, she doesn't take chances. She carries powerful binoculars and height and wind speed gadgets.'[5] The first part of the sentence—for all her fearlessness—is superfluous. Just go straight on to the next topic—not taking chances.

If you have followed the organisational principle of keeping related material together, there will be little need for superfluous or jarring link phrases. When you write such phrases you feel you are guiding the reader along, but you actually risk confusing them with clutter. Trust the relevance of the story material to guide the reader. Picking up a word or phrase from one section and using it in the next is a way of cementing the link. In Garry Linnell's profile of the swimming coach accused of drug cheating, Linnell's billboard paragraph finished by mentioning the drugs in question, which he said were uncommon in Australia but enjoyed a high reputation overseas. 'And reputation, after all, is what this case is really about', began the next paragraph, easing the reader from one section to the next.

Links can be worked even harder, according to Blundell, because many links centre on a 'blob word or phrase' that covers too much ground.[6] Can the writer replace the blob with specific images? If they have written about a situation, can they say what that situation is? In the section about Art Marsden in David Brearley's profile, he moves from his anecdote about Marsden bringing the explicitly erotic paintings into court to a new paragraph that began: 'The art is just one part of the trophy collection. Marsden is a keen observer of his own press, prized examples of which hang framed in his home.' It is a reasonable link that could have been improved to read something like: 'Press clippings about Marsden, framed and hanging on the wall, are another part of his trophy collection.' With practice, links come easily so if you find a link tortuous—and torture to write—step back and look at it carefully. Your difficulty is probably a sign of a larger structural problem that is more important to fix than an awkward link.

HANDLING QUOTES

A strong quote enlivens a feature but overuse of quotes is commonplace in features. There are four reasons to quote in features:

1. Revealing of character
2. Credibility
3. Variety
4. Punch.

REVEALING OF CHARACTER

In straight news, if a prominent figure such as the former Governor-General, Peter Hollingworth, is responding to allegations that he was more interested in protecting the Anglican Church from legal action than in protecting the victims of sexual abuse by clergy, it is important to quote his exact words regardless of whether he is eloquent. The equivalent in feature stories is the quote that reveals something about the subject's character. In an interview piece in *Rolling Stone*, Jay Kay, the lead singer of Jamiroquai, was encouraged to prattle on about the band's tour of Australia:

> Yeah, I got up to all sorts. I shagged everything that fucking moved and had a great time. It was good fun. It was proper rock & roll. But the best bit was swimming with dolphins. Because for one minute I could forget everything else. It isn't easy being at the centre of it all.[7]

Nothing he said elsewhere in the article suggested he was being ironic.

CREDIBILITY

Experts are essential for many features but must be handled with care. Writing about, say, the retirement industry, you need an expert's quote to give the piece credibility but experts can descend into jargon, which readers hate. It is your job to translate jargon into plain English or, better still, make the expert do it. If they won't or can't the result may be a quote like this: 'I have an increasingly mobile client base for whom this would provide opportunities that are cost effective.'[8]

VARIETY

Readers like variety and quotes can provide that. Commonly, paragraphs begin with a statement or assertion, which is then substantiated with information followed by a quote to provide further, varied substantiation. In its 30 December 2002 issue, *Time* magazine named three women as joint persons of the year; one of them was Coleen Rowley, the FBI agent who wrote a famous memo after the September 11 tragedy complaining of the agency's tardiness in heeding warning signs of the impending attack. Here is a paragraph from late in the story:

> Rowley half-jokingly asks everyone, from fellow agents to college students, if they'll come buy a burger from her one day if she gets fired ... And she continues to send e-mails to headquarters suggesting investigative and legal strategies. She has sent about a dozen since her

notorious memo. None have received a substantive response. "I'm sure they think I'm crazy Coleen Rowley," she says.

PUNCH

There is nothing better than a punchy quote. Marlon Brando once said of a forgettable movie he starred in: 'It makes about as much sense as a rat fucking a grapefruit.' Few are as outrageously pithy as Brando, and too many journalists, hardened by years of straight news, overuse quotes. They remain attached to their role as a reporter of important events and forget they need to tell a story. Whenever you are tempted to use more than one consecutive paragraph of quotes, see if it can be paraphrased. Not many people speak more interestingly than you can write. Ask yourself how often are you fascinated listening to people speak uninterrupted for more than a few moments. And in print, the reader does not even have the benefit of hearing a voice or watching gestures. Interview pieces are an exception to this tip, because the reader is paying to hear exactly what the famous person said. The endless string of quotes remains the weakness of interview pieces as a feature sub-genre.

Wherever possible, shear the undergrowth from people's speech to leave the strongest point most clearly expressed. In the spring/summer 2002 issue of the *Monash* magazine for the university's alumni, an article about four decades of medicine contained this quote from a Professor Murtagh: 'The Department of Anatomy teaching facility was in the original science block. The dissection room was very hot and filled with cadavers—some of the students used to faint.' It is not bad, but why is the first sentence left as part of the quotation? It is straight exposition and should be paraphrased, which would draw attention to the students fainting. The quote is also underdeveloped. Why not ask the professor to describe the smell in the room?

HANDLING NUMBERS AND ACRONYMS

Readers dislike numbers and acronyms because an act of translation is needed to understand them. Both are essential in many stories, so supply the reader with a foreign language dictionary. Spelling out acronyms on their first mention helps, and afterwards refer to, say, the union instead of repeatedly writing CEPU (for the Communications

Electrical Plumbing Union). Instead of writing that the current account deficit has risen from $516.77 billion to $593.85 billion, shave the last two decimal points. Better still, write that the deficit has risen from just over $500 billion to just under $600 billion. Those are easier numbers to get hold of. Easier still are simple multiples. Instead of writing that the number of housing loan approvals in 2002 increased from, say, 355 612 to 703 424, write that the number of approvals almost doubled to just over 700 000.

Finally, when dealing with large numbers about something removed from the reader's experience, provide an everyday equivalent. In an article about urban sprawl Rachel Buchanan wanted to give readers an idea of the size of Melbourne, one of the most widely dispersed cities in the world. She began by saying Melbourne was 90 kilometres in diameter, which means little, but then wrote that to drive around the perimeter of Melbourne takes about four and a half hours.[9] Now, you get the picture.

ATTRIBUTION

Over-attribution and under-attribution are both problems in feature stories: the former because journalists interview more people for features than for hard news yet try and squeeze in every source; the latter because journalists traditionally are chary of sourcing other media outlets or books. Journalists routinely interview 20 to 30 people for a feature; quoting and sourcing all of them is like plonking the reader in one of those playrooms filled with plastic balls. Kids love them but readers won't thank you. Break down your sources into various groups—experts, people on the floor level of the story, etc.—and use those whose comments are most relevant, and best expressed.

It may be important to give a person's exact title, but many are miles long and mean little to anyone but those in the same organisation. If I am quoted in the media, readers do not need to know I am Program Coordinator of Journalism in the School of Applied Communication within the Faculty of Art, Design and Communication at RMIT University. Usually I am referred to as a media commentator or a journalism academic at RMIT. That is enough.

Under-attribution has its roots in past practice. News organisations dislike acknowledging each other's scoops, but as discussed earlier the saturation media age means the only people who really know—or care—who got the scoop are journalists. For readers it is simply puzzling that the source of a major newsbreak is downplayed or ignored altogether. Programs such as *Media Watch* on ABC TV have raised public literacy about these little trade secrets, as has the Internet, which gives prompt access to information and news media around the world.

Journalists have for years plundered books for reference, and for the kind of details that take long research. A few years ago a high profile sportswriter penned a lengthy profile of Muhammad Ali that spoke with Olympian authority about all manner of incidents in Ali's life that only those who were there or those who had read the numerous biographies would know. The sportswriter has lived in Australia most of his life. Not one book was acknowledged. This is plagiarism and it is far too common in journalism. It stems from the historical notion that journalism is of the day and provides only the freshest information where books, by their nature, do not. Books can and do provide masses of fresh information, and can and should be acknowledged in the same way an interviewee is. I speak as a journalist who blanches at the amount of material I lifted unattributed in earlier years and as an author who has seen the amount of work that goes into researching and writing a full-length book.

DESCRIPTION

Critics search for ages for the wrong word, which, to give them credit, they eventually find.

Peter Ustinov

Getting the picture is the aim of description in features. Writing is, really, just a series of abstract black symbols on a white sheet of paper. If you can create pictures in the reader's mind, they will love you forever because one of the great pleasures of reading is the act of imagination it requires. Which is why people are so often disappointed by film adaptations of favourite books: the director's vision did not match the movie already running in their head. From previous chapters you know that good description requires more than a stenographic reproduction of everything in sight and that it is a digression from the story's action, so it is doubly important to write it well.

BE SPECIFIC

The words 'horse breeding' seem innocuous. Garry Linnell showed they are anything but in a lengthy description of the process, beginning with the teaser stallion, who is likened to a royal food-taster. 'He gets to sample this and that, but a seat at the banquet will forever be denied him.' The mare, Tempest Morn, is a virgin whose rear is wiped down with a sterilising solution by one of the four men required to hold her and guide the thoroughbred stallion, Giant Causeway, whose seed each time is worth $137 500.

> And then it starts. The stallion, fully aroused, roars and rears high as his handler rushes to one side, pulling at the rein. Then 500 kilograms of muscled horseflesh crashes onto Tempest Morn's back. Someone is yelling, "Giddup, giddup, giddup." Giant Causeway's forelegs are splayed across the back of his mount. His head is shaking and tiny bits of froth are being flung from the corners of his mouth. The four men below are moving quickly like tiny stagehands. O'Brien, the mare's tail in one hand, is reaching under the stallion, grabbing the animal's penis and guiding it to the right spot . . .
>
> For 25 frantic seconds the barn is filled with whinnying and human shouting and raucous horse farting as muscles spasm and spinal cords grind.[10]

It makes you wince, but the point of such a brutally unromantic description is to highlight the brutally unromantic nature of a multi-million dollar industry that has long been romanticised by mug punters.

Novelist and freelance journalist Helen Garner has a flair for metaphor as well as vivid description. For one story, Garner visited the morgue, watching from a raised and glassed-in viewing area as two gowned and masked technicians performed an autopsy on a hepatitis-infected young man. In a precise, lengthy description, Garner seemed to notice everything: how the pathologist moved as swiftly and lightly as a dancer; how the technician scoured out the man's hollowed skull 'using the same rounded, firm, deliberate movements of wrist and hand that my grandmother would use to scrub out a small saucepan', and how, finally, the technician hosed down the body, wiping the man's mouth, which 'moves under the force of the cloth just as a child's will, passively, while you wipe off the Vegemite or the mud'. Immediately, pictures are imprinted on the reader's mind. The contrast between an autopsy and grandma scouring a saucepan or cleaning a child's face is striking enough, but it works at another level, I think. Garner's images are from everyday domestic life; at the morgue death is an everyday event. Such images resonate in the reader's mind long after they have finished the piece.

BRING PEOPLE IN

Describing scenery or clothes or houses on their own is one-dimensional because it is static. If you want to avoid your copy reading like a real estate brochure or fashion advertisement, bring in people or show what happens in the house or scenery. John Bryson's groundbreaking 1985 account of the Azaria Chamberlain murder case, *Evil Angels*, opens with a description of the origins of Seventh-Day Adventism. (The Chamberlains were Adventists and prejudice about their religion played a key role in this notorious Australian case.) 'It was Autumn. Roadside aspens and hickories were already lean and spiky. Leaves lay in the waggon ruts, and grass in the field was still damp late in the afternoon.' In the next paragraph Bryson brings in people: 'The meadow was owned by Josiah Levitt. The Levitt family had invited friends to pass a day there, in prayer, though it was not the Sabbath but a Monday.'[11] He shows the people in action, welcoming newcomers, the children shyly holding hands. It is not Arnold Schwarzenegger-scale action, but then little is.

Gay Talese is an American journalist who in the 1960s began writing profiles that read like short stories. He was an influential figure in a loose movement that Tom Wolfe later dubbed The New Journalism.

Here is how Gay Talese began a piece published in *Esquire* magazine about Floyd Patterson's loss of the heavyweight boxing title to Sonny Liston in 1963:

At the foot of a mountain in upstate New York, about sixty miles from Manhattan, there is an abandoned country clubhouse with a dusty dance floor, upturned barstools, and an untuned piano; and the only sounds heard around the place at night come from the big white house behind it—the clanging sounds of garbage cans being toppled by raccoons, skunks, and stray cats making their nocturnal raids down from the mountain.

The white house seems deserted, too; but occasionally, when the animals become too clamorous, a light will flash on, a window will open, and a Coke bottle will come flying through the darkness and smash against the cans. But mostly the animals are undisturbed until daybreak, when the rear door of the white house swings open and a broad-shouldered Negro appears in gray sweat clothes with a white towel around his neck.[12]

Apart from noting how in the early 1960s *Esquire* referred to African-Americans as Negroes, see how Talese sets the scene then brings in a person—Patterson—off for morning roadwork. There is more to notice, which leads to the next tip.

ANIMATE THE INANIMATE

Talese and Bryson animate the inanimate: leaves lie in waggon ruts, Coke bottles are thrown out of windows. Recall that in the Blainey profile the same method is used in the lead, where the hills are stripped of their vegetation and the mine's sulphurous fumes choke new growth. American journalist Richard Preston combines all three methods of successful description in his bestselling account of an outbreak of the deadly Ebola virus. Viruses are not visible to the naked eye but Preston's description is so vivid the virus becomes almost a character, a malevolent force, in his book. Here he describes a man named Charles Monet who contracted the virus near Mount Elgon in Kenya and was put on a plane to get him to Nairobi hospital.

He is holding a sick bag over his mouth. He coughs a deep cough and regurgitates something into the bag. The bag swells up. Perhaps he glances around, and then you see that his lips are smeared with something slippery and red, mixed with black specks, as if he has been chewing coffee grounds . . . The muscles of his face droop. The connective tissue in his face is dissolving, and his face appears to hang visibly from the underlying bone, as if the face is detaching itself from the skull. He opens his mouth and gasps into the bag, and the vomiting goes on endlessly. It will not stop, and he keeps bringing up liquid, long after his stomach should have been empty. The sick bag fills up to the brim with a substance known as *vomito negro*, or the black vomit. The black vomit is not really black; it is a speckled liquid of two colours, black and red, a stew of tarry granules mixed with fresh red arterial blood. It is haemorrhage, and it smells like a slaughterhouse.[13]

This is way too much information! It is not gratuitous, however. The black vomit is loaded with the highly infective virus. Preston compares yellow fever with Ebola. The former is considered lethal, killing about one in 20 patients once they reach hospital; Ebola kills nine out of ten. Ebola, Preston writes, 'is a slate wiper of humans'.

SHOW, DON'T TELL

Each of the descriptions in the preceding section probably stirred strong emotions; they certainly did when I first read them. None of the journalists told me what to feel. They showed me. Then I felt—revulsion and fear at what the Ebola virus can do, fascinated horror as Garner watched an autopsy, and awed queasiness at the violence of horse breeding. In all likelihood this was what the journalists felt themselves when they witnessed or researched these events. They must all have had an urge to tell people what they felt but, paradoxically, if they had most readers would have said 'enough already'.

Through description and other narrative techniques they draw you into a story, enabling readers to experience in their imagination what the journalist felt and saw. The idea that you show rather than tell the reader how to react is well established among novelists, but less so in journalism where editorial writers and columnists are paid to tell readers what to think. Some columnists have a seemingly inexhaustible supply of opinions that they express with unshakeable certitude; you imagine this begins from the moment they roll grumpily out of bed, opining on the terminal decay of the appliance industry should their toast be burnt.

FREIGHT-TRAIN SENTENCES

This is a Blundell term to describe a sentence where the central subject, or a subject plus verb, pulls behind it a series of objects or clauses. Such a sentence conveys maximum information in minimum space. It is valuable for making complex explanations easily understood or at least swiftly dispatched. Here is a paragraph from the Blainey profile about his historical research into the working conditions of the Ballarat gold-miners that were one of the causes of the 1854 Eureka Stockade uprising; in draft form it read something like this:

The Ballarat goldminers were not like most prospectors because they had mine shafts that were 30 to 40 metres deep. The prospectors said they were back-breaking to dig and dangerous to work. They also said the shafts took a lot of time to dig and required a lot of capital. In the end, the shafts might yield nothing. Police checks on licences annoyed miners who had shallow-diggings, but they infuriated Ballarat miners, who had to stop work for half an hour while they climbed to the top for a 10-second inspection.

Using a freight-train construction, I rewrote the paragraph:

Unlike most prospectors, the Ballarat goldminers had mine shafts 30 to 40 metres deep that were back-breaking to dig, dangerous to work, required capital and time, and might eventually yield nothing. Police checks on licences annoyed shallow-diggings miners but infuriated Ballarat miners, who had to stop work for half an hour while they climbed to the top for a 10-second inspection.

The first version is 90 words, the second 60. That is 30 words to spend elsewhere.

RHYTHM AND PACE

Just as readers enjoy variety in tones of voice, and in proofs of an assertion, so they enjoy variety in a feature story's rhythm and pace. An article in which every sentence was exactly the same length would read like a manual for embalming, but beyond that elementary point we move into a mysterious area that begins with rhetorical devices and opens out into poetry. Editors are forever exhorting their journalists to make the words sing on the page, but few can, especially on deadline. Let's settle for outlining a few rhetorical devices.

TAKE A COMMON PHRASE AND TURN IT UPSIDE DOWN

Mark Spitz won seven swimming gold medals at the Munich Olympics, but no friends on his team. One, Doug Russell, said of him: 'It could have happened to a nicer guy.' Groucho Marx once commented of his anarchic brothers, Chico and Harpo: 'Any resemblance between these two and living persons is purely coincidental.' John Clarke once offered this definition of satire by turning the dictionary upside down: 'Satire. *noun.* a reaction to the process whereby politicans and public figures hold the community up to ridicule and contempt.'

REPETITION

By dint of the constant demands on editorial space, journalists are trained to prune any repetitions. It is good for packing the maximum amount of news into a limited amount of space, but no good for rhetoric. Think of Winston Churchill's 'We shall fight them on the beaches' speech; Churchill repeating 'we shall' eleven times in his May 1940 parliamentary speech is why it is still quoted today. On a modest scale, the piece about journalism education mentioned earlier used repetition in its lead by referring to most older journalists, most young people and most middle-aged journalists to bind the idea together in the reader's mind.

Malcolm Gladwell is a journalist whose extended articles for *The New Yorker* were published in a book, *The Tipping Point*, which became a bestseller. He has a knack for writing complex sentences with a strong rhythm that is felt as soon as they are read aloud.

> *The Tipping Point* is the biography of an idea, and the idea is very simple. It is that the best way to understand the emergence of fashion trends, the ebb and flow of crime waves, or, for that matter, the transformation of unknown books into bestsellers, or the rise of teenage smoking, or the phenomena of word of mouth, or any number of the other mysterious changes that mark everyday life is to think of them as epidemics. Ideas and products and messages and behaviors spread just like viruses do.[14]

Note how he repeats the word 'idea' in the first sentence, making his proposition seem charmingly simple when it is anything but. Note how he uses a freight-train construction in the second sentence by repeating the word 'or' four times. Note how he varies the length of the subclauses in that sentence. Note how the section beginning 'or any number' forces you to read with an upward inflection in your voice. Note how the final sentence uses nouns that summarise the detail described in the previous sentence. Finally, note how I keep beginning my sentences with the word 'note' and how it is probably driving you nuts. That's because I haven't written this passage as artfully as Gladwell has written his.

BALANCING PARTS OF THE SENTENCE

This is another form of repetition, but instead of repeating words, the same grammatical form is repeated. To achieve this effect successfully, the different parts of the passage need to have a logical connection. Thus, Raymond Chandler opens his detective novel, *Farewell My Lovely*, with an unforgettable description of Moose Malloy, part of which reads: 'He was a big man but not more than six feet five inches tall and not wider than a beer truck.' David Brearley drew a parallel between Marsden and Oscar Wilde, which he underscored by repetition and parallel sentence structure:

> Each case began with a sexual slur against a prominent gay man. Each slur resulted in a civil suit for defamation. Each suit turned on the evidence of rent-boys whose calumnies fuelled the fires of common prurience.

The third sentence is longer than the first two but it carries a weight that is driven home by the quiet alliteration—calumnies and common, fuelled and fires. In a travel story about luxury holidays on Queensland's Hayman Island published in *The Courier-Mail*, Catriona Mathewson wrote about a resort's casual approach to evening dress. 'One patron was spotted dancing in the bar not only shirtless and shoeless at well past 6 pm, but also shortless and completely shameless.'[15]

In parentheses, be careful using alliteration. If overdone, it reads like a children's storybook or a *Carry On* film. Finally, recall the quote from Tad Friend's piece about the Hollywood public relations industry, with its catalogue of publicist-speak followed by his translation into plain English. Remember how it finished with the wonderfully acid line: '"The film is not for everybody" means it's not for anybody.'

DISCUSSION QUESTIONS AND EXERCISES

1. Pick an explanatory passage from a report or book and practise writing freight-train sentences.
2. Find an interview piece or news feature in a newspaper or magazine and see how many quotes have been used. How many should be retained and how many should be paraphrased? Rewrite the piece

accordingly, and see how many words can be saved and whether you have made the piece more readable.

3. Revisit the feature story you have written and look carefully to see whether you have applied the wordcraft tips outlined in this chapter. Rewrite the feature accordingly.

POL POT PARK

by **Kimina Lyall**[16]

Desperately poor and struggling to attract foreign currency, Cambodia is developing a tourist attraction that exploits one of the lowlights of history.

You can't buy a postcard in Anlong Veng. There is no 24-hour electricity, no Internet café—not even a telephone. The few cars that blow dust down the main street belong mostly to United Nations agencies, and the town's best guesthouse charges $4 per night for a room within sleep-disturbing distance of your neighbour's snores.

Not surprisingly, Anlong Veng hasn't featured in Cambodia's glossy brochures—yet—but its 20,000 residents have something that the country desperately needs: a readymade source of tourist revenue.

Deep in the mountain jungle-scrub that overlooks Anlong Veng, in the far north near the Thai border, the ashes of the man responsible for the country's deepest pain, Pol Pot, rest beneath a corrugated iron shelter. The shelter is new, posted with a sign that declares it a historic site, but the ashes have been there since Pol Pot's former cadres unceremoniously burned his body on a pyre of car tyres on April 17, 1998.

Caution is needed to travel here. Landmines and bamboo booby traps, a final legacy of the Khmer Rouge's wars, surround the cremation site. Hundreds of men in the town have had legs blown off by the mines. And the danger is not just on the ground—the mountain's mosquitoes carry malaria, a disease that's spreading at an increasingly deadly rate.

As if to emphasise the site's authenticity, Commander Khun Lee, who served as a Khmer Rouge cadre and who now patrols the nearby Thai border, scratches around in what's left of the ashes and tyre rubber and pulls out a splinter of charred bone that he says is part of his former leader's knee. How does he know? "It's science," he says simply.

The man whose remains lie here is less ambiguously presented. Here, Pol Pot is no despot. "I look at him as my father," says Rin Aun, 35, who appears out of the forest and kneels by the spot with five incense sticks signifying parental homage. "When I live under his command, he gives me land. Now, I have nothing." Any attempt to counter such adulation with known facts sparks a flash of anger. "Don't you spoil his name!"

No matter how hard it tries, Cambodia can't quite bury Pol Pot. People who come to this site leave bottles of water, incense sticks, a biscuit—even a blank writing book and a pen—as part of a Buddhist tradition to offer in death what was enjoyed in life.

At the moment, the trail is just a trickle. It takes three bumpy hours in a four-wheel-drive from the western Cambodian city of Siem Reap just to get to the town, and another 14km up the steep Dongrek escarpment towards the border to reach the cremation site. "They mostly come to make sure if he lives or dies," says Commander Lee. "Both people who like him and hate him come here because they want to know the truth."

Now the Cambodian Government wants to profit from such morbid curiosity and expand the attraction to tourists, especially foreigners. Tourism minister Veng Sereyvuth is candid about the town's appeal.

"This is part of our history. Nobody made it up and we can't wash over it," says Veng, who in 1977 buried his nine-year-old brother in a grave he cannot now find. Insisting the scheme is part of an "overall tourist development plan", Veng points out that most of Cambodia's natural attractions—including unspoiled highlands in the east, pristine beaches in

the south and 500km of Mekong riverfront—are virtually inaccessible. Anlong Veng will do as a tourism destination simply because it is possible to get there.

The Khmer Rouge Trek, as it may be dubbed in a future backpacker's guide, would take in the remains of three houses located deep in the heavily logged jungle that were lived in by former Khmer Rouge army chief of staff Ta Mok (aka "the butcher"), and two houses lived in by Pol Pot. The frames of Ta Mok's houses remain largely intact, though the walls are scrawled with multilingual graffiti such as: "Everything is finished and I am very sorry".

Pol Pot's bunker offers an eerie insight into the ruler's last years. Its bin Laden-like remoteness suggests a ruler in internal exile and helps to explain why there were no non-cadre sightings of him through most of the 1990s. Little remains of his two-storey house except the 45 square-metre underground bunker, but the cow dung-spotted concrete slab once supported a large meeting space where he would continue lecturing against his enemies to his few remaining loyalists.

Perhaps the most bizarre site is the one least likely to survive an influx of tourists. All that is left of the house where Pol Pot died is a jumble-pile of his belongings. According to Commander Lee, the cracked toilet, empty medicine bottles and even a fragment of shirt-cloth scattered there are Pol Pot's personal possessions. The rest of his belongings and the hut were removed, piece by piece, by government and Khmer Rouge soldiers. Lee himself claimed a cane chair.

If Veng's plan works, Anlong Veng could become the spearhead of a "beyond Angkor" tourism strategy. The desperately poor country earns approximately $A437 million from tourists per year, creating 100,000 jobs, but the industry is a long way from helping Cambodia to become self-reliant. The income pales against the $13.3 billion its neighbour Thailand earns from tourism, and Cambodia still receives $1.17 billion per year in international aid donations.

About 50 per cent of Cambodia's tourist income derives from Angkor, a 400 square-kilometre site containing more than 200 temples in Cambodia's west that is referred to by the name of its largest temple, Angkor Wat. The sand-stone structures date from the 9th to the 13th centuries and were built by a series of local god-kings in honour of them-selves. These houses of religious megalo-mania—one of the most famous, the 11th century Bayon, is believed to be deco-rated with 200 smiling stone faces of Jayavarman VII, the king who commis-sioned it—attract both national worship and hard foreign currency.

In 1997, fewer than 45,000 tourists visited the temples; last year, that figure had increased to more than 210,000. But the number of tourists clambering up the dangerously steep temple stairs has sparked warnings of decay. Im Sokoithy, an archaeologist and assistant director of Aspara, the government body assigned to protect the UNESCO-listed site, says the thousands of feet are wearing away the sandstone, and some tourists defy requests not to climb to the tops of the towers. Eventually, he says, visitor num-bers will have to be restricted to perhaps half a million a year. At the current rate, the area will reach saturation point in two years' time.

The tourists are accommodated in the 145 hotels and guesthouses in the nearest city, Siem Reap—an increase of more than 100 since 1997. The region's 22,000 villagers prefer to send their chil-dren to the temples rather than to school so they can hawk postcards, sarongs and T-shirts in a desperate effort to profit from the influx. Srei Roath, a 23-year old guide, sums up the job rush. If it weren't for the industry, which also employs her older brother, she would be "maybe just growing rice". Instead, she earns $500 per month, triple that of her friends working on the front desks of hotels. "It's not so much," she says of the wage, which would be considered a fortune in the rest of rural Cambodia. "If I am sick, I do not get paid."

Angkor was one of the few Khmer cultural treasures that Pol Pot retained. The temples became part of his relentless propaganda program that asserted Khmer people were culturally superior to the Chinese, Vietnamese and other

The number of tourists clambering up the dangerously steep stairs of Angkor Wat has sparked warnings of decay. Thousands of feet are wearing away the sandstone.

ethnicities living in Cambodia at the time of his revolution. Consequently, they avoided any large-scale damage during his regime, though many of them needed to be de-mined later.

Now it is Angkor's popularity that could open the way to Anlong Veng. The Thai Government, keen to capitalise on Angkor's proximity to its borders, has embarked on an aggressive plan to take over its tourism traffic. Already, all flights into Siem Reap—from Phnom Penh as well as Bangkok—are via Bangkok Airways. The Thai strategy is to make Angkor part of a Thai, rather than Cambodian, holiday. In November, a Thai cabinet meeting pledged to build a bitumen road direct to Angkor from Thailand. One of the proposed routes would cross the Thai border at Anlong Veng. Tourism minister Veng welcomes the double-edged sword: "We have to be part of globalisation."

Asian adventure travel agent Toy Mason, of Canada's Footprints Travel, doesn't see much attraction in the Pol Pot town—until he hears about plans for the road. "I think it has a perverse appeal perhaps to some travellers who want to explore the lowlights of history. I don't think it would attract highbrow intellectual interest. You can say, 'I was there', but there's actually not much to see. But if it is on the way to Angkor Wat? Well, in that case I think people would definitely stop."

Anlong Veng is situated in the northwest Cambodian area where Pol Pot supporters fled in the wake of the 1979 Vietnamese invasion that ended the Khmer Rouge's four-year rule. Dongrek Mountain, with sweeping views over the Anlong Veng plains, became the last base from which the Khmer Rouge continued to rage against the world until 1998, when government forces seized the stronghold. While Pol Pot effectively hid here from about 1994, Ta Mok, "the butcher", was considerably more open. He built three houses, one in the centre of town, and openly ruled the area, continuing the Khmer Rouge's unskilled experiments with reservoirs by flooding the local river.

Today, central Anlong Veng's most obvious monument is a statue of "peace" erected by Prime Minister Hun Sen to mark the opening of the dirt road from Siem Reap in 2000. Many of the town's residents, however, are Pol Pot supporters, sheltered by the more gentle political acronyms of the Cambodian People's Party (CPP), led by Hun Sen and Prince Norodom Ranariddh's Funcinpec.

The area's current district chief, Yim San, welcomes the tourism plan and estimates that all he needs is $20,000 and one year to reconstruct the house that belonged to the man he calls "Grandfather Pol Pot". Yim emphasises he is now part of the "reconciliation government"—referring to a peace deal brokered by Hun Sen in 1995 that saw massive Khmer Rouge defections—but quickly insists he is "proud" of his former life as a commander with the Pol Pot regime. "I don't have any regrets for my movement," he says, sitting in his gardener's hut in a UNICEF T-shirt awaiting the completion of what will become one the town's showiest houses. "I am proud because I take part in protecting my country from US imperialism."

There isn't much evidence in these parts of the nightmare of the 1970s. For that, tourists travel to the infamous Killing Fields at Cheung Ek, where a crude monument of skulls forms a gruesome public reminder of the 1.7 million Cambodian deaths supervised by Pot Pot.

Almost all these tourists will also visit the Toul Sleng genocide museum, the former high school turned secret service prison in central Phnom Penh. Here, dozens of photographs of victims—a tiny proportion of those who perished—gaze soullessly from the walls where they were once imprisoned, starved and tortured in tiny coffin-sized cells. Ashen-faced Western tourists, in a futile attempt at comprehension, walk silently through room after room of what the Khmer Rouge codenamed S-21. A Cambodian woman breaks the silence with sobs—it is the first time she has braved a visit in 22 years. Her mother, who witnessed Khmer Rouge soldiers killing babies by whacking them into palm trees, has refused to join her.

In part, this is the inspiration for the new tourist approach. Cambodia's rulers began capitalising on its weeping past from the moment Pol Pot fled Phnom Penh in January 1979. The Vietnamese invaders who discovered Toul Sleng immediately turned it into a museum and employed locals to sift through the thousands of documents left there by the secret police.

Museum director Chey Sopheara had been a Toul Sleng student in the 1960s. Sheltered by hill tribes during the 1975-79 revolution, Chey returned in 1979, wondering why the Vietnamese soldiers were sending him to work at his old school. Not surprisingly, Chey refers to the educational benefits of the museum and supports tourism for Anlong Veng for the same reason. "There are still so many alive who remember," he says, adding that the S-21 buildings are still primarily sites for mourning rather than objective historical observation. "Anlong Veng is important to show the people the last days of the Khmer Rouge. The end of it all."

The Pol Pot nightmare hasn't quite ended for Nhem En. He joined a Khmer Rouge music troupe when he was ten because the organisation was linked to King Norodom Sihanouk. In 1977, at 15, he was posted to Beijing to learn photography. When he returned, he was sent to Toul Sleng—to photograph the prisoners on the way to their deaths. One of five photographers, he says he took 5000 pictures of the estimated 16,000 victims of the prison. Two were friends from his local village, accused of poisoning food. Prevented by fear from speaking to them, Nhem says he communicated his last remaining emotion—pity—with his eyes.

But Nhem, 41, is a complex representative of recent Cambodian history. He insists he, too, was a victim of the Khmer Rouge, yet he remained a loyal cadre until the mass defections of 1995. He carries a 1977 photograph of himself in Beijing in his pocket to "prove" his past, presumably to any doubters he meets. He says the Khmer Rouge was a "big mistake" but believes that his boss at the prison, Kang Kek Ieu, also known as Duch, was a "good man". And he still lives in Anlong Veng, though he is now a member of the royalist Funcinpec party. His wife will stand as a candidate for the party in next week's local elections.

Chhang Youk, perhaps Cambodia's leading light in the reconciliation movement, believes people like Nhem remain in Anlong Veng because they cannot go home to their villages. "They have not been forgiven," he says. "They are not reconciled. If they can be separated from the grave of Pot Pot, they will learn that he is not their grandfather, he is not their father. They need to go home to their own families."

Chhang, director of the Cambodian Documentation Centre, is preparing an estimated 600,000 documents for use as data in a forthcoming war crimes tribunal. Ostensibly agreed to by the government, the proposed tribunal has been bogged down in recent months in negotiations between PM Hun Sen and the United Nations in New York over such trivial matters as which language it will be conducted in. Two men—Duch and Ta Mok—are in jail awaiting charges that could lead them to the tribunal, but must be freed within months if the bickering doesn't stop. Another three surviving members of Pol Pot's inner circle are all frail but free in former Khmer Rouge strongholds such as Pailin, in western Cambodia.

These are the survivors most responsible for 19,440 known mass graves and 67 prison sites across Cambodia. Chhang, a political realist, is open-minded about Pot Pot's resting place, but begs for government recognition of another 77 known memorial sites throughout the country. In these, local villagers have simply bundled up skulls and bones of their relatives, forming crude monuments destined for quick erosion. "We mustn't give the impression we're willing to preserve Pol Pot's grave but not build memorials to the victims," says Chhang. "It's about justice. It's about memory."

There is an audience for on-the-edge tourism, of course. And other attractions: at an army training camp shooting range outside Phnom Penh, uniformed soldiers play snooker as they wait for customers, and offer them a "menu" price list when they arrive. This is Cambodia's "unofficial" tourism—technically illegal but not policed. London engineering student John Watt, 24, and two friends stop by on their way to the killing fields and pay $350. That buys them a chance to fire AK47, M16 and K57 machine guns into a paper target and hurl a hand grenade into a pond.

"I've got the biggest blood lust," says Watt, of the adrenalin rush that marked his adventure. "It's like bungee-jumping or skydiving—you know how dangerous it is, but you do it anyway."

His friend, 24-year-old trainee chef Andrew Crees, is more circumspect. "Once you've fired one of those guns you realise how powerful they are," he says. "So in that respect it's educational." Crees says he would travel to Anlong Veng if it were easy enough to get there—a comment both the Cambodian and Thai governments would welcome. "Every country uses its history for tourism. Why shouldn't Cambodia?

THE STORY BEHIND THE STORY

Kimina Lyall

To be successful, feature writers must be obsessed with detail. I remember Jake Young, a former editor of *Time Australia*, sending a reporter on assignment to cover the murder of New South Wales politician John Newman, who was shot in his driveway. Among his list of fired-off questions: what colour is his letterbox? Collecting those details, remembering to notice the letterbox, is, in my opinion, the key to feature writing. So, for feature writing, to the who, where, what, when, why, and how questions we could add: what colour?

Like most features, 'Pol Pot Park' was spurred by a news story—an announcement by the Cambodian government that it would look to develop Pol Pot's cremation site as a tourist attraction. I saw it as a way into a piece I had wanted to do for months, on the problems of setting up the Khmer Rouge war crimes tribunal, which had not sparked the interest of any features desk. This grisly tourist attraction was the detail that could drive a more thoughtful piece about Cambodia's reconciliation with its past.

It took one conversation to get the go-ahead from the magazine. (Arguing over the cost of the photographer became the only potential sticking point.) I allocated four days in Cambodia to research the story: two in Anlong Veng, one at Angkor to explore the irony of the complementary tourist attractions, and the last in Phnom Penh for the talking heads to broaden the picture. Such time constraints were necessary but risky. In my experience the best details appear in second interviews, visits or conversations, after a rapport has been established. But because I am firstly a news reporter, I could not afford to spend more than four days outside the breaking news loop.

There are no telephones in Anlong Veng, so the trip was pretty much 'on spec'. I flew to Siem Reap, hired a translator and a car and hoped for the best. Commander Lee happened to be at the border checkpoint (Pol Pot's grave is only metres from the Thai border) and agreed to escort us to the site. We spent about an hour there, but returned at dawn the next day because the photographer, Yvan, wasn't satisfied with the light. I can thank his diligence for the most delicious detail I obtained on the trip, for it was during this second visit that Commander Lee told us there were still many pieces of Pol Pot's bones in the ashes, and proceeded to dig around for them.

The biggest challenge in the story was translation. While the local person I had hired was excellent at helping track down people and places, he left a lot to be desired in translation skills. There were few quotes in the story from local residents, and all were difficult to get. I often needed to ask the same question over and over. One example was the interview with Nhem En, the Khmer Rouge photographer, who was required to document prisoners on their way to their deaths. I asked if he ever took a picture of someone he knew and he said yes. Did he talk to them? I asked. No, came the answer—you were not allowed. I then tried to ask whether he attempted to communicate a message with his body language, perhaps his eyes? It took three or four tries before my translator understood what I wanted and got a reply. It was worth the patience, but I had almost given up before the answer came.

Obviously, this was a language problem, but I do find with features, it is necessary to be persistent and keep asking the question until you get the quote or the fact you need to slot into a specific component of the story. One of the great skills of any interviewer, particularly a feature interviewer, is to convince people to relinquish the piece of information they may think is not important but that actually provides a necessary piece of light or movement for the piece.

The Pol Pot grave itself would have worked as a simple 'quirky' feature from a faraway place. But I wanted to broaden it out, to go from the specifics to the general and answer a question I think every feature should answer: what does this mean? The bigger question—why? Details are well and good, but they must colour, or explain, a greater truth. So the next part of my trip involved visits to Angkor, to explain Cambodia's burgeoning tourism industry and its hazards, and on to Phnom Penh to describe the progress on the war crimes trials.

It was important to conduct the interview with Chhang Youk face to face, as I not only got a sense of the masses of documents he has been collecting, but also I saw for the first time the other grave sites—crude memorials of piles of skulls across the countryside—from photographs on his desk. Unfortunately, I ran out of time to visit them (already it was day four) but I did return with some photographs the magazine elected not to use. I still believe the detail of these other gravesites helped explain the enormous paradox of the Pol Pot legacy. The other advantage of interviewing Chhang Youk last was I was able to get reactions to some of my earlier material, in particular the habit of Anlong Veng locals of calling Pol Pot 'grandfather'. That produced the exceptional quote about those people needing to go home and be forgiven by their real families.

Finally, I decided to end the story with an example of 'on-the-edge' tourism. The shooting range outside of Phnom Penh is listed in guidebooks and I had slated it down as a potential pic story for another day, but I decided it too would help to illustrate the rawness of contemporary Cambodia. Getting the material was again, a challenge. Sticking to my Media Entertainment & Arts Alliance code of ethics, I told the soldiers I was a reporter and they told me I was not allowed to interview any customers. As the place was empty, I played dumb (sometimes it helps not to speak the language) and sat down and ordered a Coke. They didn't seem to have any objection to this, nor me copying their 'menu' of shooting prices into my notebook. Eventually, some yobbos arrived, and I simply watched them have their fun and waited for them to leave. Then I jumped in my car and chased them down the road. It was the only interview for the piece conducted after a pull-over! Thankfully, the boys were happy to talk.

My story didn't bring down any institutions or ruffle any feathers (except Rin Aun's!) but I hope it did manage to achieve what it set out to—provide a realistic picture of contemporary Cambodia's struggles with reconciliation, through a series of small but significant details.

12 EDITING YOUR STORY AND WORKING WITH EDITORS

In 1915 The Washington Post *reported that President Woodrow Wilson had taken his fiancée, Edith Galt, to the theatre but rather than watch the play the president 'spent most of his time entering Mrs Galt'. They meant 'entertaining'.*

Robert Hendrickson, *The Literary Life and Other Curiosities*

CHAPTER SUMMARY

The importance of journalists editing and proofreading their own work before giving it to editors is stressed. Three kinds of editing are outlined: filling in gaps, reading the article for structure and rhythm, and the laborious line-by-line editing. A case study of the editing of a profile piece is presented to demonstrate the value of editors helping journalists improve stories.

You have finished writing the feature. Good stuff. I knew you could do it. If the piece is not needed yesterday, save the file and take a break. You have earned it. Reporting and writing a 2000-word plus feature is a lot more work than it looks. Or it should be. If you are not at least a little tired afterwards you are either a consummate craftsman or you did not put much effort into it. Readers have little understanding of the work required to produce a good piece of writing. They think because a piece is easy to read it must have been easy to write. I wish. It was Red Smith who said, sure writing is easy—all you have to do is sit down at the typewriter and open a vein.

Smith was an outstanding American sportswriter until his death in 1982. His columns may be decades old now but he really was a consummate craftsman. There are moments, of course, when you are on song and what a buzz that is, but there are times when you don't feel like writing at all, and even times when, as Stephen King puts it, 'you're doing good work when it feels like all you're managing is to shovel shit from a sitting position'.[1]

Many features are written against a hard deadline, but one of the aims of the planning process is to build in time to edit and proofread. Just as you should take charge of your professional life by generating the bulk of story ideas, so you should edit the feature before handing it over to the editor who commissioned it. Editors appreciate clean copy because they have to rescue so much that isn't. It is not simply a matter of running the computer spellcheck over it; spellcheck is a problem I will come back to.

There are four stages of editing that feature writers can do:

1. Filling the gaps
2. Reading it out loud
3. Editing line by line
4. Proofreading.

FILLING THE GAPS

After a break, the first step is to read through the feature to see if there is anything left out. The act of writing clarifies the mind and propels it forward. Even well-organised feature writers finish a story and see changes to be made. You write and edit in two different frames of mind. As John Gould, a local newspaper editor, told Stephen King during an early stint as a journalist: 'When you write, you're telling yourself the story. When you rewrite, your main job is taking out all the things that are not the story.'[2]

Look at what you promised the reader and whether you have kept your word. As discussed earlier, it is easy for feature writers, immersed in their story, to overlook the bleeding obvious question. It is also easy to overlook small matters. Readers will put up with one unanswered question, maybe two, but much beyond that they will register annoyance and turn the page. For instance, in a profile of film-maker Michael Moore that appeared in *The Sunday Telegraph*, Moore's earlier tenure as editor of the left-leaning magazine *Mother Jones* was covered but there was only a cryptic reference to why he quit after only five months. Given that Moore is left-wing and the magazine has a strong reputation for the kind of journalism for which Moore subsequently made his name, it was puzzling.[3] It is also easy to clutter stories with unimportant characters and events.

If you think there is a contradiction between answering nit-picking questions and stripping out clutter you are half right. There is no contradiction, but it feels as though there is. Writing a good feature requires clear thinking skills of a high order because you need to provide enough information to answer relevant questions readers might have about the topic, but not so much as to overwhelm them. This is why at all stages of the research and writing, you keep tacking back to the question, what is this story about? You have to be clear-eyed in pruning out material that is not relevant to the story; simultaneously you are always looking for more and better quality relevant information.

Do final checks at this stage. While writing, you may have chosen not to check a particular fact because it would have interrupted the flow. Fair enough, but as you sweep through your material to see if there is anything important left out, check facts too. It is easy to misspell someone's name in the rush of writing. It is easy to misspell names full stop. Even a simple name like John Brown can be spelt Jon Browne. Particularly check numbers, quotes and anything that smells of a potential lawsuit. If in doubt about the latter, talk to the editor or consult a good textbook, such as Mark Pearson's *The Journalist's Guide to Media Law*, 2nd edition (Allen & Unwin, Sydney, 2004).

READING IT OUT LOUD

Look at the story's structure, its lead and close. Does the structure tell the story well? Does the tone match the content of the piece? Is the lead polished and diamond-sharp? How do you react when you read the close? Does the pace vary? Is it quick when it needs to be and not when it isn't? Does the piece read well? The best way to check is to read it out loud. You may feel like a dag doing this in a newsroom, although senior writers like Gary Tippet are known for regaling colleagues with passages as they write them. Read it under your breath if you are self-conscious. Find a good reader among your colleagues; by good reader I don't mean a member of a book club, but someone who will read the feature carefully and offer honest, constructive criticism. It has to be honest, otherwise they are wasting your time or worse; it has to be constructive, to help you improve the piece.

EDITING LINE BY LINE

This is the hard part. You need to prune your feature, to which you have become inordinately attached. You have put so much effort into it, this story is so important, it is almost poetry. It is okay to feel this way. It is your work and if you are not passionate about it, it is unlikely anyone else will be. But the story has to fit into a space, it is competing with dozens of others, and, hey, this is journalism; the whole newspaper is created top to bottom every day and when it is done, you come in the next day and do it all again. Magazines go through the same process weekly or monthly.

You need to begin looking at your beloved feature through the eyes of an editor; if you don't the editor will and their comments will make you feel as if you have been king-hit with a case of king prawns. Stephen King's early mentor, John Gould, who King credited with teaching him more about writing in ten minutes than he learnt in years of English literature classes, had a formula: final version = draft − 10 per cent. This is good advice; almost every draft of a feature (or novel or textbook, for that matter) can be trimmed by 10 per cent. The question is: how?

Begin by getting into the right frame of mind. The English writer and critic Sir Arthur Quiller-Couch said, 'Murder your darlings.'[4] It is an alarming image, necessarily so. The darlings are those little pieces of literary self-indulgence that are not about the story but you showing off. Close your eyes if need be, but plunge a stake through your darlings' hearts or they will suck the story dry. Try thinking of it this way: imagine your feature was written by a complete arsehole. Now set to work on it.

PROOFREADING

Mistakes are unavoidable in journalism because, despite all technological advances, a newspaper or magazine is, in the end, a handmade object. Technology is only as good as the people who invented it, which brings me back to the computer spellcheck program. By all means use it, but it is not, repeat not, a substitute for proofreading your story word by word for the simple reason that a word may be spelt correctly (spellcheck gives it a tick) but may be the wrong word (spellcheck gives it a tick—D'oh!). A student handed in an assignment in which the word 'loose' was used at least a dozen times when they really meant 'lose'. Full marks for spelling, none for proofreading.

Reading for errors is different to reading for sense, let alone pleasure. It is not fun and it takes time, but few error-prone journalists survive long in the industry. You read slowly, focusing on each word to see if it is spelt correctly, to see if the sentence is punctuated correctly, if a report title is named consistently throughout the piece, a person's age has not changed between paragraphs seven and 21, and so on. To see this process in action, begin by reading this profile I wrote of Australian author Robin Klein, published in *The Weekend Australian Magazine*.[5]

THE FLEETING MEMORY

By Matthew Ricketson

[Precede] A stroke has left Robin Klein, one of Australia's most popular children's authors, with vivid long-term recall but a tenuous grasp on today.

[1] Hunched over her desk at 12.20 one spring night in 1999, Robin Klein pursued the scurrying figures on her computer screen as they built fortifications for their next battle in 'Age of Empires'. The game was light relief from the spade work of writing, although one of its medieval scenarios helped inspire the starting point for the plot of her latest novel. She writes up to a dozen drafts of a book before showing it to her editor, and this one was only a couple of drafts away.

[2] Klein was engrossed in the action when without warning a searing pain gripped her, as if someone had struck a match inside her head. The 63-year-old children's author cried out and her daughter Ros, who lived at home in the Dandenong Ranges outside Melbourne, found her clutching the left side of her head. 'Call an ambulance', was all Klein could manage.

[3] She had suffered a cerebral aneurism, a type of stroke. Some strokes come from a blood vessel bursting in the brain, others from a clot in the blood supply. An aneurism is a weakness in the wall of an artery that makes it balloon out, rather like the flawed inner tube of a bicycle. It may be brought on by the effects of smoking or hypertension, but it is often a congenital weakness, as it appeared to be in Klein's case. Some aneurisms rupture early, others not until later in life. It is an uncommon condition and victims have no idea of the time bomb ticking away—the aneurism simply sits there, causing no discomfort.

[4] Klein spent three weeks in intensive care. Aneurisms can be killers and the doctors feared she would succumb. But very slowly, watched by friends and her four children, Klein began to recover. Klein spent a further month in hospital, before being moved to a rehabilitation centre called Dunelm.

[5] Visiting family and friends were puzzled by Klein's mental state. She had little short-term memory, but could recall childhood events of 50 years before. Her imagination seemed to be roaming ceaselessly. Dunelm, with its nurses, rules and patients, conjured

thoughts of her father who had been wounded during battle in World War I and of her daughter Ros, who had been training recently in the Army Reserve. Klein's novel-in-progress had a martial theme. At Dunelm she began thinking the novel could revolve around an 11-year-old growing up in an army training camp run by his parents.

[6] Fiction writers have rich imaginary lives; children's writers also have an ability to recall the textures of childhood. Klein appeared to be not just recalling hers, but re-experiencing it. Would this make her novels more authentic?

[7] For two months Klein's mind drifted between her memories, her imaginings and reality. Those close to her were distraught. She was no longer in danger of dying but she was no longer the Robin they knew. The Robin they knew loved writing; she had once told her editor at Penguin, Julie Watts, she felt ill if more than a few days passed without her writing.

[8] Klein still saw herself as a writer, but no longer of novels. She told her longtime agent, Tim Curnow, when he visited: 'I'm sorry I can't write books for you. I've got to write army training manuals now.' In all likelihood, though, Klein will not write any training manuals, either. The aneurism's scrambling of short-term memory cripples her as a writer. She may still be able to recall perfectly her father's throaty laugh, but she can watch the same movie two days running and not remember she has already seen it. Imagination may be crucial to writers, but not if they are unable to connect thoughts and analyse them.

[9] When *The Weekend Australian*

Magazine interviewed Klein recently she had still not written anything since being struck by the aneurism. 'I remember being very confused,' she recalls now. 'One minute I was a little kid rocking a doll to sleep, the next minute I was getting married in a church in all my wedding finery. I remember thinking, "what's going on? I'm bumping all over the place." I knew something had happened but not really what had happened. It was a bit like watching yourself on a film.'

[10] She has recovered enough to move out of Dunelm and in with her son Michael and his family in nearby Menzies Creek. We meet at her old home, where Ros now lives alone. To a stranger, there are no physical traces of Klein's condition. A small birdlike woman with a surprisingly unlined face, she chats in the lounge room of the old timber cottage with its views of the lush Dandenongs while her daughter brings in coffee and muffins. She slips into the sharp-edged banter she and Ros exchanged for the many years they shared the family home after the other three children moved out.

[11] Later, though, watching an education video made about Klein in 1997, I am struck by how she actually looks better now than before her illness. Since the aneurism she has shed weight, no longer suffers from migraines and, most remarkably, has sloughed off the arthritis that plagued her for many years. Where it had once hurt her fingers so badly just to type that she experimented with a voice-activated computer, now the fire-like pain has gone.

[12] These are not typical reactions to an aneurism, although it is unclear whether Klein's short-term memory loss

means she does not notice these conditions or reflects the still limited understanding of the mysteries of the brain. 'So, that aneurism was a good thing,' she says, seemingly without irony. Ros laughs bitterly; Michael Klein, who has driven his mother over for the interview, shifts his seat on the couch.

[13] She shows no signs of anxiety about being interviewed, something that once would have given her a conniption. She is naturally reclusive and grew more so with time, granting interviews only if her publisher insisted. Although she enjoyed the adulation of her young readers, she always looked for an excuse to call off a school visit. 'Can't we say my arm's in plaster and I won't be able to sign any autographs, so I'd best not come,' Ros recalls her mother saying on several occasions.

[14] Klein's shyness is one reason she is not as well known as she could be—she is out of step with the current demand for writer as performer. Adults rarely take notice of children's books, which is another reason why few outside her immediate circle know about Klein's illness. J.K. Rowling's Harry Potter series is a rare phenomenon—children's literature that has crossed over to the adult world.

[15] The best-selling Australian children's author, Paul Jennings, believes Klein has 'contributed more to helping Australian children read than J.K. Rowling, yet you hardly ever see her name in the newspaper'. The hype surrounding Rowling's books and the film adaptations disguise the general invisibility of the children's book world.

[16] Other children's authors are treated as if they really do live at the bottom of the garden and eat fairy bread, according to Nadia Wheatley who has won prizes for her books for teenagers but is best known for her biography of Charmian Clift.

[17] Klein is one of Australia's most popular children's authors, alongside Jennings, John Marsden, Emily Rodda and Andy Griffiths. In Australia her books, published by Penguin, have sold more than a million copies. Her Penny Pollard series, published by Oxford University Press, has also achieved healthy sales. Her books have been translated into seven languages.

[18] Klein's career predates the other authors'. She started writing relatively late, nearing 40, and as one of her editors, Rita Hart, recalls: 'She just wrote and wrote. She was so full of ideas.'

[19] Jennings remembers being 'really impressed and overwhelmed' when he began visiting schools in 1986 to promote his first book, 'because every kid's desk seemed to have a copy of Penny Pollard on it'. They still do: figures released last year showed eleven of the top 100 books held in Australian school libraries were written by Klein.

[20] She has written at least 50 books since 1978, as well as more than 100 short stories and school readers. Many of her books are still in print, which is increasingly rare in the modern publishing world with its shrinking back lists. Klein's best known books are *Hating Alison Ashley* (published in 1984 and regarded as a classic of Australian humour), and the Penny Pollard series, the first instalment of which was published in 1983. The sixth instalment was published in 1999 and is Klein's most

recent book—and probably her last.

[21] Klein has also won numerous awards, including two Children's Book Council gold stickers, a NSW Premier's Literary award in 1992, and six of the awards voted for by children. Appealing to both children and judges of literary awards is uncommon.

[22] Mark Macleod, children's publisher at Hodder Headline, believes Klein would have won more literary awards if not for an apparent bias against humorous books. *Hating Alison Ashley* was shortlisted and should have won, says Macleod, but no humorous novel won a CBC gold sticker until Nick Earls' *48 Shades of Brown* in 2000.

[23] *Hating Alison Ashley* is written from the perspective of grade six girl Erica Yurken, whose unfortunate name prompts a rash of nicknames that constantly undercut her desperate desire to rise above her inelegant surroundings at Barringa East primary and prepare for a glittering career on the stage.

[24] The book has not dated because its appeal has little to do with a stenographic rendering of the latest kidspeak and everything to do with children's experience of school, teachers and other kids. Erica hates the beautiful, composed new girl Alison Ashley because she is everything Erica aspires to, but the book turns on how each girl learns more about themselves by shedding their prejudices about the other.

[25] Children's author, Judith Clarke, wrote recently of Klein's unrivalled understanding of 'the adolescent yearning for the perfect, the lovely and romantic, beyond the mundane world of everyday'. Clarke says Klein portrays compassionately the way young people come to terms with their dreams, learning to distinguish between fantasy and truth and discovering the possibilities of both the real world and themselves.

[26] The source of Klein's empathy seems to be her bone-deep recall of her own childhood, a quality she shares with many outstanding children's writers. Born in the northern New South Wales town of Kempsey in 1936, Klein was the eighth of nine children. Her father, Lesley McMaugh, received a war veterans' pension and ran a small family farm. She recalls the family's poverty: 'I remember walking along the main street on a Saturday morning, shopping and looking in the shop windows with the pretty dresses, and I was just consumed with sadness that we couldn't get them.'

[27] She and her sisters were teased about their clothes. 'Oh, you're wearing that funny old dress again,' they would say. 'You'd just keep your face perfectly straight, without flinching a muscle, to show that you didn't care. Underneath, of course, you're dying, but you never show the other kid that.'

[28] There were books in the house, scrambled from second-hand sales, and all the children were early and avid readers, but there were not enough to satisfy their curiosity. Their parents told them to write their own books, and Robin in particular took them at their word, starting with *The Beautiful Widow of Perrin's Creek* in primary school. She grew up thinking everyone wrote their own books, telling herself stories at night or plunging into the imaginary worlds that others like Ethel Turner and, later, Shakespeare and William Golding had created.

[29] Her love of stories made her an oddity; she did not enjoy her office jobs and it was only after she married Karl Klein at the age of 20 and began raising their four children that she found her passion a source of enjoyment and power. She loved cuddling on the couch, reading to the kids or making up her own stories; one became her first published book. A light went on in her head when she realised it was possible to make a living from it.

[30] Few do, but Klein is a gifted storyteller. For several years she worked as a teacher's aide at a primary school in a housing commission area in Melbourne's south-east. Many of the students would not be seen dead with a book, but soon the teachers knew that if they sent the aide down the back of the excursion bus her exotic stories of army captains in the war would settle the natives. Those experiences, she recalls with a laugh, resurfaced years later when writing *Hating Alison Ashley*.

[31] If Klein's memories of a decade ago are still sharp, she is blithely unaware that more than once in a 90-minute interview, she retells the same story. She is confused about Dunelm, describing it as an army camp. Her son Michael says: 'It was never an army camp.'

'But the army put me in, didn't they?'

'No they didn't. It was just a hostel where you stayed to recover.'

'And they did get me recovered, did they? Am I a lot better?'

Says Ros: 'You're a lot better than you were.'

'Oh thank you . . . you liar. You're lying, aren't you?'

'No, I'm not,' Ros replies.

Her mother laughs and says: 'When she gets that smirk on you know she's lying about something. So I am safe to let out on my own?'

'Maybe,' says Ros with a half smile.

'Oh, god! She's a bitch isn't she,' she says, laughing again.

'I learnt it all from you, Mum.'

[32] Their banter continues. Its robust wit is a feature of the strong family she raised and of Klein's writing. Though there may never be a new book, that skill and empathy endures in every Australian school library.

In the next few weeks the magazine published three letters, all of them positive. One, from an Anna Renzenbrink, read:

Reading about author Robin Klein's stroke reminded me of the sadness I felt on hearing that Roald Dahl had died . . . I am very sorry that there may never again be a novel from this fantastic children's author. Hating Alison Ashley has one of the best punchlines I have ever read in a novel, and I enjoy it even more now at age 24 than I did at age ten. Klein's books are entertaining, engaging and essential reading for any literate Australian childhood.

The magazine's editor, Helen Anderson, was happy with the piece, readers liked it and I was reasonably satisfied. Would it surprise you to learn the original article was rejected by another magazine editor? Perhaps not if you knew the original was nearly 4000 words long and not especially good. This is a case study in the value of editing, both by the journalist and the editor.

The impetus for the story came from Julie Watts at Penguin, who edits both Klein's and Paul Jennings' books. She told me about Klein's aneurism; I wanted to write the story because of the peculiar mental state Klein found herself in, and because she is an outstanding author who has not received the recognition she deserves. I pitched the idea along those lines to the editor of *Good Weekend*, Fenella Souter, and she liked it. It took a long time to do the story, partly because it was difficult to set up interview times with Klein and partly because I was juggling it with university work. I also did too much research for a magazine profile, probably a hangover from having recently written a book.

These details of my life are only relevant because they help explain why the original version was nearly 4000 words (it is reprinted in the appendix beginning on p. 254). When I finally sent it to Fenella Souter she had forgotten she had even commissioned it, meaning I had neglected my own advice of keeping in touch with editors, and in any case she did not think the story worked. This upset me; I had put a lot of effort into the piece. Stupid editors, what would they know? Well, she was absolutely right. Nearly 4000 words on a relatively unknown writer is too much, and I had failed to properly bring out the poignancy of Klein's situation.

I took the idea to Helen Anderson at *The Weekend Australian Magazine* and she too liked it but agreed only to look at the story. I went back and pruned it to 2912 words. What was cut and on what grounds? The main cuts were:

- Understanding Klein's condition was complicated by her story-teller's habit of exaggerating—one paragraph.
- Detail on the number of Harry Potter books sold in Australia—one sentence.
- Detail on the number and type of awards she has won—one paragraph.
- Comment on her writing across a variety of genres—one paragraph.
- Material about a teenage novel Klein wrote about a drug addict—one paragraph.

- Details about the games she and her sisters played as children—one and a half paragraphs.
- One of the quotes about the family's poverty—one paragraph.
- Material about her mother having no time to cuddle her children—one paragraph.
- Exaggerated stories her parents told her—one sentence.
- Details about Klein's early working life—one paragraph.
- Material about letters Klein receives from fans—six paragraphs.

The reasons for the cuts were that there was far too much information and analysis of Klein's writing for a feature in a general interest magazine, there was too much biographical material about someone who is hardly an A-list celebrity, and sifting fact from fiction in Klein's stories of her past was a diversion from the main theme of the story. All the cut material would be included in a biography of Klein; that is, the material itself was not rubbish, just in the wrong place at the wrong time.

Anderson emailed, saying she liked the story and wanted to run it. She had a few queries that required new material but she wanted to trim the piece to 2700 words. She sent me a version that she had already worked on to make space for the new material. She cut:

- One paragraph from a two-paragraph precede I had written.
- Several references to Klein's daughter Ros amounting to two paragraphs.
- Another detail about sales of the Harry Potter series.
- Two paragraphs about *Hating Alison Ashley* and another Klein book, *The Listmaker*.

Anderson continued the cutting I had already begun, with an important addition. She drastically reduced the role of Klein's daughter, Ros, in the story because she was secondary. My problem had been that Ros was the conduit to her mother and much of my contact had been through her. As a writer it was natural to include her; an editor has never met the source and simply asks whether they are central or peripheral to the story action. In her accompanying email, Anderson said more material was needed on aneurisms.

At the moment you don't even give a brief description of what it is, or more detail about how it affects this person. How does it affect most sufferers; are Robin's symptoms common; is it common, for example, for conditions such as arthritis to be 'cured' after an aneurism? To me the intrigue of this feature should rest on how a strange, unexpected explosion in the brain affects—in negative and positive ways—the two most vital characteristics of a passionate writer: imagination and memory. I think you need to develop that as the main focus of the feature. If Robin had been a doctor, say, or a scientist, the tragedy might be less poignant, or poignant in a different way. I feel the potential of this side of the story, but it's not there at the moment.

You don't make it clear why she hasn't written since the illness. We have no idea what her capabilities are now. At one stage I thought the notion of living more frequently in childhood memories would be an odd advantage for a children's writer—obviously not, but you don't tell us why. In general, I'd like to read more about the slippery nature of memory and imagination, in relation to the illness afflicting this writer. Otherwise, I'm afraid, it's just a story about another writer.

This is a stellar example of the writer missing the bleeding obvious question. Of course the nature of aneurisms was central to the story. Why hadn't I seen that? I had seen it at the outset when Julie Watts told me about Klein's stroke but lost it while reporting and writing. I then interviewed Klein's doctor and another doctor I knew and put in the new material. It was only four paragraphs (numbers three, six, eight and twelve in the published story) but it improved the piece greatly.

Finally, Anderson felt the ending did not quite work. She wanted to trim the dialogue between the Kleins. Originally, it ran for a few more lines with Robin scolding Ros before she added: 'It's nice to have a daughter who's one of your best friends, though.' After which I had written a closing line: 'It would be even nicer, for her family, her colleagues and for thousands of children around Australia, if she was fully recovered and writing again.' In a phone conversation shortly before the piece was sent off to the printers, Anderson and I agreed this ending was a touch sweet and substituted the one that was published.

This case study should help you see how easy it is for journalists to get lost in the thickets of a story and how important editing and editors can be.

DISCUSSION QUESTIONS AND EXERCISES

1. Find a colleague and read each other's feature stories. Provide honest, constructive criticism for each other. How easy or hard do

you find it to be completely frank with colleagues or to consider their comments about your work?

2. Take your feature story and reduce its length by 10 per cent without losing anything important.

3. Proofread a page of a newspaper or a magazine feature article and list every grammatical or typographical error. If you cannot find any, keep reading carefully until you do.

13 LOOKING AHEAD . . . TO LITERARY JOURNALISM

'Tis strange—but true; for truth is always strange. Stranger than fiction.

Lord Byron

CHAPTER SUMMARY

Literary journalism is news that stays news. It has its roots in journalism, but draws on the techniques of fiction to tell true stories more fully. The defining elements are outlined of a kind of journalism that is growing in the United States and the United Kingdom and to a lesser extent in Australia. The potential benefits and drawbacks of literary journalism are discussed.

The poet and critic, Ezra Pound, once said literature is news that stays news. He could have been talking about literary journalism.[1] Most journalism, we know, lasts no longer than the kitty litter it soaks up days after publication, but outstanding works of literary journalism, such as John Hersey's *Hiroshima* and George Orwell's *Homage to Catalonia*, are still in print 50, even 80 years after their release. Literary journalism is not journalism about literature; it uses the techniques of fiction in factual writing. Isn't that what feature writers do? Partly.

A core message of this book has been that journalists are storytellers. Stories may be presented in that grey block of a form—hard news—but equally often they are presented as a feature, and draw upon the techniques of fiction, at least the elementary ones. Most daily newspaper features contain large chunks of straightforward exposition. The bodybuilding piece quoted in the introduction is, as I said, an advanced feature. By the standards of daily journalism, the lead paragraphs are long and sophisticated, combining description, anecdote and suspense, with a stunning punchline.

Literary journalism draws more fully on fictional techniques. It is well beyond routine daily journalism, but its roots are journalistic. Think of the who, what, when, where, why and how questions as ice cubes that melt into the fictional techniques that comprise literary journalism:

Who becomes Character
What becomes Action
Where becomes Setting
When becomes Chronology
Why becomes Motive
How becomes Narrative.[2]

Where the standard feature story uses exposition, garnished by quotes and anecdotes, literary journalism renders the material into a short story, with scenes, dialogue and characters' points of view embedded in the narrative. Sometimes a character's thoughts and feelings will be rendered in an interior monologue, which is the most controversial and certainly the most difficult fictional technique for the literary journalist. Tom Wolfe used it in *The Right Stuff* to put readers in the space rocket with the astronauts as they made their historic flights. So realistically and intimately did these passages read that it was not surprising Wolfe was accused of inventing them. He replied they were all drawn from detailed interviews in which he asked the astronauts exactly what they were thinking and feeling during the flights; the astronauts later independently backed Wolfe's accuracy on the flight passages.[3] Garry Linnell used similar methods in his piece about the cancer ward at the Royal Children's Hospital reproduced at the end of this chapter and, as you will see from his story behind the story, gained the material in a similar way.

It is worth your while knowing about literary journalism because you can benefit from seeing the possibilities inherent in your chosen vocation and because literary journalism offers an alternative to the superficiality that, by definition, characterises much daily journalism. Most people benefit from role models, and journalists are poorly served because of their industry's preoccupation with the here and now and because, as you have no doubt noticed, journalists have what the PRs call an image problem. Newspaper journalists routinely finish well down the list of most trusted professions. Such surveys partly reflect the nature of journalistic work, which is to pry into and uncover stories that powerful people want to remain hidden, and which the public may well not want to hear. Journalists' unethical behaviour undoubtedly contributes too. Journalists invade people's privacy, sometimes without good reason, and as the ABC's award-winning investigative reporter Chris Masters has argued, too many journalists, cowed by the nation's restrictive defamation laws and by political and corporate intimidation, turn away from scrutinising powerful interests and intimidate ordinary people instead.[4]

Many working in the news media are acutely aware their stories only glancingly connect with their audience. Some have sought to reconnect by producing civic or public journalism. Some commentators have urged journalists and proprietors to match their power and influence with greater accountability. Literary journalists nod respectfully at public journalism and accountability, then place their faith in providing deeply researched, well-written pieces that use the techniques of fiction to fully engage the reader's mind and emotions.

One of the best journalistic books I have read in recent years is *Newjack* by American literary journalist Ted Conover, who spent a year working undercover as a guard in New York's notorious Sing Sing prison. It sounds like the ultimate in hairy-chested journalism and at one level it is, but Conover is no Hunter S. Thompson constantly drawing attention to himself in the narrative. The United States locks up more of its citizens per head than any other country on earth, making prisons a topic of legitimate and urgent public interest. Conover requested permission to see inside the prison system but was rebuffed, so he decided the only way to do the story properly was to work undercover.

Newjack offers a deeply disturbing picture of lives wasted in the prison system that is grounded in acute first-hand observation, thorough secondary research and an unobtrusive but highly effective literary style. After passing officer training Conover is assigned to work in the massive B Block. He describes his first shift in detail; there are far too many inmates for him; he is working with a similarly inexperienced colleague; he knows the rules but not the real rules; and he struggles to get inmates to follow even his simplest requests.

> Most ignored me, or seemed to. But I persisted, and in five minutes maybe half the inmates had disappeared from the gallery, presumably into their cells. I made my way from one end to the other, saying "Excuse me" to inmates in the way, and repeated my mantra. "Step in, guys—time to step in." One of them imitated me but then smiled when I stared at him. I began to grow irritated at a handful who continued to ignore me; at an upstate prison, I knew, this would never be tolerated. I decided to make it personal with one, who I felt was making a show out of ignoring me.

"Time to step in, pal. Five minutes ago."

"Pal? You're not my friend."

"Step in anyway. It's time."

"Time for you, maybe, not time for me."

"No?" I said, on the verge of anger.

Suddenly he grinned. "Chapel porter, CO [Corrections Officer]. I was just leaving."

"Chapel porter?"

"Yeah, I go every morning. The regular officer knows. Or you can call Officer Martinez over in the chapel."

"Maybe I will," I said, jotting down the name.

He'd either bamboozled me or had a little fun, neither of which was the outcome I'd hoped for. I had just decided to approach the next guy who was still out when an inmate called to me from his cell.

"CO! CO! They didn't call me down for my medication."

"Yeah? What are you supposed to get?"

I waited half a minute while the man doubled over with a deep chest cough. He started to speak again, then coughed in my face.

"TB pills, man, gotta take my TB pills every day."

I wiped my face. He didn't seem to have coughed on me intentionally; he was just heedless. "What's your name and cell number?"

He told me his name and then pointed out the cell number painted by the door lock. "You're new here, right, CO?"

"How can you tell?" I said ruefully.

"You know who you look like? You look like that guy on *Three's Company*, CO. Know who I mean?"

I nodded.

"Anybody ever tell you that?"

"No," I said. "I'll get back to you." [5]

When one of the training officers inspects B Block, Conover suffers a tirade for failing to keep the log book up to date and for not checking the condition of inmates' cells, but he wants the officer to stick around because he commands a modicum of respect from prisoners.

I turned to wend my way through the large number of inmates responding to the announcements for gym and yard runs—I hadn't even heard them—when a tall, lanky, black inmate in a muscle shirt yelled, "Hey, CO!" As I turned to face him, the short, bulky man at his side went through nine tenths of the motion of landing an uppercut on my chin. He stopped maybe an inch away, and as I jumped reflexively backward, the two of them dissolved into laughter and strolled off down the gallery. 102.10, I thought, threats to an officer. But was it a threat if they were only kidding, if they were just trying to make a fool out of me? I tried to calm my pounding heart and wondered if I should have pulled out my baton. I wondered how I'd last five more hours.[6]

My heart was pounding too when I read that passage. The question I kept asking was what would I have done in his shoes? Conover achieves this effect by recreating the scene, by rendering speech as dialogue rather than quotes and by letting the reader share his thoughts and feelings. Not that literary journalism must concern itself with serious topics. John McPhee once wrote a book about oranges and Hunter S. Thompson's gonzo journalism can be uproariously funny.

Literary journalism is more common in magazines and books than in daily news and the style is growing in the United States, the United Kingdom and, to a lesser extent, Australia. Journalism and fiction occupy different domains but there has long been a relationship between the two. Journalism is about covering real events and issues and people in the news media; fiction is about inventing stories. The primary task of journalism is to gain accurate information about a news event. A novelist's primary task is to tell a compelling story. The two activities share a core belief in the necessity and virtue of constructing the world into a narrative. The difference is that the journalist's story is true.

Novelists ask readers to willingly suspend their disbelief. They use coincidence sparingly in plotting, for fear of straining the reader's credulity. Conversely, when a true story is told in an extended narrative it carries the power of the real. As McPhee, a respected American literary journalist, once said: 'Things that are cheap and tawdry in fiction work beautifully in non-fiction because they are true.'[7] For instance, the pardoning of Lindy Chamberlain for the 1980 murder of her daughter in central Australia happened only after a truly remarkable coincidence; a travelling English backpacker, David Brett, tried to climb Ayers Rock (now known as Uluru) at dusk in 1986, slipped and fell to his death. When police found his body eight days later they stumbled across Azaria's missing matinee jacket, a crucial piece of evidence that would have buttressed Lindy Chamberlain's claim at the trial that a dingo had taken her baby. 'Were it fiction, no new and risky character would appear so late, but the ways of unruly fact drew in David Brett,' wrote John Bryson in an afterword to the American edition of *Evil Angels*.

It is widely believed, thanks to the rhetorical force of Tom Wolfe's 1973 manifesto, *The New Journalism*, that the use of fictional techniques in journalism was his idea, but it has a much longer history. Novelists and journalists have been borrowing from each other since at least the 18th century. Novelists envy journalists the power of the real and journalists resent the limitations of news, both its rigid form and the shadow of restrictive libel laws. Literary journalists aim to go beyond journalism's facts but stop short of fiction's creations; they fuse the role of observer and maker to find a third way of depicting reality.[8] Some writers have used fictional techniques to examine historic events, with electrifying effect. John Hersey's *Hiroshima* has been mentioned already. When it was originally published it sold out within hours. Broadcast companies in several countries cancelled regular radio broadcasts on four successive evenings to read aloud the whole article, and the US army ordered reprints for its education service.

Today important newsmakers are guarded by thickets of advisers and flacks; accordingly, many literary journalists opt to explore historic events through the lives and struggles of ordinary people, as Australian writer Anna Funder did in examining the fallout of the collapse of the communist regime in East Germany. Funder documented the Stasi secret police service's obsession with surveilling and controlling citizens' lives; there was one Stasi officer or informant for every 63 people compared to one KGB agent for every 5830 citizens in communist Russia, and Stasi agents collected in bottles samples of people's smell in the bizarre belief that smells, like fingerprints, could be used to identify alleged criminals. In a series of remarkably empathic interviews with ordinary East Germans, Funder showed the devastating effect on their lives. She told the story of a woman forced to choose between informing on a man helping others to get over the Berlin Wall and reuniting with her severely disabled baby boy, who was receiving treatment in a West German hospital. She refused to be an informer, was tortured, then imprisoned for four years. Funder comments:

> It is so hard to know what kind of mortgage our acts put on our future. Frau Paul had the courage to make the right decision by her conscience in a situation where most people would decide to see their baby, and

tell themselves later they had no choice. Once made though, her decision took a whole new fund of courage to live with. It seems to me that Frau Paul, as one does, may have overestimated her own strength, her resistance to damage, and that she is now, for her principles, a lonely, teary guilt-wracked wreck.[9]

Frau Paul helped numerous people escape to West Germany but did not see herself as brave, which to Funder was the most tragic element of her tragic story: 'that the picture she has of herself is one that the Stasi made for her'.

Magazines are the seedbed of literary journalism; they provide a bridge between daily journalism and books, giving writers the time and space to learn the narrative skills needed to hold a reader's interest through 10 000 or 15 000 words. The United States has long had a strong culture of magazine journalism. So too has the United Kingdom; *Granta*, as Oxford literature professor John Carey noted, has published 'some of the most powerful journalism of recent years, transmitting excitement and intelligence that would be hard to match'. It is common for lengthy magazine articles to be expanded into books, such as Malcolm Gladwell's *The Tipping Point*, and increasingly common for literary journalists to conceive book-length projects. Barbara Ehrenreich's *Nickel and Dimed: On (not) Getting by in America* (2001), and Julie Salamon's *Facing the Wind: A True Story of Tragedy and Reconciliation* (2001) are two recent examples.

Australia has a vibrant magazine industry but, because of the country's vastness and its small population, has been unable to sustain support for the kind of publications that run literary journalism. Magazines such as *Australian Society* and *The Independent Monthly* and weekly newspapers such as *Nation Review* and *The National Times* (all defunct) sometimes ran literary journalism but either did not have the money to support the research time literary journalists need or the know-how to train journalists in this demanding form. It has largely fallen to individual journalists to do their own experiments. Evan Whitton and Craig McGregor were influenced by the New Journalists and their efforts in the 1970s to transplant it to Australia rewarded them both with Walkleys but spurred only a small number of imitators and successors. The rising popularity of literary journalism overseas during the past fifteen years has sparked a renewed resurgence of interest in the form in Australia.

A few writers have published books that could be termed literary journalism, notably John Bryson and Anna Funder, both mentioned earlier, and, controversially, Helen Garner, in her extraordinary but flawed *The First Stone*.[10] A growing number are publishing books, of greater or lesser literary quality. As of 2003 Stephen Mayne's Crikey.com.au website listed more than 200 books written by Australian journalists. In the past decade, newspapers such as *The Age*, *The Sydney Morning Herald*, *The Financial Review* and *The Australian* have run only a few pieces of literary journalism but have made greater use of narrative to tell the stories of major news events in a way that makes sense of them for readers. *The Age* has done this most often, notably with a Walkley award-winning narrative of the Port Arthur tragedy in 1996. *The Australian* has set up a regular feature, 'Inside story', to run less ambitious but still narrative-driven pieces that background news events.

A body of critical literature has been emerging in the past fifteen years or so, developed by practitioners such as Jon Franklin and Mark Kramer as much as by critics. Between them, they have delineated the following elements of literary journalism:

1. Documentable subject matter chosen from the real world as opposed to 'invented' from the writer's mind. This means no composite characters, no invented quotes and no attributing thoughts to sources unless they can be verified.
2. Exhaustive research, whether through conventional sources such as documents and interviews, or by 'saturation' reporting; that is, by immersing yourself in the world of your subject, often for weeks or months at a time, to get beneath surface realities. This implies a higher standard of accuracy.
3. Novelistic techniques, where a bedrock of research makes it legitimately possible to use a range of techniques borrowed from fiction, such as creating whole scenes, quoting passages of dialogue, describing the social milieu in detail and writing interior monologues for subjects (based on interviews with the subject). Literary journalists are restricted mostly to techniques drawn from socially realistic fiction.
4. Voice, which gives the writer freedom to be ironic, self-conscious, informal, hectoring, self-aware, etc. It is mainly through the authorial voice that literary journalists can move beyond a socially realistic portrayal of events and people. Daily journalism is tyrannised by the

institutional voice. Hunter S. Thompson is an extreme example of the individual voice. Sometimes indulgent, he can be highly effective too; one of George McGovern's advisers said Thompson's account of the 1972 presidential campaign was the least accurate and most truthful he had ever seen.[11]

5. Literary prose style, both in the attention paid to structuring the narrative and choosing the words themselves.

6. Underlying meaning. The purpose of all this work and style is to go beyond the constraints of daily journalism and find the underlying meanings in issues and events. This implies greater intellectual rigour in mounting an argument about the subject, even if that argument is embedded in an artfully constructed narrative.[12]

What emerges from this list of elements is that literary journalism stands or falls on the quality of the reporting and research work. Without that, all the finest prose in the world has little meaning. In literary journalism the research is the iceberg, the polished prose its tip. Everybody sees the tip and it can be a truly impressive sight. Bulking below the surface is the iceberg, unseen and largely unknown.

Literary journalists themselves understand the need for strong research. John Hersey interviewed about 40 A-bomb survivors in Japan before choosing six as representative for his *New Yorker* piece; John McPhee traversed the United States several times with geologists before writing *Basin and Range* (1980); John Bryson said his account of the Azaria Chamberlain case occupied him 'day and night' for four years; Adrian Nicole Blanc tracked the chaotic life of a teenage drug-addicted prostitute over two years for a piece in *The Village Voice*; Gay Talese interviewed hundreds of *New York Times* people during two and a half years for his 1969 book, *The Kingdom and the Power*; Ian Jack took the best part of a year to research and write for *Granta* his 20 000-word account of the killing of three IRA terrorists at Gibraltar in 1987; and Ryszard Kapuscinski journeyed 60 000 kilometres through remote villages in the Soviet Union as it collapsed for his 1993 book *Imperium*.

If the reporting work earns literary journalists the freedom to borrow fictional techniques to write the story, there is just one problem: how does the reader know that the events described are real? The simple answer is they do not; they must trust the writer. But some writers are not trustworthy. They envisage all those months of research, gaining people's trust, hanging around waiting for things to happen, recording minute details, asking endless questions and they start to think, 'Why don't I simply make it up?' Or else, they amass all the material and are horrified by the gaps and lumps and mess of real life and are tempted: 'Why don't I make this read better?' The freedom of literary journalists to borrow from fiction to tell their true stories better comes at a price; to keep faith with the reader.

Postmodern literary theory shows us it is important to question notions of the inviolability of objective truth.[13] It is important for journalists to be aware that they bring cultural and psychological baggage to every assignment. It is important to understand that the act of story-telling frames the world in a particular way and portrays people through a particular lens. But all this does not mean journalists should give up trying to find out what is going on in the world and striving to make sense of it and communicating it as widely and strongly as possible.

Paradoxically, literary journalists have more time than colleagues on daily deadlines to ensure a higher standard of factual accuracy surface and to plumb underlying meanings in events, as is shown in Conover's *Newjack* or Funder's *Stasiland*. The key point is that fictional furnishings are built on factual foundations. Labelling a work correctly becomes more important. If a writer wants to blur fact and fiction because they could not get the full story or because it suits their literary purposes, then they should label their work accordingly, and not call it a true story. Muddying these waters confuses or angers readers. As Norman Sims, an American journalism professor, wrote:

> As a reader, I react differently to literary journalism than to short stories or standard reporting. Knowing this really happened changes my attitude while reading. Should I discover that a piece of literary journalism was made up like a short story, my disappointment would ruin whatever effect it had created as literature.[14]

The use of fictional techniques in journalism offers readers much more than they customarily get and the best literary journalists create pieces that, unlike most daily journalism, stand the test of time. George Orwell's *Homage to Catalonia* is as engaging to read today as it was on publication over half a century ago. But literary journalism requires considerably more skill and work than most daily journalism. It is hard for journalists to master its demands, and it requires substantial time and resources; two things that are increasingly squeezed in newsrooms. If literary journalism seeks to get at the underlying meanings of issues and events, it also makes it far harder for readers to determine what is fact and what is fiction, making it all the more important that its practitioners keep faith with their readers. In a world where spin doctors put more turn on the truth than Shane Warne could ever muster on the cricket field, literary journalism does not pretend to have all the answers. It does, however, ask good questions, and with a persistence and flair that is easily lost in the helter-skelter of daily journalism.

DISCUSSION QUESTIONS AND EXERCISES

1. Where does fact end and fiction begin? Does it matter? Can fact and fiction be blended and if they can what rules, if any, apply?
2. Choose two works of literary journalism, such as Ted Conover's *Newjack* and Anna Funder's *Stasiland*, and ask what the reader gets from these works that is mostly not provided in daily journalism?

HOPE LIVES HERE

by Garry Linnell[15]

While you are driving to work, or mowing the lawn, or picking the kids up from school, a few kilometres from the city, life in Ward 6 East is carrying on as usual. It's a place where lives are fought for, where children laugh and play, and sometimes, they die.

This is the moment you dread the most. Time to go. The day just goes too damn quickly. One minute you're busy working, trying to figure out how to get that bloody wrench unstuck, working out a way to remove the rivets from that gas pump, yarning with your mates, talking about what the Blues might have done this year if Kernahan hadn't copped that hammy and Diesel hadn't been done over by the tribunal again. And then it all stops. Time to go and let the emptiness rise up and take over once more. So you go through the routine. You clock off. You wave goodbye to the others and then you climb into your car and go home. You could just about do this drive in your sleep. The road is flat, the paddocks and fenceline never changing. Nothing to look at, nothing to keep that emptiness at bay. And you know that when you get home Lisa will be feeling the same. You'll walk in the door and say hi and kiss her and she'll ask you how your day was and then she'll go back to being busy, filling in the time, looking for something else to do.

She might go back to painting one of the rooms, making it come alive with color. Or she could be doodling away on some other project, always keeping herself active. Perhaps if she's lucky one of her sisters will ring and they'll sit and talk for ages. But she won't ring herself. It's too hard. She even hates the thought of picking up the receiver and punching in the numbers. Better to wait and let it ring.

Maybe you might go and work out the back. You've started building coffee tables, anything to keep your hands busy. You might take the dog for a walk. Perhaps you'll tell yourself that the car was making a strange noise on the way home, so you'll pop the hood and tinker away.

But it's so damn quiet, isn't it? You walk down the hallway, the passage that Lisa just finished painting a beautiful rich yellow with stencils high up the sides, and there's not a bloody toy to stand on or trip over. There's no cartoons blaring on the television. And when you go outside and get the ladder out to check something just beyond your reach, there's no one to scramble up it before you, to see what the world looks like from six feet up, no one tugging at your trousers wanting you to look at that snail over by the rock, no one wanting to hold

a hammer like you do, to punch a nail into some wood. No one wanting to be just like you.

There is a spa outside. It's one of your pride and joys. You used to sit there with him and enjoy the rhythmic push of the water. You couldn't get him out of the bloody thing, could you? He could stay in there for what seemed like hours until his skin wrinkled up. You'd sit there and talk about all sorts of stuff, just you and him.

The boys. For months Lisa couldn't even stand looking at the spa. She moved her eyes away whenever she had to walk past it.

But sometimes at night you go outside and turn it on. All alone, you slide into the warm water and let it wrap itself around your hefty frame. Then you look up into the night and you talk to him. You tell him about the day you had, about all the things you did to fill in the time, about all the thoughts that flashed through your mind, their noise filling the void and cancelling out the quietness.

How long has it been? Two, three months? You and Lisa do whatever you can to get by. But at night there is no escaping it. In the darkness you lie next to each other and listen to the sound of one another breathing. And as you drift off, you wonder: How long does it last? How long will it take before this aching emptiness fades, even a little?

But you know the answer even before you fall asleep. When you wake the next morning, it will still be there. It always is.

Why the hell does he keep touching him there? Thomas is lying on the bed, half scared, half curious. Graeme and Lisa Bottoms keep exchanging nervous glances. The doctor continues pushing and prodding the three-year-old boy's body. He bends Tom's knee, checks his hips. But always he keeps returning to his stomach, pressing on its left side, looking more concerned with each passing minute.

Last night they were celebrating Graeme's birthday when Tom's limp had come up in the conversation. Ever since early August, when he went down with the flu for a week, he hadn't been his usual self. He'd started favoring one leg but, as usual, he never complained. He didn't seem to be in pain but then, you never could tell with Tom, anyway. He was a tough little kid. He could fall over and hurt himself and, like any three-year-old, have a quick cry. But a cuddle would soon repair the damage and he'd be off again, captivated once more by everything going on around him.

They had been up to Moama just recently. Graeme had gone fishing and, as usual, Tom had tagged along. These, thought Graeme and Lisa, were the best of times, even if your fishing line ended up a tangled mess. It was getting hard for the two of them to remember what life had been like before Tom had been born. It was true what they said. When you had a child everything changed. Those dreary, mundane things that envelop adulthood, the hassles at work and the bills stuck on the fridge, no longer seemed that important. No perfume in the world could compare with the scent of your own son. Fleeing from the terrors of a toddler nightmare, he would wedge himself between the two of you in bed and fall asleep, his soft breath falling gently on your face. And you would hold him there, protecting him from the darkness, even as his knees dug into your ribs.

The limp refused to go away. The local doctor had ordered an X-ray on his knee but that failed to find anything. On the Saturday night in early September, as they celebrated Graeme's birthday, a relative said it probably wouldn't hurt to take him to the Royal Children's Hospital. Now, here they were the next day, and things were going from bad to worse. At first they had suspected a slight hip displacement. And then the doctor had suggested that, while they waited for the X-rays, he should give Tom a closer examination.

That's when he found the lump in his stomach. The next few hours passed by in a blur. Late in the afternoon, Graeme and Lisa were taken aside and told Thomas would have to be admitted to the hospital's Department of Oncology and Haematology. The words were unfamiliar to them. They asked what it meant. It was, they were told, the cancer ward for children.

The large lift took them to the sixth floor and a new kind of hell. There, they turned right and entered 6 East. It was late on Sunday afternoon when they led them into room 2 and found a bed for Thomas. Lisa looked around. Across the room, a young girl with a bald head was jumping up and down on her bed. Apart from the baldness, Lisa thought she looked fine. Perhaps things were not as bad as she thought. The girl kept jumping. Higher and higher she leapt, until her nightie flew up around her. And that's when the sense of dread building within Lisa Bottoms reached critical point. "Oh my God," she thought. The girl had a tube sticking out of her stomach.

Over the next few days they pummelled and prodded Thomas's body to find out what was wrong. There were more ultrasounds and blood samples taken, and a bone marrow aspiration where a nurse had to curl Tom into a ball while a doctor inserted a needle into a bone in his hip to take a sample. Lisa didn't know whether to walk right up and pull the nurse off her boy, or leave the room.

By Wednesday they knew enough. They called Lisa and Graeme into a small room overlooking Royal Park and told them what was wrong with their boy. He had stage four neuroblastoma, with a tumor the size of a softball, and its cancerous cells had spread throughout his body. There was only a 20 per cent chance of Thomas making it into remission.

That night, Lisa and Graeme took Tom home with them. Uncomplaining as usual, he drifted off to sleep between them.

That was then. This is now. June, 1997, and a place where hope begins, and sometimes ends. In a darkened room with the curtain drawn around their bed, the mother sleeps with her daughter. The girl is young, barely turned two and still carrying baby fat in her face. She is at one end, lying awkwardly with her head off the pillow, breathing heavily. At the other end of the bed, the mother is drawn up in a foetal position, dark hair hanging loosely across her face, head slumped on her left arm.

The sun is yet to rise and the lights are low in 6 East. Mother and daughter, scared and exhausted, sleep deeply. For the past two days since her daughter's diagnosis with leukaemia, the mother has given the staff more concern than the child. Throughout the day she sits by the side of the bed, child in her arms, and rocks back and forth, staring out the windows. Family members come, sit in silence, and then go. She says little, and cries a lot.

This morning, though, someone else is crying. In the bed on the other side of the room, Thomas is whimpering. Huddled beneath a blanket, a cap warming his bald head, he sobs, and it seems every shudder sends a ripple through his body. Graeme, slumped in a chair next to the bed, rubs his reddened eyes, leans over and picks up his son. The blanket falls away and for a moment you catch your breath. His legs are like sticks, crudely poking out from the nappy he has been forced to wear when the treatments and tubes running in and out of his body made going to the toilet impractical.

The fight has been going on for more than nine months now. In January surgeons removed the tumor and one of his kidneys. The tumor, they discovered, was crusted and effectively dead. Repeated courses of chemotherapy had almost killed it off and, for the first time, there was hope. Tom started the first term of kindergarten and seemed to be getting back to his old self. But if there was one thing Lisa couldn't do with Tom, it was to convince him to give up sucking a dummy. Tom called them his "nings" and he boasted an impressive collection.

She'd had to put her foot down on the first day of kinder and there had been a scene. Tom wanted to take a ning with him. Lisa remained steadfast. No nings.

She had worried that, with his bald head and frail arms and legs, the other kids might single him out and pick on him. But he seemed to have no problems until the morning he declared he was not going back to kinder.

"I'm not going," he'd said, defiantly.

"Why?"

"They called me a baby."

Lisa was horrified. It was the bald head, after all. But Tom's appearance had nothing to do with it. Instead, he'd craftily found a way to smuggle a ning to kinder without her knowledge, hiding it in his shoe. And under the rules of the pre-school playground, only babies sucked dummies.

For a short time Graeme and Lisa Bottoms dared to dream that it was over. Somehow, between surgery and the constant chemotherapy, Tom had managed to be home for Christmas, his fourth birthday, Easter and now the first term of kinder. Maybe their luck had changed. But by April things had collapsed again. A bone marrow rescue had left him with ulcers in his mouth, right through his gut. The pain was intense. By the end of the month he had come down with a form of pneumonia and spent a week in the intensive care unit (ICU), drugged out and on a respirator. They almost lost him then. But he'd fought back and now, in June, he was hanging in there.

So, too, were his nings. Spread around his bed were four or five of them. Some of the nurses in 6 East didn't like them. But the nings had stayed, their comfort level far outweighing any danger of germs.

On the wall behind his bed hung a large piece of paper, covered in stickers. Each sticker represented a trip to the ward's treatment room. Now, early on this June morning, he had to go in there again. The hurting room, he called it. As the ward came to life and the staff cleared away breakfast trays and uneaten pieces of toast, Graeme picked Tom up and carried him across the ward to the hurting room. There were fears he might be getting the flu. In 6 East, with chemotherapy lowering your immune system, even a cold could be dangerous. They gathered in the treatment room and Graeme held his son down on a bed. A nurse inserted a tube into his nasal passage and, with Tom kicking and squirming, they kept him down while they attempted to take a sample of mucus to be tested.

When it was over Graeme carried a sobbing Tom back to bed. Not even the offer of another sticker from the unit's manager, Mary McGowan, could produce a semblance of a smile.

Mary McGowan knew all about death. She had grown up in Mohill, a small village in Ireland where everyone knew everyone else. Set among postcard green hills, the McGowans were well known and liked. Harry and Noeleen had done well raising their brood of nine. Mary was the fourth to arrive and had quickly shown the same McGowan pluck and spirit possessed by the clan.

When someone in the village died, a black ribbon was hung on the front door as a sign of respect, as well as a notice to those around that death had visited. Noeleen McGowan, famous for her cooking (she'd been a home services teacher before the job of rearing a large family interrupted her work), was always one of the first to think of the grieving family. Here, she'd say to one of her children. Take this batch of cakes down the street and help out the family. Sometimes Mary would tag along with her parents to visit what they called the corpsehouse. The body was usually kept at home until the funeral, on display for all to pay their respects.

But while she loved the village, Mary McGowan wanted more than Mohill could provide. So, after finishing a nursing course in Dublin specialising in paediatrics, she travelled to Australia. It would be a short, working visit, she thought. Two years at most.

She is still there 19 years later and no one can remember a time when her formidable presence has not been felt in 6 East. "Mary," says someone who works closely with her, "is 6 East." No-one argues with the assessment. As unit manager, she is responsible for budgets, nursing rosters and the well being of a ward that, at times, can house up to 17 patients. But there are things Mary McGowan feels responsible for that form no part of her job description. You can spend days hanging around 6 East, talking to the staff, chatting to the patients and, occasionally, turning away with a feeling of utter helplessness. But every time you look back, Mary McGowan is there, watching and listening.

She holds a conversation with a visitor while overhearing a progress report on a patient. On a bad day, when one of the doctors has had to tell parents that their child is likely to die, or even worse, when they lose a kid after months of working hard to save them, McGowan is on the phone, quietly warning a wife that her husband is on his way home after a bad day in the office and may need some help to get over it.

And sometimes, despite all her bravado and understanding of death, Mary McGowan needs a shoulder to cry on, too. It hasn't happened that often. But, unmarried and with her family on the other side of the world, McGowan has established a support network that is there when she needs it. She has close friends among the coterie groups that help fund 6 East, organisations like Challenge and My Room, as well as a staff that understands when to stay away, and when to buy you a coffee and cry with you.

Two years ago she endured one of the worst moments of her career. Three teenage brothers she had known for more than 10 years died within 10 months of each other, all victims of the same bone-marrow disorder. She keeps a photograph of the boys in her office. In the constant stream of children who enter 6 East and momentarily touch the lives of the close-knit staff, many long-lasting relationships are formed. Barely a day passes without a former patient dropping by, celebrating another milestone in their remission. In an age of improving medical techniques, winners seem more common than losers. But how we deal with death is just as important as how we cope with life. And those three boys, whose parents later separated and who only ever called Mary "Big

Mac", touched McGowan more than she even knew at the time. It was one of the twins who was the last to go, and who broke her heart. At the end he weighed just 20 kilograms, his face beset by a tumor. But at night, Big Mac made her way out to his home and spent hours massaging and rubbing his frail body. "That's all he wanted," she says. "He just wanted to be touched."

Mary McGowan falls silent. For a brief moment she is back there again. And then, when you ask another question, a phone rings in the distance. A beeper goes off in the hallway. Someone else has called her name. She deals with a query from a nurse and turns back to you. And quickly changes the subject.

In the old days it was sometimes easier, says Dr Keith Waters. Back then, even 20 years ago, you expected everyone to die. If a patient survived leukaemia, or any of the myriad types of childhood cancers, it was a bonus. But in the past two decades remarkable advances have changed the field of oncology and haematology enormously. Generally, 70 per cent of children who suffer lymphatic forms of leukaemia survive. The introduction of chemotherapy, coupled with a greater understanding of how the disease infiltrates and takes over the body, has been one of the great break-throughs of modern medicine. "But," says Waters one morning in his office, "that still leaves 30 per cent . . ."

Waters, bearded and with a soft voice, came to the RCH as a junior resident in 1967 and, apart from a few stints working in the United States and England, has been here ever since. His father was a child of the Depression who worked a variety of jobs to keep his family going, working from seven in the morning and not getting home until midnight. When Keith matriculated, he was not sure what he wanted to do with his life. His mother dragged him around to vocational counsellors where, she was told, he could possibly pursue a career as a doctor. Don't be silly, his mother told them. No one from this family had been to university.

Keith Waters became the first. He decided early to move into the field of paediatrics: "Children were much nicer creatures to deal with," he wryly observed from beneath his beard one day. Then he fell into haematology and oncology by chance. His career has paralleled the huge advances in the field, as well as the human side.

He recalls, as a young registrar, the enormous debate that raged within the hospital about whether to tell a 14-year-old girl suffering acute myeloid leukaemia that her chances of making it were slim. "It was a big meeting and eventually the decision was taken to tell her."

Since then, and depending on the circumstances, most terminal children at the hospital are told they are unlikely to get better. Over the years, Waters says he has learnt how to build a wall around himself when dealing with the dark side of his job. "I'm fairly lucky I can turn things off these days," he says. "But every staff member has had their experiences, where one child or family has been their favorite. Everyone has."

For David Sutton, that one favorite came along a year ago and triggered one of the worst times of his life.

He slouches in a chair in the staff room in 6 East, nursing a cup of tea and rubbing the sleep out of his eyes. Sutton, one of the deputy unit managers of 6 East, is in his mid-40s with three teenagers. There is a touch of middle-age spread about him and a head of hair that looks like it could turn completely unruly with just a breath of wind. Born in England, he grew up near Liverpool. When he was 14, the old man decided the family should move to Australia, away from the chemical industries and densely populated streets. When Sutton left school after matriculation he joined the railways, working in the accounts branch with a group of other men who talked about footy a lot and went to the pub.

Then, at 26, his wife left him for another man. As he started getting his life back together he decided it was time for a change. He enrolled as a nurse and wondered why he hadn't done it sooner. Now, what had once seemed like a chance roll of the dice has become a fully-fledged mission. He is working on a Master's degree in paediatric palliative care. And what he has seen over the past 19 years will form the basis of it.

"The kids themselves don't really stress you," he says. "You've just got to learn to deal with it. You put it on like an overcoat in the morning and then you take it off at night, it's a little like putting up a wall. We build up little defensive things, all of us, little ways to deal with it. But sometimes you get these holes in the wall. And some kids, they just don't see that line, they just come crashing through and you've got no control over it. There's absolutely nothing you can do about it ... it's no problem when they're winners. But when they're losers, if they have a rough time, that's when it really hurts."

After a time, says Sutton, you get good at knowing when a kid comes your way who plans to crash through that defensive wall. "There's kids that just get under your skin. I suppose it's like friends. Why do you click with some people and not others? And you can't turn away. How could you? You have to accept it. If they go, it's going to hurt."

And along she came. She was six years old and had been through 6 East the year before with leukaemia. The treatment appeared to have worked fine. But her immune system was low. She arrived back at the hospital suffering a fungal infection. It had begun with just an innocent red, sore eye. Within days the untreatable fungus had eaten into her nose and begun working its way towards her brain. "The surgical options were to take her face off, which for a six-year-old really wasn't an option," he says. "She needed a lot of analgesia and sedation."

Sutton promised her parents he would not let her suffer. On the Wednesday, three days before she died, she wrote Sutton a letter. "Dear David," it said in its scrawled, first grade handwriting. "Thank you for looking after me so good."

It was, says Sutton, the most precious thing he had ever been given. By Friday she was totally blind. Her parents told her she was not going to get any better. "We talked a lot about hastening the end," says Sutton. "People bury their heads in the sand when they talk about kids and dying. There's no way the legal world is capable of handling it. It was a shit experience. One of the hardest things I've ever had to do."

The girl's death was just the beginning of a crisis for Sutton. After returning home from a nursing conference in Vienna with his wife, his father collected them from the airport. When they got home, his father got out of the car and dropped dead in the driveway from a massive heart attack.

Each year Sutton made the trip to Warrnambool to go camping with a large group of family and friends. As they did on many nights, a group of them gathered in a large communal area that summer to share a beer on a warm evening. There was a guy sitting there they didn't really know. The conversation had turned to a series of police shootings and the stranger, fuelled by a few too many beers, was ranting about how, in some circumstances, police should be allowed to shoot first, and ask questions later.

Sutton lost it. Almost two decades of living and working alongside death, of watching a helpless six-year-old girl die, of being unable to do a damn thing, boiled up inside him. He railed into the night, abusing the stranger.

Did he have any idea, demanded Sutton, what it cost, emotionally and physically, to stand by and help someone to die? Didn't he realise what effect it had on your soul? Shoot first and ask later? A person's life, and how it ended, should not be decided on the spot.

The room fell quiet as Sutton stood there, his anger spent. Then, after a few more moments of awkward silence, they started talking about the weather and

the cricket. Sutton went back to brooding and wrestling with his demons.

Early on a chilly morning, as the lights of the cars begin to slowly fill Flemington Road, Mary McGowan takes you into the Batcave. Nicholas Marian is dying in there, and he wants to go home.

For almost two years, the 11-year-old has been fighting a desmoplastic tumor. Largely untreatable, he has spent almost all that time in and out of hospital. Even the chemotherapy has been rough. A drug that in recent years has taken away the side effect of nausea from most patients had no effect. How often had his mother, Margaret, spent nights in a chair next to him, listening to his breathing, waiting for its rhythm to change and then, instinctively, holding out a bowl in front of him to catch his vomit? At home, she and his father, Tony, have a series of videos recording the past two years. There he is, just nine years old, a few days after coming home from school complaining he wasn't feeling well, about how his T-shirt no longer fitted him. Just a few days after his diagnosis, he has a couple of friends around to play computer games. He lifts his T-shirt to the camera and shows off his stomach, his friends looking on curiously. There, sticking out on the left side, is a large tumor pressing against his belly. He shrugs his shoulders, pulls his shirt back down and the trio of young boys turn back to the video game.

Fast forward. Here he is as his first chemo treatment takes effect. Look how he can pull lumps of hair out of his head. Then, just a week later, he is almost bald, standing in the kitchen, sucking the helium out of balloons with a family friend and laughing uproariously at the squeaky voices he can manufacture.

A life flashes by. He arrives at school one morning in a police car, courtesy of the Make A Wish Foundation. Then he's at Moorabbin Airport, taking a ride in a helicopter.

But in the Batcave in 6 East this morning, a specially-sealed area with treated air to lessen the risk of infection, he finds it hard to smile. An hour ago, Margaret had sat with him in his darkened room and talked about how he wasn't going to get any better. Did he want to stay here, or did he want to go home? "I want to go home," he said, softly. "I've got things to do."

Margaret stepped outside the Batcave soon after. Maureen Mash, one of 6 East's auxiliary staff and a constant presence in the ward, walked up and instinctively put her arm on Margaret's shoulder. "How is he?" she asked.

"He's OK. I've told him he's not getting any better. He had a tear in his eyes then he noticed a birthday present someone had given him ... he wanted to get into that. He's okay. He knows."

Now Mary McGowan is in Nick's room. If he's going to go home, then he will need to take a special pack with him he can wear around his hip. It will automatically inject a painkiller into his system to keep the agony away. Nick isn't too sure. But when Mary tells him it's just like a Walkman, he brightens. He'll take it. There's a basketball match on that night he wants to see. And besides, he needs to get home. Has to. There are things that an 11-year-old boy has to do.

Mary steps out of the Batcave and walks back to the nurse's station. There's a message waiting for her. They're calling from downstairs. They have another child waiting to be admitted. Do they have a bed? "Oh, God, here we go again," she mutters. Mary looks up at the board already filled with names, and starts making mental calculations. She needs to find another bed. Can they wait until Nick leaves?

Wednesday, 18 June. Late afternoon. Lisa Bottoms is at home, trying to rest, when the phone rings. "I think you'd better come up," says Graeme. "They're going to put Tom in ICU."

Lisa feels her stomach tighten. She had known this moment might come, but not now. On Monday he had been struggling with his breathing. And even though he had just turned four, he sensed that the struggle could not go on for much longer. He'd managed to lean over and tell her: "I'm not going to get any better, Mummy." The fight had taken too much out of him. The results from his swab showed an infection, and on Tuesday he'd been moved into an isolation room, away from the other kids.

By early Wednesday afternoon, Dave Sutton was growing impatient. Mary was in the United States looking after a group of teenagers in remission on a trip sponsored by Challenge, the children's cancer support network. Sutton was in charge, and he needed to get Thomas to intensive care. But, as usual, they were waiting for a bed.

At home, Lisa jumped in the car and rushed towards the hospital. She would barely remember the journey later; whether she went through red lights, or how she got to the hospital in record time, weaving her way through the traffic, oblivious to everything except this urge, this need, to be with Tom.

She got there with moments to spare. Tom had barely moved in his bed in the past 24 hours. But as Lisa rushed into the room, he felt her presence and moved, instinctively, toward her. She leaned over and kissed him. And as he leaned back, Graeme and Lisa watched the life of their four-year-old boy seep away. He was gone.

For a moment they didn't realise what had happened. "Why does he look so funny?" Lisa asked Sutton.

A code-blue alert went out around the hospital, the signal that a patient's heart had arrested. Clarion bells sounded. Doctors rushed through doors and within moments a team was at work on his lifeless body. Sutton picked Tom up and rushed him into the hurting room, bumping past a bewildered man, standing there with his young, leukaemic son waiting to be admitted to the ward. For 40 minutes they worked on Tom, injecting him with adrenalin, pumping his tiny chest, putting a tube into his lungs to help him breathe, pleading with him to come back. At one stage they got his pulse going, but it faded again.

It was the most public of deaths. 6 East was at its busiest, filled with visitors just after dinner time. Now it was quiet, the ward stunned by the suddenness of it all. There was no chatter. Even the constant hum of televisions and radios seemed to have disappeared.

Dave Sutton helped clean Tom up and remove his tubes. Then he left Graeme and Lisa with their boy. For the next few hours they sat with him and said goodbye. Graeme dressed his son in his nicest clothes, making sure his nings were nearby.

Lisa didn't want to leave him there like that. In all the long months they had spent since that first, horrible Sunday at the hospital, Tom had hardly been left alone. One of them had always been nearby. She didn't want to leave him alone, not down at the morgue. It was no place for a four-year-old boy to be on his own.

But finally they left. Graeme and Lisa Bottoms went home to an empty house and that hole inside them began to grow.

The next morning, Sutton arrived at work to find Danielle, a seven-year-old leukaemia patient, waiting for him in the hallway.

"Where's Tom?" she asked.

"He's gone to another place," replied Sutton.

"Where?"

"Well, he died and he went to Heaven last night."

"No he didn't. He went to ICU."

"No," replied Sutton. "He was very sick yesterday. And there wasn't anything else we could do for him to help him. He died and went to Heaven."

Sutton walked into Mary McGowan's empty office and slumped into a chair. "She already knew he was dead," he announced, staring out the window, looking at nothing, feeling tired and down, like everyone else. "If she hadn't known, she wouldn't have asked the question. They won't ask you a question like that if they don't really know the answer because they're frightened what the answer might be."

Sutton ran a large hand through his hair and pondered the minds of the young kids in the ward outside. "If they're going to ask you something tough, kids pick the moment when you are at your weakest, your most vulnerable. You might be rushing past them, someone might have soiled their bed or thrown up all over the place, and you're trying to clean it up, and some kid sitting up in bed or walking past will say: 'Am I going to die?'

"And they'll look for that one flashing sign, that one moment when you even hesitate for a brief second. And then you say, 'No, of course not.'"

Outside, 6 East was the quietest it had been in weeks. Some of the young nurses, just fresh out of university, remained stunned at the previous day's events. The unit's social workers were about to hold a meeting of parents to talk about Tom's death, and how they should deal with it.

Dave Sutton looked as though the last thing he wanted to do was walk out that door and go back to work. He stopped talking for a moment and glanced out the window again. It was a cold morning in Melbourne and there was a hint of fog in the distance.

"You know," he said, shaking his head and bunching the corners of his mouth into a tight crease, "It's an enormous amount of time and energy . . . and it feels like it was wasted. Someone is just dead. And you think of some of the arseholes out there walking around healthy."

Tom's funeral. What do you say about a life that lasted four years? You tell them what a life it was. You tell them what the last nine months have been like, not just to remind them of the pain Tom endured, but how tough, how courageous, your son was.

A large bus is parked outside the funeral parlour. It has travelled from Geelong, carrying many of Graeme's workmates from the Shell oil refinery, where he works as an instrument technician. A raffle at work has helped pay for the funeral.

Graeme looks around at this big crowd and forces himself to keep speaking. Don't lose it now, he tells himself. Make it through.

"Thomas, if your mummy and I decide to have a child in the future it is not because we are replacing you, because you are irreplaceable. And it is not because we have forgotten you, for you have left us with many memories that could never be forgotten, memories that your mother and I will carry forever.

"You are at peace and rest now, son. No more hospitals, no more needles, no more drips, no more pain. Rest well."

Nick Marian lasted longer than everyone thought. Margaret and Tony had set up a bed in the lounge room so they could all be with him. They took turns keeping him company, including Petah, their 14-year-old daughter. Every so often, Dave Sutton dropped by on his way home to check on Nick's progress.

Sutton had always been impressed with Nick's ability on the computer. In 6 East, Nick had been known for his fascination for anything with a knob or a switch. Right through school he had always been ahead of everyone else when it came to computers. It was something handed down from Tony, a high school information technology teacher.

But a week into July, Nick's ability to concentrate on anything had diminished. He was hallucinating, and Margaret, a nurse before Nick's sickness was diagnosed, gave him something to lessen the stress. Some nights the two of them would curl up in bed and have a cry. But in his last couple of days, his wretched body reduced to stick-like proportions, he hadn't had the strength for anything.

One night as they sat with him, Margaret said: "Don't worry. Pop's going to look after you." It was a reference to her father, who had just died at Christmas after his own battle with cancer.

"Yeah, I know," said Nick. "I've seen him. He's come down the stairs."

It was not an uncommon experience. Several kids who had endured cancer, and lost, had reported seeing other kids they had met in 6 East. There was the time one boy lay at home dying, and suddenly announced he had to go outside and play with the children in the yard. His parents could see no one out there, but they let him go and stand out there anyway. He passed away a short time later.

Nick died at home at 9.30 in the morning, taking a couple of slow breaths before going. Close to 200 turned up at the funeral and after the service, the temperature suddenly plunged several degrees as a cold front swept in. "That's Nick, fiddling with the buttons," someone quipped.

Dave Sutton couldn't make it to the funeral. But he signed a note in a remembrance book. A few weeks after Nick's funeral, Margaret pulled the book out of a large set of drawers and opened it to the page where Sutton had left his final message for Nicholas Marian.

"Before you start twiddling and fiddling with the knobs of destiny, come and see me," wrote Sutton. "There are a few things I'd like changed."

Each week Beth Dunn, a music therapist at the Royal Children's Hospital, joins the children in 6 East for a singalong. Every Thursday morning they struggle in to the playroom, some hooked up to machines, others in gowns and the youngest cradled in the arms of their parents.

Sometimes Dunn has to work hard to get the rhythm going. When you're five years old, bald and bruised, it's tough to get excited about an opportunity to bang a drum. But as Beth Dunn peels off the songs on her acoustic guitar, they gradually warm to the occasion.

On a recent Thursday morning they gathered once more in the play room and Beth, seated in a small child's chair, took them through their paces. The sound of percussion and strings echoed into the hallways of 6 East and everyone not in the room, the auxiliary staff, the nurses and some of the parents, stopped and listened.

"Goodbye . . . goodbye . . . goodbye," sang Dunn, her soft voice carrying the choir of wispy-haired, pale-faced children around her.

". . . goodbye . . . we'll see you again."

In the crowded doorway, nurses, parents and helpers stood and smiled and joined in the chorus.

THE STORY BEHIND THE STORY

Garry Linnell

I had been deputy editor of *The Sunday Age* for more than two years by 1997 and I was starting to get the itch to write again. The paper's editor, Jill Baker, had seen an American documentary about a hospital ward where the children had cancer and she wanted us to do a similar story. She approached two of the feature writers who said no, which is rare. They felt the subject was too difficult. One morning Jill and I were talking about the story and I said why don't I have a go.

Just about the only time you see kids with cancer in the media is the annual Royal Children's Hospital appeal where you see pictures of smiling, bald children. It projects a strange, clean, sterile view. Like, it's okay because I'm having my photo taken with an AFL footballer. And it is not like that at all. You walk into that ward and there is a child crying in the corner and someone else has shat their bed.

I set up a meeting with the head of the nursing department and the hospital's PR officer; they were interested and I went in the following week and just stood watching, lurking, trying to be invisible. I was gobsmacked by what I saw. For the next four weeks I would snatch a morning here, or an evening when I could get away from the paper. I became just this guy who was always there, which is what you need. There were no deadlines for the piece, which was the beauty of it. There was no rush, because the story was not tied to a particular event.

All the time you are meeting children and their families you are looking for a good storyline to follow and I felt really ghoulish about it, but I did not get one family knocking me back for an interview, which is unusual. But I think it was because the parents are at the hospital all the time and they are so stressed and they are just craving to tell someone about how they feel and about their child who is the most important thing in the world to them.

Something came up at work that distracted me from the story for a couple of weeks and in that time the two children—Tom and Nick—had died and so I had to go back and reconstruct how they had died. I went out to see their families and I spent hours with them. I would interview them and then I'd turn off the tape and they showed me round the house and what Tom used to do. That was when I got all these really strong details, like about the father sitting in the spa at nights and Tom climbing the ladder and the mother distracting herself from the silence in the house by decorating all the time. One family showed me all these home videos. The other family I saw about two weeks after their son had died and talking to them really affected me. I was driving home in the car and I was crying most of the way. As soon as I got home I sat down and wrote 700 to 800 words and that is the first section of the story. It just poured out.

At this point, though, I was starting to suffer information overload. I knew I had to write the whole story. I had to get away from home and take the phone off the hook, so I disappeared down the coast and started writing at 10am and finished at 1am. Then I had a few hours sleep, got up and did the editing and refining. The key to it was finding the right voice. Too often journalists kill terrific stories by overhyping them. They try and manipulate the reader by reminding them all the time how sad things are. I tried to almost understate the tragedy—I never wanted to use that word in the story. I just really wanted people to feel like I did.

There were things I had to leave out because I had collected so much material. I had interviewed half a dozen other families so I knew that the families I had written up were representative and that they had the strongest stories to tell. But also, the issue of child euthanasia came up. I knew I could have had a news story but I also knew one news story would wipe out the whole feature. That sounds a strange thing to say, but I knew that if I got right into that issue, it would take over the whole story and then after a few days it would all disappear because that's what happens in the media. I didn't want there to be any question marks hanging over the deaths of the children and I felt I owed that to the families. This story was about two ordinary children who died of cancer and that is terrible and let's think about what that means for them and their families.

Anyway, I talked over this issue with Jill Baker and a couple of other senior writers and they agreed with me. Jill liked the story and wanted to run it in the paper's new magazine, *Sunday Life!*, which is a lifestyle magazine but we wanted it to have some serious journalism as well. The editor-in-chief, Steve Harris, told Jill he felt it was too much of a downer to have in the magazine and wanted to run it in the 'Agenda' section. Anyway, the story ran in the magazine and it had an amazing response. I received 30 to 40 letters, which is more than I have ever received before or since (except for a *Good Weekend* piece I wrote about creationists—enough said). People said they were physically moved and cried. A couple of people said they couldn't even finish it, which some might take as a compliment but I was disappointed because as a journalist you want them to finish your article!

It is a harrowing piece to read, and early on I wondered whether to include a story about a child going into remission, but in the end I decided that would muffle the impact of the story. While the piece was being edited, actually, Lisa Bottoms (Tom's mother) rang to tell me she was pregnant and I decided against putting that in too, because it was very early in the pregnancy and how would it be if she miscarried, and also because I didn't want the easy way out. The piece ends quite downbeat. The music therapist is singing with the kids, but the singing is pretty desultory. I wanted it to be like the ending of that Beatles song, 'A Day in the Life', which is a long piano note that goes on and just finishes, like that.

APPENDIX

A PROFILE OF ROBIN KLEIN
(Unedited version of published story on pages 218–22)

CHILDREN love jigsaw puzzles, the pleasure of sifting and sorting all the pieces, the satisfaction of seeing it all finally fall into place. Occasionally, though, someone will come along and upend the whole thing, scattering pieces all over the place.

Robin Klein is one of Australia's best loved children's authors; two years ago she suffered an aneurism in her brain and has not written a word since. She has slowly retrieved some pieces of her mental jigsaw but not all. Some may be lost forever.

HUNCHED at her desk at 12.20 one spring night in 1999, Robin Klein watched the scurrying figures on her computer screen as they built fortifications for their next battle in 'Age of Empires'. She was not as expert in the game as her 32 year old daughter Ros, but she couldn't resist its temptations, playing for four hours at a stretch.

The book she was writing actually drew on her fascination with castles and in one of the computer game's scenarios a boy living in a medieval castle had to rescue a princess imprisoned in the castle by invaders. She would write up to 25 drafts of a book before showing it to her editor at Penguin, Julie Watts, and this one was only a couple of drafts away.

Suddenly, Klein let out a cry and clutched the left side of her head as a searing pain gripped her. It was as if someone had lit a match inside her head. Klein was 63 and her four children were all grown up but fortunately the youngest, Ros, still lived at home. She came quickly into the study of their home in the Dandenong Ranges on Melbourne's outskirts; her mother was in pain but with no obvious cause she was unsure what to do. If it had been a gunshot wound to the stomach, Ros wryly thought, she would have known as shortly before she had been training for the Army Reserve.

'Call an ambulance,' Klein said and they arrived soon after the call was made, rushing her to intensive care at the Alfred hospital where she spent three weeks. Initially the family feared she might die but she gradually began recovering, spending a month in the William Angliss hospital in Ferntree Gully before being transferred to a specal accommodation home, Dunelm.

Family and friends who visited her during this period say Klein had little short term memory, even though she could still recall childhood events of 50 years before. She actually seemed often to be mentally back in her childhood, as she recalled recently in an interview with *Good Weekend*: 'I remember being very confused. One minute I was a little kid rocking a doll to sleep, the next minute I was getting married in a church in all my wedding finery.

'I remember thinking, "what's going on? I'm bumping all over the place." I knew something had happened but not really what had happened. It was a bit like watching yourself on a film.' In this film, she was still a writer, her imagination ceaselessly roaming, and sometimes taking a storyteller's licence; her recollection of wedding day finery exaggerated her then modest means.

But she would not be able to write novels any more, as she told her longtime agent, Tim Curnow, when he visited her after the aneurism. 'I'm sorry I can't write books for you. I've got to write army training manuals now.'

Living in the special accommodation home, with its nurses, rules and patients heightened Klein's imagination. Her father had fought in the first World War and been wounded and her daughter Ros recently had been training for the Army Reserve. Her novel-in-progress had a martial theme. She began thinking the novel could revolve around an 11 year old growing up in an Army training camp run by his parents.

Perceptions of her state were blurred further by her storyteller's habit of exaggeration; her recollection of a fine wedding day dress were at odds with her meagre means at the time.

For several months Klein's mind drifted between her imaginary world, her memories and the real world. Those close to her were distraught. She was no longer in danger of dying but she was no longer the Robin they knew. The Robin they knew loved nothing better than writing; she had once told Julie Watts she used to feel ill if more than a few days passed without her writing anything.

When the *Good Weekend* met Klein in 2001 for the first of two interviews, she had not written anything for months. She has recovered enough to have moved out of Dunelm and in with her son Michael and his family in Menzies Creek near her former home in Belgrave. She could not move back home because she needed full-time care and Ros was a full-time student.

We met at her old home, where Ros still lives, now alone. 'Rose Cottage' is an old timber house set on a steep slope; what looks like a single storey house is two storeys, with the second level built down rather than up. Sizeable windows on all sides offer views of the lush Dandenongs.

To a stranger, Klein shows no signs of the effects of her aneurism. A small birdlike woman with a surprisingly unlined face, she chats in the lounge room while her daughter brings in tea and muffins. She slips back into sharp-edged banter she and Ros engaged in for the many years they shared the house after her other three children had left home.

Weeks later, though, watching an education video made about her in 1997, I was struck by how she actually looks better now than then. Paradoxically, since the aneurism she has shed weight, no longer suffers from migraine headaches and most remarkably of all, has sloughed off the arthritis that plagued her for many years. Where it had once hurt her fingers so badly just to type that she experimented (unsuccessfully) with a voice activated computer, now the fire-like pain has gone.

'So that aneurism was a good thing,' she says seemingly without irony. Ros laughs bitterly, while Michael Klein, who has driven his mother over for the interview, shifts his seat on the couch.

She shows no signs of anxiety about being interviewed, something that once would have given her kinniptions. She is naturally reclusive and grew more so as the years went on. She would do interviews only if her publishers insisted, and although she enjoyed the adulation of her young readers, she always looked for an excuse to call off a school visit. 'Can't we say my arm's in plaster and I won't be able to sign any autographs, so I'd best not come,' Ros recalls her mother saying on more than one occasion.

Her shyness is one reason she is not as well known as she could be—she is out of step with the current yen for the writer as performer—but the other, more important, reason that few outside her immediate circle know of Klein's illness is that adults rarely take any notice of children's books—with the obvious exception of a certain bespectacled trainee wizard. J.K. Rowling's *Harry Potter* series is that rare phenomenon, a children's book that has crossed over into the adult world, selling 120 million copies worldwide in just four years.

The all-encompassing hype surrounding Rowling's books and the film adaptation disguise the invisibility of the children's book world before and even since *Harry Potter*. Other children's authors are treated as if they really did live at the bottom of the garden and eat fairy bread, according to Nadia Wheatley who has won prizes for her books for teenagers but is best known for her biography of Charmian Clift.

If it is not surprising then that few people have heard of Klein, what is surprising is that bestselling Australian children's author Paul Jennings believes Klein 'has contributed more to helping Australian children read than J.K. Rowling yet you hardly ever see her name in the newspaper.'

This is a big claim, and may not be supported by raw numbers—more copies of the first *Harry Potter* book were sold in Australia last year than any other title in any other year, according to Australian Publishers Association figures—but it is certainly true that Klein has written many popular books over many years and deserves far more recognition in the wider community.

To begin with, Klein is prolific. Her first book was published in 1978 and she has since written at least 50 more, as well as 100-plus short stories and school readers. She started writing relatively late, when she was nearing 40, and as one of her editors, Rita Hart, recalls: 'She just wrote and wrote. She was so full of ideas.'

Next, Klein is one of Australia's most popular children's authors, alongside Jennings, John Marsden, Morris Gleitzman, Gillian Rubinstein, Graeme Base and Andy Griffiths. In Australia her books published by Penguin have sold over a million copies. Her *Penny Pollard* series, published by Oxford University Press, has also sold well, and her books have been translated into at least seven other languages, including Italian, Spanish and Chinese.

Klein's popularity has endured. Her career predates the other authors. Jennings recalls that in 1986 when he began visiting schools to promote his first book, *Unreal*, 'I was really impressed—and overwhelmed—because every kid's desk seemed to have a copy of *Penny Pollard* on it.' They still do; when the federal government released figures earlier this year about the number of copies of books held in school libraries, 11 of the top 100 books were Klein's.

Many of her books are still in print, which is increasingly rare in the modern publishing world of shrinking back lists. Klein's best known books are *Hating Alison Ashley*, published in 1984 and regarded by children's literature experts like Mark Macleod as a classic of Australian humour and the *Penny Pollard* series, whose first instalment was published in 1983. The sixth instalment was published in 1999 after a 10 year gap; it is Klein's most recent book—and probably her last.

Klein has also won numerous awards, including two Children's Book Council gold stickers, for *Thing* in 1983 and for *Came back to show you I could fly* in 1990. *All in the blue unclouded weather* won a New South Wales Premier's Literary award in 1992. Some of her stories have been adapted for film or television, notably *Halfway across the galaxy and turn left*. She has also won six of the awards voted for by children, including the inaugural YABBA (Young Australians Best Book Award) in 1986 for *Hating Alison Ashley* and most recently one for *The Listmaker* in 1998.

Appealing to both children and judges of literary awards is uncommon, and Pam Macintyre, the editor of *Viewpoint*, a magazine about youth literature, says Klein's willingness to experiment in many different genres, from picture books to books for older teenagers, and from science fiction to poetry, is also uncommon.

Mark Macleod, now children's publisher at Hodder Headline, believes Klein would have won more literary awards if not for a seeming bias against humorous books by the Children's Book Council judges. *Hating Alison Ashley* was shortlisted and should have won, says Macleod, but no humorous novel won a CBC gold sticker until Nick Earls' *48 Shades of Brown* in 2000.

Hating Alison Ashley is, basically, a hoot from beginning to end, written from the perspective of grade six girl Erica Yurken, whose unfortunate name prompts a rash of nicknames—'Erk', 'Yuk' and 'Gherkin'—that constantly undercut her desperate desire to rise above her inelegant surroundings at Barringa East primary and prepare for a glittering career on the stage.

The book has not dated because its appeal has little to do with a stenographic rendering of the latest kidspeak and everything to do with children's experience of school and of certain kinds of teachers and kids. Mention the name Barry Hollis to anyone who has read the book and they're guaranteed to roll their eyes and laugh, because Barry Hollis is a kind of walking pre-testerone minefield who is forever defacing school property, disgracing the schoool on excursions or handing in assignments scratched on the back of an old envelope: 'I never been to a theaer in my hole life and I don't wantto. If I knew any guy lerning ballay I would bash him.'

Erica hates the beautiful, composed new girl Alison Ashley because she is everything Erica aspires to, but the book turns on how each girl learns more about themselves by shedding their prejudices about the other. Alison's life seems perfect, but there are glimpses of problems at home where her professional working single mother can't spare any time for her, while Erica bemoans her chaotic home life, until eventually seeing the genuine affection lurking beneath the casual air of mum and her truckie de facto.

The book's tone is predominantly humorous because the reader is always encouraged to see the gap between reality and Erica's florid self-dramatising. A similar theme is dealt with more poignantly, though, in a more recent book by Klein that is intended for slightly older readers, *The Listmaker*.

Another Australian children's author, Judith Clarke, wrote recently of Klein's unrivalled understanding of 'the adolescent yearning for the perfect, the lovely and romantic, beyond the mundane world of everyday.' Clarke said Klein portrays compassionately the way young people come to terms with their dreams, learning to distinguish between fantasy and truth and discovering the possibilities of both the real world and themselves.

Sometimes Klein peers at these struggles through the prism of comedy and sometimes through drama, the latter most memorably in *Came back to show you I could fly* in which a shy, lonely boy develops an awkward but valuable friendship with a bright but brittle older teenage girl who is a drug addict.

The source of Klein's empathy seems to be her bone-deep recall of her childhood, a quality she shares with many outstanding children's writers. She has retained this despite the aneurism; she remembers her father's throaty laugh perfectly, but, says Ros, could watch the same movie two days running and not remember she had already seen it.

Born in the northern NSW town of Kempsey in 1936, Klein was the eighth of nine children; she had six sisters and two brothers. Her father, Lesley McMaugh, had been wounded while serving in the First World War. He received a war veteran's pension and ran a small family farm, but the family struggled throughout Klein's childhood.

As she breaks off a piece of the muffin to eat, Klein recalls the games she and her sisters made up, like 'Rin Tin Tin with a Rusty Sword' where they would grab the stick from the copper pot, dunk it in the outside dunny and charge around trying to mark each other on the legs.

The game appears in her autobiographical novel about the Melling sisters, *All in the blue unclouded weather,* as does a comment from the sister who most resembles Robin as a child: 'Oh, it was hateful to be poor!' Asked about it, Klein nods emphatically. 'I remember walking along the main street on a Saturday morning shopping and looking in the shop windows with the pretty dresses and I was just consumed with sadness that we couldn't get them.

'Other kids at school would have this lovely kilt dress that was in the window and I knew that would just never happen to us, never. I remember feeling so angry with God for making the world like that. I used to try and work out why God had made the world the way he did, with such unfairness in it.'

She and her sisters were teased about their clothes. '"Oh, you're wearing that funny old dress again," they would say. You'd just keep your face perfectly straight, without flinching a muscle, to show that you did not care. Underneath of course you're dying, but you never show the other kid that.'

The family's poverty left her mother, Mary, little time for showing her children affection. Klein recalls an aunt giving her a cuddle when she was around five or six. 'I thought, "this feels really nice. Why don't mum and dad do this?"'

They did tell their children stories, whether exaggerated accounts of spying missions in the war (Lesley) or the continuing adventures of Mrs Many Children (Mary). There were books in the house, scrambled from second-hand sales and all the family were early and avid readers but there were not enough books to satisfy their curiosity.

Lesley and Mary McMaugh told their children to write their own books, and Robin in particular took them at their word, starting with 'The Beautiful Widow of Perrin's Creek' in primary school. She grew up thinking everyone wrote their own books. She only realised she was different one day in the playground when she replied to a child accusing her of doing nothing, 'Yes I am, I'm trying to work out a story,' and the girl looked at her as if she was mad.

She took refuge from her surroundings by telling herself stories at night or plunging into the imaginary worlds that others like Ethel Turner, and later, Shakespeare and William Golding had created.

Her love of stories made her an oddity in the world; her first job was office work in a grocery wholesaler. She was bored by the routine and the other girls' constant chatter about preparing glory boxes for their wedding day. She would read during her lunch hour, to her workmates' disgust.

After she married Karl Klein, a mechanical engineer, in 1956 (they separated 22 years later, in 1978) and began raising their four children, she found her love of stories a source of enjoyment and power. She loved cuddling on the couch reading to them or making up her own stories; one became her first published book, *The Giraffe in Pepperell Street*. A light went on her head: you mean you can earn a living writing stories.

Few, in fact, can, but fortunately Klein is a gifted storyteller. Between 1979 and 1981 she worked as a teacher's aid at a primary school in a housing commission area in Melbourne's south-east. Many of the students would not be seen dead with a book, but soon the teachers knew that if they sent the aid down the back of the excursion bus her exotic stories of army captains in the war would quell the natives. She laughs as she recalls that her experiences at the school resurfaced in *Hating Alison Ashley*.

This memory prompts another, of later trips on trains where she sat reading her book but was irresistibly drawn to the whispered conversations of nearby teenagers. 'You can't help yourself as a writer, and you never forget a word. You don't feel like you're prying. It's just part of the job.'

Another part of the job has been writing replies to the many letters that children send her; Klein may prefer writing stories to almost anything else and has sometimes found it a chore to set aside a weekend day to write to children, but she feels humble on receiving a letter from a child who says they have taken three of her books to get through a hospital visit.

Ros Klein goes into the study to get a book her mother published some years ago collecting the most memorable letters from children. Some would gladden any writer's heart: 'Our teacher read us your *Penny Pollard* books. It was like an oases in a desert of boredom.' Others were simplicity itself: 'Please write me a story because I have nothing to read.'

A few candidly admitted they were only writing because they had to for a school project, while some children had their teachers pegged: 'Our teacher didn't like Penny Pollard's attitude at first. She usually reads stories with good attitudes in them ("attitude" is her favourite word next to "quiet").' And one child touched on every writer's fear: 'When your mind is wordless, do you get your children to help you?'

Occasionally, she has corresponded with readers. One boy, Jon Appleton, started writing to her from Sydney in 1985 when he was a precociously bookish and bullied 11 year old and received her last letter just months before her aneurism. The letters—there are 36 in all—start with standard author-fan exchanges, but Klein was quick to reassure Appleton that there is nothing wrong with him being different from other boys at school.

'I wish I'd known something when I was your age that I know now and that is: I used to feel such a misfit and so lonely because I didn't fit in, but now I've realised that the state of being lonely is only hungering for your own kind. That's why kids who are popular at school always have plenty of mates around them—there are a lot of them with similar tastes. If you're marching to the sound of a different drum, it takes longer to find kindred spirits because they are in the minority.'

As Appleton grew up, beginning to write himself, going to university and then finding work in publishing (he is now commissioning children's editor for Hodder Headline in the United Kingdom), her anxiety about him eased and she wrote the chatty, casual, candid letters of a friend. It is a beautiful correspondence that Appleton feels privileged to have. Klein laughs as she recalls a day a decade or so ago when Appleton came to Melbourne and she invited him to stay for a few days.

If Klein's memory of a decade ago are still sharp, the edges blur closer to the present. She remains confused about Dunelm, the special accommodation home she stayed in, describing it as an army camp. Michael Klein says, 'It was never an army camp.'

'But the army put me in, didn't they?'

'No they didn't. It was just a hostel where you stayed to recover.'

'And they did get me recovered, did they? Am I a lot better?'

Ros Klein says: 'You're a lot better than you were.'

'Oh thank you . . . you liar. You're lying, aren't you?'

'No, I'm not,' Ros replies.

Her mother laughs and says: 'When she gets that smirk on you know she's lying about something. So I am safe to let out on my own?'

'Maybe,' says Ros with a half smile.

'Oh, god! She's a bitch isn't she,' she says laughing again. 'Some people say to me, how do you get on with your daughter Rosalind? She's a nastly little piece, and she always has been.'

'I learnt it all from you mum.'

Robin turns to me. 'When she was five she used to walk along shopping with me and it'd just be a list of orders that she'd give me on the way up to the shops. "Now you shouldn't wear that blue dress, it makes your legs look bad. You haven't got very good legs anyway." Oh, I used to cop it all. I used to think it was funny so I put up with it.' A pause. 'It's nice to have a daughter who's one of your best friends, though.'

It would be even nicer, for her family, her colleagues and for thousands of children around Australia, if she was fully recovered and writing again.

GLOSSARY

Billboard paragraph: A paragraph placed high in a feature that sets out briefly and clearly the reason why the piece is worth reading. Sometimes the billboard extends over two paragraphs.

Breakouts: Small blocks of text sitting in a box alongside the body of the feature story that provide additional information or explanation about the feature topic. Strong quotes can be broken out from the body of the story too, and reprinted in larger type as a way of drawing readers in.

Briefs: One to two paragraph news items, often gathered in a briefs column.

Close: The end of the feature; in contrast to a hard news story, the close of a feature is an integral part of the story and should not be cut.

Hard news: Fact-based timely information written in formal, neutral language.

Hostile profile: A profile written without the consent of the subject.

Inverted pyramid: The inverted pyramid formula is a way of organising newsworthy information so that the most important information is put in the first paragraph, the second most important information in the second paragraph and so on until the final paragraph.

Lead: A lead is the first paragraph or paragraphs of any piece of journalism, whether hard news or feature story. The aim is always to capture the reader's attention, but where hard news wins readers by providing the most important available information as quickly as possible, features win readers by using a range of storytelling techniques. Once a journalist has decided on the lead for a news story there is only one way to write it; conversely, there are many ways to write a feature lead.

Precede: A few lines sitting between the headline and the lead that are aimed at enticing the reader into the feature story. Sometimes known as the standfirst.

Spill: Some articles begin on one page of the newspaper or magazine and then 'spill' to a later page or pages. In the United States spills are known as 'jumps'.

Standfirst: See precede.

Sub-headings: Like breakout quotes, sub-headings are in larger type than the rest of the feature story and are aimed at making it more appealing visually by breaking up the text.

NOTES

INTRODUCTION

1 D. Conley, *The Daily Miracle*, second edition, Oxford University Press, Sydney, 2002, p. 55.

2 N. Coleman and N. Hornby, eds, *The Picador Book of Sports Writing*, Picador, London, 1996, pp. 275–94, and G. Stout and D. Halberstam, eds, *The Best American Sports Writing of the Century*, Houghton Mifflin, New York, 2000, pp. 574–92.

CHAPTER 1

1 M. Stephens, *A History of News*, second edition, Harcourt Brace, New York, 1997, pp. 246–7.

2 M. Schudson, *The Power of News*, Harvard University Press, New York, 1995, p. 57.

3 For good discussion of this issue, see Stephens, *A History of News*, pp. 246–55, and D. Mindich, *Just the Facts: How 'Objectivity' Came to Define American Journalism*, New York University Press, New York, 1998, pp. 64–94.

4 M. Stephens, *A History of News*, p. 247.

5 Personal communication from Media Entertainment & Arts Alliance secretary Chris Warren, 2002.

6 *Communications Update*, issue 164, April 2002, Media Ownership issue, prepared by the Communications Law Centre.

7 M. Ricketson, 'Newspaper feature writing 1956-1996', in *Journalism: Print, Politics and Popular Culture*, A. Curthoys and J. Schultz, eds, University of Queensland Press, Brisbane, 1999, pp. 168–84. I have also regularly taken random samples of metropolitan daily newspapers from each capital city during 2002 and 2003.

8 F. Bonner, 'Magazines', in S. Cunningham and G. Turner (eds), *The Media and Communications in Australia*, third edition, Allen & Unwin, Sydney, 2002, p. 188.

9 Quoted in 'Small, but perfectly formed', by S. Jackson, *The Australian*, 'Media' supplement, 11 July 2002.

10 F. Bonner, in *The Media and Communications in Australia*, p. 188.

11 B. Griffen-Foley, *The House of Packer*, Allen & Unwin, Sydney, pp. 88–100.

12 M. Day, 'Lies, damn lies and women's mags', *The Australian*, 'Media' supplement, 9 January 2003.

13 J. Schauble, 'China Buries a deadly secret', *The Age*, 31 July 2002.

14 S. White, *Reporting in Australia*, second edition, Macmillan, Melbourne, 1996, p. 11.

15 S. Dickers, ed, *Our Dumb Century*, Crown Publishing Group, New York, 1999, p. 143.

16 H. Garner, *True Stories*, Text, Melbourne, 1996, pp. 145–53 and 223–9.

17 K. Keogh and N. Toy, 'He's the showbiz host who draws the ghost', *The Daily Telegraph*, 3 August 2002.

18 B. Lane, 'History breakers', and D. Cassrels, 'The evolution of Manne', *The Weekend Australian*, 28 December 2002.

19 Quoted in S. White, *Reporting in Australia*, p. 20.

20 C. Pryor, 'Flowers on the bench for man who spent 25 years at a bus stop', *The Australian*, 28 September 2002.

CHAPTER 2

1 M. Fyfe, 'Cruising the red carpet—in search of vital facts on Penelope and Tom', *The Age*, 20 December 2001.

2 C. Tatman, 'Holding on to Hope', *The Bayside Advertiser*, 30 October 2000. Tatman commented on the readers' response in a personal communication with the author in 2002.

3 R. Riley, 'Seb shines', *Sunday Herald Sun*, 17 June 2001.

4 S. Godwin, 'Couple pursues lost herd', *The Weekly Times*, 24 July 2002.

5 C. Egan, 'Inquiry puts justice on trial', *The Australian*, 29 June 2002.

6 M. Steketee, 'Party in a state of confusion', *The Weekend Australian*, 27 July 2002.

7 S. Nolan, 'The rise and rise of lifestyle journalism', *Desktop*, February 1998, pp. 76–80, plus lecture material provided by Sybil Nolan to journalism students at Royal Melbourne Institute of Technology (RMIT).

8 S. Krum, 'Spears chuckers', *The Australian*, 3 January 2003.

9 F. Wheen, 'The deserted village' in S. Glover, ed, *Secrets of the Press: Journalists on Journalism*, Allen Lane, London, 1999, p. 8.

10 No byline, 'The rough with the smooth', *The Guardian*, 4 September 2002.

11 K. Halfpenny, 'Bringing up baby', *Who Weekly*, 17 June 2002, pp. 48–51 and A. Sampson, 'Islam in the suburbs', *The Courier-Mail*, 30 November 2002.

12 Ruth Lamperd, 'Hits and misses', *Herald Sun*, 16 November 2002.

13 I. Jack, ed, *The Granta Book of Travel Writing*, Granta Books, London, 1998, pp. vii–xii.

14 V. Walker, 'Seen but not heard', *The Australian*, 26 October 2001.

15 Barber's journalism has been collected in two books, *Mostly Men*, Penguin, London, 1992, and *The Demon Barber*, Penguin, London, 1999.

16 T. Kunkel, *Genius in Disguise: Harold Ross of The New Yorker*, Random House, New York, 1995, passim, and B. Yagoda, *About Town: The New Yorker and the World It Made*, Scribner, New York, 2000, pp. 133–45.

17 J. Hamilton, 'Father, I never knew you', *Herald Sun*, 21 April 2001.

18 K. Moor, *Herald Sun*, 26, 27 and 30 July 2001. The series was presented under the 'Insight' dinkus and contained several articles on each of the three days.

19 P. Williams, *The Financial Review*, 5-8 March 1996. The book was *The Victory*, Allen & Unwin, Sydney, 1997.

20 A. Rule, 'Geoff Clark: power and rape', *The Age*, 14 June 2001. The news story appeared under the headline 'Rape claims' in *The Warrnambool Standard* on the same day. The comment by the editor, Michael Gawenda, was reported in M. Ricketson, 'The strange case of the stalemated story', *The Age*, 13 December 2001.

21 Quoted in Z. Heller, 'Girl columns', in *Secrets of the Press*, p. 15.

22 P. Bone, 'A harsh sting in the tail', *The Age*, 9 June 1995.

23 Quoted in M. Ricketson, 'The personal columns', *24 Hours*, April 1997, p. 63.

24 Z. Heller, 'Girl columns,' in *Secrets of the Press*, pp. 10–11.

25 H. Marsh, 'Pupils can lose their shine in elite schools', *The Sydney Morning Herald*, 26 July 2002.

26 M. Ricketson, 'Media' column, *Australian Book Review*, July 2001, p. 8.

CHAPTER 3

1 To paraphrase Bono's song 'Dirty Day' from U2's 1993 album, *Zooropa*.

CHAPTER 4

1 J. Cassidy, *Dot.con: The Greatest Story Ever Sold*, Allen Lane, 2002, p. 11.

2 M. Stephens, *A History of News*, second edition, Harcourt Brace, New York, 1997, p. 214.

3 Nobel Prize-winning economist Herbert Simon, as quoted in J. Cassidy, *Dot.con*, p. 116.

4 Fiona Hudson, personal communication with the author in 2002 when she was working as deputy chief of staff at the *Herald Sun*.

5 S. King, *On Writing: A Memoir of the Craft*, Hodder and Stoughton, London, 2000, p. 164.

6 R. Johnson, *Cash for Comment: The Seduction of Journo Culture*, University of New South Wales Press, Sydney, 2000, p. 49.

7 M. Stephens, *A History of News*, p. 4.

8 J. Magnay, 'The bigger they are, the faster he goes?', *The Age*, 28 August 1999.

9 C. King, 'The love machine', *Good Weekend*, 14 August 1999, pp. 55–7.

10 C. Stewart, 'Bandits on the superhighway', *The Australian*, 3 August 2002.

11 N. Bita, 'Illegals wear thin Europe's welcome mat', *The Australian*, 29 July 2002.

12 M. Adams, M. Coyte and R. Luck, 'Dial "M" for Malkovich', *Empire*, May 2003, pp. 52–6.

13 M. Loupis, 'Comedy by design', *Herald Sun*, 14 October 2000.

14 K. Fuller, 'The seven wonders that weren't', *The Weekend Australian Magazine*, 13 October 2001, pp. 27–31.

15 D.D. McNicoll, 'Knowing when to stop', *The Weekend Australian*, 28 August 1999.

16 G. du Venage, 'The lion weeps tonight', *The Australian*, 21 May 2001.

17 D. Graham-Rowe, 'Depleted uranium casts a shadow over peace in Iraq', *New Scientist*, 19 April 2003, pp. 4–6.

18 A. Rule, 'Broken Lives', *The Sunday Age*, 17 October 1999.

19 C. Johnston, 'John's place', *The Age*, 11 August 2001.

20 M. Gross, 'How to get an autograph', *Good Weekend*, 11 August 2001, pp. 32–5.

21 S. Skelly, 'Home truths', *Good Weekend*, 27 July 2002, pp. 36–9.

22 M. Gunn, 'Babysitter's big night in', *The Australian*, 8 June 1999.

23 C. Stewart and V. Carson, 'Winners and losers', *The Weekend Australian*, 24 March.

24 M. Mottram, 'Palmed off: how secret bank business strangled a growing enterprise', *The Sunday Age*, 12 August 2001.

25 D. Brearley, 'To Mammon with love', *The Australian's Review of Books*, March 2001, p. 13.

26 The cartoon by David Sipress was published in the 13 May 2002 issue.

CHAPTER 5

1 For this point, I am indebted to Sybil Nolan, formerly an editorial executive at *The Age* and a journalism lecturer.

2 P. Boyer, 'The emperor of ice', *The New Yorker*, 12 February 2001, pp. 59–69.

3 J. Madden, 'Silver service from now on for super-roo LuLu', *The Australian*, 23 September 2003.

4 W. Blundell, *The Art and Craft of Feature Writing*, Plume, New York, 1988, p. 20.

5 B. Montgomery, 'The man who killed smallpox', *The Australian*, 21 August 2002.

6 L. Younes, 'Autism: families living in limbo', *The Canberra Times*, 3 August 2002.

7 W. Blundell, *The Art and Craft of Feature Writing*, pp. 27–9.

8 This section draws on W. Blundell, *The Art and Craft of Feature Writing*, pp. 69–76, and on the teaching work of a RMIT colleague, Sybil Nolan.

9 G. Linnell, 'Stand and deliver', *Good Weekend*, 2 November 2002, pp. 18–22.

10 P. Bone, 'This man raped two little girls. His victims were forced to relive what happened to them over and over again. This is called justice', *The Age*, 10 August 2002.

CHAPTER 6

1 *The Economist* (no byline), 'Bilked at birth, scarred for life', reprinted in *The Australian*, 28 September 2002.

2 Quoted in M. Ricketson, 'When we are myths: the quest for Ali the man,' *The Age*, 25 March 2002.

3 M. Ricketson, 'Survivors of the Holocaust', *The Age*, 20 February 1995.

4 P. Ellingsen, 'The true story of true crime,' *The Age*, 30 October 2002.

5 G. Orwell, *The Road to Wigan Pier*, Victor Gollancz, London, 1937, reprinted by Penguin, 1962, p. 39.

6 B. Weaver, 'The computer as an essential tool', in *Journalism: Investigation and Research*, Stephen Tanner, ed, Longman, New South Wales, 2002, p. 62.

7 J. Waterford, 'The editor's position,' in S. Tanner, *Journalism: Investigation and Research*, Allen Lane, London, 1999, pp. 45-6.

8 M. Simons, 'Using public records', in S. Tanner, *Journalism: Investigation and Research*, p. 97.

9 B. Weaver, in S. Tanner, *Journalism: Investigation and Research*, p. 59.

10 A. Davies, 'Dear John—fix it! Yours, Alan', *The Sydney Morning Herald*, 5 August 2000.

11 R. Kirkpatrick, 'The glory of the revelator: historical documents as a resource', in S. Tanner, *Journalism: Investigation and Research*, p. 145.

12 V. Laurie, 'The collected Lindy', *The Weekend Australian Magazine*, 2 June 2001, p. 30-3.

13 T. Conover, *Newjack: Guarding Sing Sing*, Charles Scribner, New York, 2001. Conover's book raises ethical questions, given the scale of his deception in working undercover. In the book he discusses his acute anxiety about these issues. Conover had applied to New York's Department of Correctional Services for access to the prison and prisoners but had been rebuffed. He decided that on public interest grounds the deception was warranted. He also changed the names of guards and prisoners so they could not be identified. He still felt uncomfortable about the level of secrecy required.

CHAPTER 7

1 C. Silvester, *The Penguin Book of Interviews*, Viking, London, 1993, p. 49.

2 M. Stephens, *A History of News*, p. 233

3 Quoted in C. Silvester, *The Penguin Book of Interviews*, p. 2.

4 Quoted in C. Silvester, *The Penguin Book of Interviews*, p. 4.

5 L. Barber, 'The art of the interview,' in *Secrets of the Press: Journalists on Journalism*, p. 200.

6 J. Brady, *The Craft of Interviewing*, Vintage Books, New York, 1977, p. 56

7 R. Wilson, *A Big Ask: Interviewers on Interviewing*, New Holland, Sydney, 2000, p. 86.

8 J. Malcolm, *The Journalist and the Murderer*, Bloomsbury, London, 1990, p. 3.

9 J. Malcolm, *The Journalist and the Murderer*, p. 6.

10 C. Masters, *The Inside Story*, Angus & Robertson, Sydney, 1992, p. 26.

11 J. Brady, *The Craft of Interviewing*, p. 32.

12 G. Haigh, personal communication with the author, 2002.

13 J. Schembri, personal communication with the author, 2002.

14 M. Stephens, *A History of News*, p. 253.

15 These points were made by Michael Smith, head of the firm, Inside PR, in a lecture to journalism students at RMIT University on 28 April 2003. As a former editor of *The Age* who has worked in public relations for almost a decade, Smith was well placed to comment.

16 For details of Stone's career, see R. Cottrell, *Izzy: A Biography of I.F. Stone*, Rutgers University Press, New Jersey, 1992.

17 T. Friend, 'This is going to be big', *The New Yorker*, 23 September 2002, pp. 38–46.

18 Material about types of questions and types of listening draws on G. Killenberg and R. Anderson, *Before the Story: Interviewing and Communication Skills for Journalists*, St. Martin's Press, New York, 1989, chapters three and four, pp. 47–119.

19 B. Yagoda, *About Town: The New Yorker and the World It Made*, Charles Scribner, New York, 2000, p. 190. Hersey wrote the piece for *The New Yorker*, which devoted an entire issue to the 31 000-word story. It was soon published in book form and *Hiroshima* has not been out of print since. The magazine's editor, Harold Ross, was famous for his editorial queries; in this case, his query spurred Hersey to include critical information about the victims dying from radiation burns, which had until that time been denied by the United States military.

20 G. Killenberg and R. Anderson, *Before the Story*, p. 93.

CHAPTER 8

1 M. Ricketson, 'I coulda been a contender . . .', *The Sunday Age*, View magazine, 11 June 1995, pp. 4–7.

2 C. McGregor, *Headliners*, University of Queensland Press, Brisbane, 1990, p. 190.

3 M. Ricketson, 'The Brown Lowdown', *The Sunday Age*, 10 September 1995.

4 M. Frayn, *The Tin Men*, Fontana Books, London, 1966, pp. 99–100.

5 Tippet said this during a training session on feature writing run by the author for journalists at *The Age* in June 2001.

6 C. Fussman, '11-9-2001', reprinted in *The Age*, 9 March 2002.

7 From Wolfe's introductory essay to *The New Journalism*, an anthology edited by Wolfe and E.W. Johnson, Harper & Row, New York, 1973, p. 68.

8 J. Carey, ed, *The Faber Book of Reportage*, Faber, London, 1987, p. xxxiii.

9 W. Harrington, *Intimate Journalism: The Art and Craft of Reporting Everyday Life*, Sage, California, 1997, p. xxx.

10 W. Harrington, *Intimate Journalism: The Art and Craft of Reporting Everyday Life*, p. xxxiv.

11 H. Garner, *The First Stone*, Pan Macmillan, Sydney, 1995, p. 25.

12 J. Carey, ed, *The Faber Book of Reportage*, p. xxxii.

13 C. Overington, 'Facing up to Humphries', *The Age*, 9 November 2002.

14 D. Brearley, 'The Passion of John Marsden', *The Australian*, 26 June 2001.

CHAPTER 9

1 B. Tuchman, *Practising History*, Papermac, London, 1983, pp. 20–1.

2 Gideon Haigh, personal communication with the author.

3 W. Blundell, *The Art and Craft of Feature Writing*, Plume, New York, 1988, pp. 97–100.

4 W. Blundell, *The Art and Craft of Feature Writing*, pp. 94 and 101.

5 J. Franklin, *Writing for Story*, Plume Books, New York, 1986.

6 M. Ricketson, 'On the ball', *The Sunday Age, View* magazine, 17 September 1995, pp. 6–8.

7 M. Cave and A. Hepworth, 'Public v. private: the great salary divide', *The Weekend Australian Financial Review*, 10 August 2002.

8 S. Guy and D. Crofts, 'Piggy banks', *Reader's Digest*, August 2002, pp. 22–32.

9 M. Ricketson, 'Monitoring the monitors,' *The Australian*, 'Media' supplement, 3 June 1999.

10 C. Wockner, 'Evil August', *The Daily Telegraph*, 3 August 2002.

11 Hersey's *Hiroshima* is discussed in detail in B. Yagoda, *About Town: The New Yorker and the World It Made*, Charles Scribner, New York, 2000, pp. 183–93, and in T. Kunkel, *Genius in Disguise: Harold Ross of The New Yorker*, Random House, New York, pp. 369–74.

12 P. Barry, *The Rise and Rise of Kerry Packer*, Bantam, Sydney, 1993, pp. xiii–xiv.

13 M. Simons, 'The burning question . . . why?', *The Age*, 30 November 2002.

14 M. Ricketson, 'Lone wolf', *The Weekend Australian Magazine*, 11 December 1993, pp. 18–25.

15 S. Weale, 'Would you microchip your child?' *The Guardian*, 4 September 2002.

16 D. Webster, 'Celebrity big bother', *Who Weekly*, 19 August 2002, pp. 46–51.

17 S. Calechman, 'Mum knows best', *Men's Health*, August 2002, pp. 72–5.

CHAPTER 10

1 Associated Press correspondent, 'Judge sends Oscar nominee down for drugs', *The Australian*, 10 December 1997.

2 T. Squires, 'Andrew Denton goes blah, blah, blah', *The Age*, 8 March 1994.

3 P. Lloyd, 'A Hardy tradition that spans 150 years', *The Advertiser*, 12 April 2003.

4 M. Ricketson, 'A twist in the tale', *The Age*, 'Green Guide' supplement, 3 June 1999.

5 M. Maiden, 'Media giants face off over pay TV merger', *The Age*, 15 June 2002.

6 B. Wilson, 'Tables turn on Diana's tattler', *Herald Sun*, 25 November 2000.

7 S. Hattenstone, 'An author unmasked', *The Guardian*, reprinted in *The Age*, 3 June 2002. The article was published to coincide with the release of Morton's biography of the singer Madonna.

8 M. Ricketson, 'How to school a scribe', *The Australian*, 'Media' supplement, 31 May 2001.

9 J. Mayer, 'The accountants' war', *The New Yorker*, 22 April 2002, pp. 64–72.

10 E. Griswold, 'A day in the life of a 14-year-old hitman', *Marie Claire*, August 2002, pp. 36–40.

11 P. Toomay, 'Clotheslined', *SportsJones*, 21 December 1999, reprinted in G. Stout, ed, *The Best American Sports Writing 2000*, Houghton Mifflin, New York, 2000, p. 246.

12 M. Davis, 'Corrigan still blazing a familiar trail', *The Financial Review*, 2 August 2002.

13 I. Sheddon, 'Dishing it up', *The Weekend Australian*, 'Review' section, 14 September 2002.

14 G. Linnell, 'In the deep end', *Good Weekend*, 21 July 2001, pp. 20–4.

15 M. Cowley, 'The thoughts of Thorpe', *The Age*, 30 July 2001.

16 W. Blundell, *The Art and Craft of Feature Writing*, Plume, New York, 1988, chapter five, pp. 94–126.

17 D. Brearley, 'Judge finds Marsden lied, then awards him $600,000', *The Australian*, 28 June 2001.

18 W. Blundell, *The Art and Craft of Feature Writing*, p. 143.

CHAPTER 11

1 W. Strunk and E.B. White, *The Elements of Style*, third edition, Macmillan, New York, 1979, p. 70.

2 No byline, 'Scientists seek "super-soldiers" formula', *The Age*, 6 January 2003.

3 M. Doman and S. Brook, 'Industry prepares to end slump', *The Australian*, 'Media' supplement, 2 January 2003, pp. 4–5.

4 S. Junger, 'Slaves of the brothel', *Vanity Fair*, July 2002, pp. 70–5 and 120–4.

5 J. Hall, 'Home on the range', *The Weekend Australian*, 'Review' section, 30 November 2002.

6 W. Blundell, *The Art and Craft of Feature Writing*, Plume, New York, 1988, p. 159.

7 I. Watson, 'Brit mega-shagger can't get enough "bearded clams"', *Rolling Stone*, November 2002, p. 114.

8 H. Matterson, 'Dream schemes take holiday', *The Weekend Australian*, 4 January 2003.

9 R. Buchanan, 'The fringe dwellers', *The Age*, *Saturday Extra*, 17 August 1996.

10 G. Linnell, 'Stand and deliver', *Good Weekend*, 2 November 2002, pp. 18–22.

11 J. Bryson, *Evil Angels*, Viking, Melbourne, 1985, p. 3.

12 G. Talese, 'The loser', reprinted in B. Lounsberry and G. Talese, eds, *Writing Creative Nonfiction: The Literature of Reality*, HarperCollins, New York, 1996, p. 107.

13 R. Preston, *The Hot Zone*, Random House, New York, 1994, pp. 46–7.

14 M. Gladwell, *The Tipping Point*, Little Brown, New York, 2000, p. 7.

15 C. Mathewson, 'Taste of the extreme', *The Courier-Mail*, 12 April 2003.

16 K. Lyall, 'Pol Pot Park', *The Weekend Australian Magazine*, 26 January 2002.

CHAPTER 12

1 S. King, *On Writing: A Memoir of the Craft*, Hodder Stoughton, London, 2000, p. 82.

2 S. King, *On Writing*, p. 56.

3 C. Graham, 'In the line of fire', *The Sunday Telegraph, Sunday Magazine*, 1 December 2002.

4 Quoted in S. King, *On Writing*, p. 323.

5 M. Ricketson, 'The fleeting memory', *The Weekend Australian Magazine*, 27 July 2002.

CHAPTER 13

1 Quoted in K. Kerrane and B. Yagoda, *The Art of Fact: A Historical Anthology of Literary Journalism*, Charles Scribner, New York, 1997, p. 20.

2 This idea comes from Rick Zahler of *The Seattle Times*, quoted in C. Scanlan, ed, *The Best American Newspaper Writing 2000*, Poynter Institute, Chicago, 2001, pp. 398–9.

3 W. McKeen, *Tom Wolfe*, Twayne's United States Authors series, No. 650, Twayne Publishers, New York, 1995, pp. 92–111.

4 C. Masters, *Not for Publication*, ABC Books, Sydney, p. 196.

5 T. Conover, *Newjack: Guarding Sing Sing*, Charles Scribner, New York, 2001, pp. 72–3.

6 T. Conover, *Newjack: Guarding Sing Sing*, p. 76.

7 Quoted in N. Sims, ed, *The Literary Journalists*, Ballantine Books, New York, 1984, p. 3.

8 T. Connery, 'American literary journalism at the turn of the century', in N. Sims, ed, *Literary Journalism in the Twentieth Century*, Oxford University Press, New York, 1990, p. 18.

9 A. Funder, *Stasiland*, Text Publishing, Melbourne, 2002, p. 221.

10 For a fuller discussion of Helen Garner's journalism, see M. Ricketson, 'Helen Garner's *The First Stone*: hitchhiking on the credibility of other writers', in J. Mead, ed, *Bodyjamming*, Random House, Sydney, 1997, pp. 79–100.

11 Quoted in E.J. Carroll, *Hunter: The Strange and Savage Life of Hunter S. Thompson*, Plume, New York, 1993, p. 153.

12 For details of the literature cited, see M. Ricketson, 'Helen Garner's *The First Stone*', p. 84 and endnote on p. 282.

13 T. Eagleton, *Literary Theory: An Introduction*, second edition, Basil Blackwell, London, 1996, pp. 190–208.

14 N. Sims, ed, *The Literary Journalists*, p. 5.

15 G. Linnell, 'Hope lives here', *Sunday Life!* magazine, *The Sunday Age*, 5 October 1997.

SUGGESTIONS FOR FURTHER READING

Just about every writer or writing teacher says you should read a lot. But what, exactly? You can learn from lousy writing as well as good, but time is short and the number of available newspapers, magazines and books is long, and getting longer by the hour. I have been reading journalism daily for more than 20 years and reading about journalism for ten. I could provide an exhaustive list but that would prove exhausting. Instead I offer a highlights reel.

These suggestions are organised by category; many are anthologies, which has long been the only way of saving good journalism from its secondary use as fish'n'chip wrappings. Today, newspapers and magazines keep archives of stories that are available online for a small fee per article. Many of the books listed below are recently published and may still be in print; others are not but should be available in secondhand shops, an increasing number of which operate online.

1. BOOKS ABOUT WRITING—TO BE TAKEN IN SMALL DOSES, BEFORE MEALS

Jon Franklin, *Writing for Story*, Plume, New York, 1986.

An excellent book about advanced features. Particularly useful is Franklin's paragraph by paragraph annotations on his Pulitzer Prize-winning piece 'Mrs Kelly's Monster'.

Stephen King, *On Writing: A Memoir of the Craft*, Hodder and Stoughton, London, 2000.

Aimed at novelists, this book still has much value for journalists. By weaving instruction into memoir, King shows good writing is about far more than good grammar. That a book about writing can be such an engaging story shows the power and value of storytelling.

William Zinsser, *On Writing Well*, HarperCollins, New York, fifth edition, 1994.

A model of clarity and wit, Zinsser demystifies writing, which, he says, is not an innate gift but 'thinking on paper, or talking to someone on paper'.

2. BOOKS ABOUT INTERVIEWING—YOUR QUESTIONS ANSWERED ABOUT Q&A

Christopher Silvester: *The Penguin Book of Interviews*, Penguin, London, 1993.

This anthology of interviews with the famous (Sigmund Freud, Marilyn Monroe) and infamous (Adolf Hitler, Joseph Stalin) makes wonderfully entertaining—and informative—reading. It perfectly illustrates the interview's universal appeal—a sense of being there in the room with the famous one. The lengthy introduction illuminates the interview's history.

Ruth Wilson: *A Big Ask: Interviewers on Interviewing*, New Holland, Sydney, 2000.

This is an Australian collection of interviews with interviewers. Many, but not all, are journalists; you can still learn from comedian H.G. Nelson, and police interviewer Bill Dowton. The most valuable journalistic interviews are with Caroline Jones, Phillip Knightley, David Leser and Sarah Macdonald.

3. AWARD-WINNING JOURNALISM—BE INSPIRED BY COLLEAGUES, PAST AND PRESENT

The annual Walkley awards, the most prestigious in the Australian news media, have been around since 1956. The Walkleys cover all media and are listed on the Media Entertainment & Arts Alliance's website. Earlier winners were written up in John Hurst's *The Walkleys: Australia's Best Journalists in Action* (John Kerr, Richmond, 1988).

A list of the Best Australian Journalism of the Twentieth Century, as judged by a panel of journalism educators and senior industry people, can be found at the ezine Fifth Estate—<http://fifth.estate.rmit.edu.au>.

4. JOURNALISM OVERSEAS—WHERE TO START

The Week is an excellent international digest of the best of the world media, providing a handy round-up of major news events worldwide, an authoritative background briefing on the issue of the week, excerpts from outstanding columnists and quirky tidbits, such as the section 'It must be true . . . I read it in the tabloids'. Published in England, *The Week* is available in Australia by subscription. Its website is <www.theweek.co.uk>.

5. HUMOUR AND SATIRE—AN ENDANGERED SPECIES WORTH PRESERVING

Begin with two satirical newspapers, *The Onion* and *The Chaser*. The former is American, the latter Australian. Both are presented as a straight newspaper, but the content is anything but. Typical headlines: 'Michael Jackson undergoes complete blackendectomy' (*The Onion*) and 'Marsden to sue himself: says court case damaged his own reputation' (*The Chaser*).

Watch John Clarke and Bryan Dawe's mock interviews on ABC TV's *7.30 Report*; the scripts are available as *Great Interviews of the Twentieth Century*, *More Great Interviews . . . etc.*, as are the scripts of their fly-on-the-wall mockumentary *The Games* about the Sydney Olympics.

6. SPORTS JOURNALISM—TOO MUCH SPORTS JOURNALISM IS NEVER ENOUGH

Alongside cliché-sodden hacks, Australia also has outstanding sports journalists. Their best work has been collected in anthologies such as *The Best Australian Sports Writing 2003*, edited by Garrie Hutchinson (Black Inc., Melbourne). English and American sports writing traditions can be tapped through *The Picador Book of Sportswriting*, edited by Nick Hornby and Nick Coleman (Picador, London, 1996) and *The Best American Sports Writing of the Century*, edited by Glenn Stout and introduced by David Halberstam (Houghton Mifflin, New York, 1999).

7. FILM ADAPTATIONS—GO BACK TO THE SOURCE

Many films based on true stories bear little resemblance to the truth; not so the books on which they were based. *A Perfect Storm* (Fourth Estate, London, 1997) and *A Civil Action* (Century Books, London, 1995) were originally well reviewed books written by American journalists, Sebastian Junger and Jonathan Harr respectively. *Alive: The Story of the Andes Survivors* (Secker and Warburg, 1974), by novelist Piers Paul Read, has been filmed twice.

8. THE NEW YORKER—DUMBING UP CAN WORK

America has several journalism-driven magazines, including *Atlantic Monthly*, *Harper's* and *Vanity Fair*. *The New Yorker* is my favourite among them. Its current editor, David Remnick, has overseen numerous thoroughly researched, elegantly written pieces, offering rare perspectives on subjects. Readers are responding; in 2002 circulation hit 900 000, the highest in the magazine's history. Below are a dozen examples from Remnick's editorship.

'Last words: what Ernest Hemingway didn't want us to read', by Joan Didion, 9 November 1998.
'Big guns: the lawyers who brought down the tobacco industry are taking on the gunmakers and the N.R.A.', by Peter J. Boyer, 17 May 1999.

'The demon in the freezer: the return of the deadliest disease in history, and why we're now powerless to stop it', by Richard Preston, 12 July 1999.

'Deadline: a desperate bid to stop the trashing of America's historic newspapers', by Nicholson Baker, 24 July 2000.

'The hardest test: drugs and the Tour de France', by Julian Barnes, 21 August 2000.

'The trouble with fries: can fast food be made safe?', by Malcolm Gladwell, 5 March 2001.

'The great terror: in northern Iraq, there is new evidence of Saddam Hussein's genocidal war on the Kurds—and of his possible ties to Al Qaeda', by Jeffrey Goldberg, 25 March 2002.

'Wasteland: Robert Mugabe's thug rule', by Philip Gourevitch, 3 June 2002.

'The talent myth: why smart people are bad for business', by Malcolm Gladwell, 22 July 2002.

'Honest, Decent, Wrong: The invention of George Orwell', by Louis Menand, 27 January 2003.

'Lost in the Jihad: Why did the government's case against John Walker Lindh collapse?', by Jane Mayer, 10 March 2003.

'Vox Fox: How Roger Ailes and Fox News are changing cable news', by Ken Auletta, 26 May 2003.

9. TRAVEL WRITING—ARMCHAIR SIGHTSEEING

Everybody has favourites in this perennially popular genre. Get into the good stuff through *The Granta Book of Travel* (Granta Books, London, 1998), which includes a thoughtful introduction by editor Ian Jack, and *The Best American Travel Writing*, an annual series that began in 2000.

10. PROFILES—GOOD WRITING ABOUT GOOD, BAD AND UGLY PEOPLE

Another popular genre, easily approached through anthologies. David Remnick collected *The New Yorker*'s outstanding profiles in *Life Stories* (Random House, New York, 2000). In Australia, see Craig McGregor's best profiles from the 1970s and 1980s in *Headliners* (University of Queensland Press, Brisbane, 1990) and David Leser's in *The Whites of their Eyes* (Allen & Unwin, 1999).

11. ANTHOLOGIES—CAPTURING THE BEST BEFORE IT GOES IN THE RECYCLE BIN

NB. Don't skip the excellent introductions to these anthologies.

Ian Jack, ed., *The Granta Book of Reportage*, Granta Books, London, 1998.

John Carey, ed., *The Faber Book of Reportage*, Faber, London, 1987.

William Howarth, ed., *The John McPhee Reader*, The Noonday Press, New York, 1976.

Robert Love, ed., *The Best of Rolling Stone: 25 Years of Journalism on the Edge*, Straight Arrow, London, 1993.

David Remnick and Patricia Strachan, eds, *The Second John McPhee Reader*, The Noonday Press, New York, 1996.

Norman Sims, ed., *The Literary Journalists*, Ballantine Books, New York, 1984.

Norman Sims and Mark Kramer, eds, *Literary Journalism: A New Collection of the Best American Nonfiction*, Ballantine Books, New York, 1995.

Tom Wolfe and E.W. Johnson, eds, *The New Journalism*, Harper & Row, New York, 1973.

12. LITERARY JOURNALISM—news that stays news (with apologies to Ezra Pound)

Classics

Begin with Kevin Kerrane and Ben Yagoda's *The Art of Fact: A Historical Anthology of Literary Journalism*, Scribner, New York, 1997—a feast of compelling reading.

Truman Capote, *In Cold Blood*, Hamish Hamilton, London,1965.

John Hersey, *Hiroshima*, Penguin, London, 1946.

Norman Mailer, *The Fight*, Penguin, London, 1975.

George Orwell, *Homage to Catalonia*, Secker and Warburg, London, 1930.

Lillian Ross, *Reporting*, Jonathan Cape, London, 1966.

Gay Talese, *Fame and Obscurity*, Ballantine Books, New York, 1993.

Hunter S. Thompson, *Hell's Angels*, Random House, New York, 1966.

Tom Wolfe, *The Purple Decades*, Farrar, Strauss and Giroux, New York, 1982.

Recent must-reads

Bill Buford, *Among The Thugs*, Mandarin, London, 1991.

Ted Conover, *Newjack: Guarding Sing Sing*, Scribner, New York, 2000.

Barbara Ehrenreich, *Nickel and Dimed: On (not) Getting By in America*, Metropolitan, New York, 2001.

Philip Gourevitch, *We Wish to Inform You that Tomorrow We will be Killed with our Families*, Picador, London, 1998.

Ryszard Kapuscinski, *Imperium*, Granta Books, London, 1993.

John Lahr, *Dame Edna Everage and the Rise of Western Civilisation*, Bloomsbury, London, 1991.

Janet Malcolm, *The Journalist and the Murderer*, Bloomsbury, London, 1990.

Ron Rosenbaum, *Explaining Hitler: The Search for the Origins of his Evil*, Macmillan, London, 1998.

Australian

Geraldine Brooks, *Nine Parts of Desire: The Hidden World of Islamic Women*, Anchor Books, Sydney, 1994.

John Bryson, *Evil Angels*, Viking, Melbourne, 1985.

Les Carlyon, *True Grit*, Text, Melbourne, 1998.

Anna Funder, *Stasiland*, Text, Melbourne, 2002.

Helen Garner, *True Stories: Selected Nonfiction*, Text, Melbourne, 1996.

Gideon Haigh, *Mystery Spinner: The Jack Iverson Story*, Text, Melbourne, 1999.

Margaret Simons, *Fit to Print: Inside the Canberra Press Gallery*, UNSW Press, Sydney, 1999.

Pamela Williams, *The Victory*, Allen & Unwin, Sydney, 1997.

INDEX